This collection lays down a sympathetic challenge to Critical Legal Studies and Critical Race Theory: to continue the critique to the point of overturning the last remnants of the rationalist primacy of mind over body still haunting many rethinkings of justice. Thinking Through the Body of the Law *echoes Spinoza's pronouncement that 'we do not yet know what a body can do'. The body, that is, is not brute matter given form by rational activity. It contains, in its own right, positive potentials for collective growth and connection that outstrip its rationalized regulation. Can an ethics be based on an affirmation of those as yet unexpressed potentials, rather than their regulatory reduction? Can justice? Essential reading for those interested in questions of ethics and justice (as they clash or converge), in the context of theories of embodied existence attuned to politics of gender and race.*

Brian Massumi
University of Queensland

Legal studies has made experimental sallies into interdisciplinarity before; here it joins cultural studies in a sparkling set of deconstructive takes on embodiment and difference. Timely and topical, this is also the most successful effort I've seen to get human rights back on the radical agenda at the level of theoretical sophistication they deserve.

Bruce Robbins
Rutgers University

THINKING THROUGH THE BODY OF THE LAW

Edited by Pheng Cheah, David Fraser
and Judith Grbich

NEW YORK UNIVERSITY PRESS
Washington Square, New York

Cover photograph and design by Kajri Jain

First published in 1996
Allen & Unwin Pty Ltd

First published in the USA in 1996 by
New York University Press
Washington Square
New York, N.Y. 10003

Library of Congress Cataloging-in-Publication Data

Thinking through the body of the law / edited by Pheng Cheah,
  David Faser, Judith Grbich
        p.   cm.
    ISBN 0-8147-1544-3 (cloth). — ISBN 0-8147-1545-1 (paperback)
    1. Law—Philosophy. 2. Critical legal studies. I. Cheah, Pheng.
  II. Fraser, David John, 1953- . III Grbich, Judith.
  K235.T55 1996
  340'.1—dc20   95–44549
                                                     CIP

Set in 10/11 Sabon by DOCUPRO, Sydney

10 9 8 7 6 5 4 3 2 1

Contents

Acknowledgments

'Of Pleasure and Property: Sexuality and Sovereignty in Australia' by Elizabeth Povinelli is a revised version of 'Sexual Savages/ Sexual Sovereignty: Australian Colonial Texts and the Postcolonial Politics of Nationalism' which appeared in *Diacritics*, Spring/ Summer 1994, vol. 24, nos.1–2. The editors are grateful to *Diacritics* and to The Johns Hopkins University Press for permission to publish. Moira Gatens' chapter 'Spinoza, law and responsibility' first appeared in her 1996 collection of essays *Imaginary Bodies: Ethics, Power and Corporeality* published by Routledge.

The editors also wish to thank Ms Fran Smithard for her tireless and cheerful efforts in bringing the manuscript to fruition and Dr Kathryn McMahon for her help in letting this book see the light of day.

Notes on Contributors

PHENG CHEAH has degrees in Philosophy, Literature and Law and is currently a doctoral student in the Department of English, Cornell University. He works on philosophies of culture, decolonisation and neocolonialism. Some of this research is published in *Social Text* and forthcoming in *Diacritics and Public Culture*. He has also published on feminist theory and the philosophy of law in *Law in Context*, the *Australian Feminist Law Journal* and the *Sydney Law Review*. He is currently co-editing and contributing to a collection of essays on rethinking the cosmopolitical.

ROSALYN DIPROSE teaches Philosophy at the University of New South Wales. She is co-editor with Robyn Ferrell of *Cartographies: Poststructuralism and the Mapping of Bodies and Spaces*, Allen & Unwin, 1991. Her most recent publication is *The Bodies of Women: Ethics, Embodiment and Sexual Difference*, Routledge, 1994.

DAVID FRASER works at the University of Sydney where he teaches a course on 'the Holocaust, Moral Responsibility and the Rule of Law'. He has published several works on law and popular culture and is currently working on a book on the Holocaust.

MOIRA GATENS is a Senior Lecturer in Philosophy at the University of Sydney. She is author of *Feminism and Philosophy: Perspectives on Equality and Difference* 1991, and *Imaginary Bodies: Ethics,*

Power and Corporeality, 1995. She is a regular contributor to feminist anthologies.

JUDITH GRBICH works in the School of Law and Legal Studies at La Trobe University in Melbourne and teaches in the Women's Studies and Law and Legal Studies Programs. She has written in the areas of cultural representations of economic value, historiographies of exertion measurements, feminist legal theory, and taxation narratives.

ELIZABETH GROSZ teaches critical theory at Monash University. Most recently she is the author of *Space, Time and Perversion*, Routledge/Allen & Unwin, 1995, and is the co-editor with Elspeth Probyn of *Sexy Bodies*, Routledge, 1995.

ROSANNE KENNEDY teaches Women's Studies and English at the Australian National University in Canberra. She has written in the areas of cultural representation, feminist theory and law in litera-ture. She is currently working on a project on the representation of Australia in the United States.

FRANCES OLSEN is Professor of Law at the University of California at Los Angeles. She is the author of numerous articles and is a leading feminist legal theorist in the United States.

PAUL PATTON is a Senior Lecturer in Philosophy at the University of Sydney. He has translated and written about the work of several French philosophers, including Foucault, Deleuze and Baudrillard. He edited *Nietzsche, Feminism and Political Theory*, Allen & Unwin 1993. His interest in bringing aspects of post-structuralist theory to bear on Australian political issues will be pursued in *Difference*, forthcoming from Melbourne University Press.

ELIZABETH POVINELLI is an Associate Professor of Anthropology at the University of Chicago. Her writings include *Labour's Lot: The Power, History and Culture of Aboriginal Action* (Chicago 1993). She has also worked with the Australian Aboriginal North-ern Land Council on land rights issues. She is currently writing a book on the cultural history of sexuality and sovereignty in the construction of 'native title' in Australia.

TERRY THREADGOLD is a Professor of English at Monash Uni-versity in Melbourne. Her research interests include Critical Legal Studies, performance studies and issues related to critical and feminist pedagogy. Her publications include (with E. Grosz) *Gunther Kress*; (with M.A.K. Hallliday) *Semiotics—Ideology —Language*, 1986; and (with A. Cranny-Francis) *Feminine/*

Masculine and Representation, 1991. Her book *Feminist Poetics* will be published in 1996.

CATHRYN VASSELEU lectures in Philosophy at the University of New South Wales, Sydney. She has made a film and published papers on a variety of contemporary imaging technologies and is currently completing a book, *Textures of Light*, on vision and embodiment in the work of Irigarary, Levinas and Merleau-Ponty.

Introduction: the body of the law

Pheng Cheah, David Fraser and Judith Grbich

While many disciplines in the humanities and social sciences are experiencing a crisis of reason, the discipline of legal studies seems to continue in its solipsistic state of professional training. The primary reason for this may be that the epistemological and ontological frameworks of legal knowledge largely remain structured around obsolete forms of philosophical understanding, particularly that of rationalist positivism which dogmatically assumes that the methods of legal reasoning are unquestionable because the law is a function of enlightened reason. Indeed, it is a commonplace to say that in the received history of Western consciousness from Plato through Aquinas, Hegel to Hart and Dworkin, the institution of law as *nomos* has always been predicated as the function and effect of a universal or at least, collective mind or Reason.

Based on and departing from social contract theory (whether liberal individualist or communitarian), mainstream legal theory is committed to an ontology which sees each human individual as possessing the fundamental traits of reason and natural liberty. Specific pre-civil rights are derived from this original freedom and autonomy. Generally speaking, it is said that rational social concensus is formed in order to protect and maximise basic personal or property rights or dispositions such as the right to personal safety and property (Locke), the right to life, the propensity towards moral freedom (Kant) etc. As a result, rationalist legal theory defines legal obligation as the acceptance of state coercion as legitimate or rationally justified by each individual subject who then internalises the state's legal rules. While morality and legality are not identical, the political morality or justice of a state, the moral basis of a legal system, is also measured in terms of the self-evidence of the moral criteria or norms embedded in rules of law to the atomistic legal subject's power of reason. This predication of justice in terms of individual autonomy and universal rationality leads to formal or procedural justice and distributive justice as the egalitarian sharing or equal partitioning of resources in a given society.

In the past two decades, however, legal theory of a critical and political persuasion has attempted to interrogate these assumptions of mainstream legal thought as part of a larger questioning of the justice of existing legal structures and institutions. Political legal theories advocating social or substantive justice are quick to remind us that the legal subject is a rational abstraction which does not exist. One thinks here of the Critical Legal Studies (CLS) movement in North America and the innovations of feminist jurisprudence. Arising out of the general contestation of the normative assumptions of American culture in the period of the 1960s, CLS formulated and articulated generalised critiques of American legal culture. Most importantly, CLS attacked the apolitical nature of legal theory and practice in the United States by situating the legal subject in a phenomenonological account of the actual oppressions operating within the world of the legal system. The ideological catchcry of early CLS interventions was the aphoristic 'law is politics'. In a number of concrete instances ranging from the ideology of legal historical categories such as the subject of tort or contract law to the disempowering effect of legal discourse on collective movements in the fields of labour law and anti-discrimination law, CLS analyses attempted to combat the political and moral notion of the inherent worth of the rule of law by demonstrating that both the ideology and practice of law and legal theory in the United States carried metaphysical assumptions and precepts which undermined not just the internal claims of legal theory to a self-evident status of inherent moral worth but which also served as a fundamental impediment to the vaguely articulated emancipatory ideals and goals of the American Left.[1]

Thus, in the Gramscian turn which characterised much CLS writing on the body of American law, the critique of rights became the normative claim against the dominant legal normativity. CLS scholars offered complex and often compelling accounts of the alienating and disempowering effects of claims by the socially marginalised to justice as rights to be accorded or recognised in terms of legal discourse. The linguistic turn in progressive legal theory and practice epitomised in the critique of rights was informed by a belief that the hegemonic nature of American democracy was such that all attempts to achieve substantive and ameliorative justice through judicial activism and claims to rights would always/already be accompanied not only by the elasticity and apparent openness of democracy but by the equally dangerous possibility that claimants seeking justice would actually perceive themselves as real embodiments of the abstract principles and characteristics of the legal subject and would therefore limit their claims to sovereignty to the normative parameter of the very system of abstraction and alienation their claims were meant to contest. In other words, the CLS critique of rights perceived the body of legal rules upon which all claims to 'rights' must be grounded as operating in reality to maintain the ideological and political integrity of the body politic of the United States. Thus, any apparent victory gained in the struggle over civil rights or abortion rights through a change in the body of legal rules actually served to reinforce the more fundamental claims of mainstream legal and political theory to law's status and function as *nomos*.

But while the CLS critique of rights directly contested the normativity of liberal positivistic legality, thereby opening up the body of legal knowledge to new challenges and newer discourses, it did not remain unchallenged. Both inside and outside the organisational structures of CLS, feminist legal theorists attacked the critique of rights for ignoring the reality of the oppressive effects of existing legal norms on the corporeal reality of women's lives. Rape law, sexual harassment, pornography, abortion restrictions, unequal wage structures etc. all had real impacts, not just on the physical bodies of women which were the objects of real oppressions and violence, but on the very idea of woman as legal object. The abstract and the real position of the legal subject in liberal legality were even more alien to women who could aspire only to the status of object. To deny or to diminish the real struggles against gender-based oppressions through the abstract and normative claims which necessarily grounded the CLS critique of rights was, for many feminist legal theorists, yet another example of dis-incorporation of woman in the body of the law.

Similarly, scholars of colour in the United States, while recognising the path-breaking nature of much CLS scholarship, reacted against the critique of rights by arguing that it basically misunderstood and perhaps infantalised people of colour in many ways. In the view of the body of scholarship and political intervention which now stands under the rubric of Critical Race Theory (CRT),[2] the CLS critique of rights reflects the concerns of a white, largely male elite with traditional ideas of the false consciousness of the masses, and does not offer an understanding of the real experiences and politics within various communities of colour of the complexities of the civil rights struggle. CRT proponents argue that the communities in question in fact have a deep and embodied understanding not only of the limits and dangers of a legal strategy but of the history of slavery, colonisation and racism which informs the politics and the legality of race in America.

It is important to note, however, that the debates which circulate within the body of legal knowledge circumscribed by CLS, feminist legal theory and CRT are not one-dimensional. Within CLS, for example, the exact role, extent and importance of the critique of rights has always been contested and refined. In a similar way, feminist legal theory is in no way one-sided. While early debates centred on the construction of 'woman' as legal object/subject and her absence from the body of the law, interventions quickly turned to issues of the ways in which the female body was in fact present in the body of the law. This sameness/difference debate posited competing ideas on and about fundamental normative claims to 'equality' as well as raising key questions on issues of autonomy, the ethic of care, the self and, very importantly, on the role of the actual physical embodiment of the female subject in her status as legal subject.

Indeed, all of these debates continue to circulate, in different embodiments, in the interstices of CLS, feminist legal theory and CRT today. With the arrival of post modernism and a renewed interest in the conjoined effect of domination and contingency within these bodies of legal scholarship, issues of the politics of identity, the potential liberation of female bodies and sexuality through the dangerous mode of feminist pornography and the contingent impossibility of all calls to justice, have taken legal theory beyond the body of the law. Now there is open contestation between MacKinnonite factions who seek to ban pornography to po-mo proponents of Madonna as the new liberating legal theorist par excellence, just as there are calls within CRT for more careful consideration of the ways in which, for example, the intersectionality of race and gender and now sexuality are or are not embodied, not just within the group's internal debates but within the body of the law as it operates in complex and subtle ways on the bodies of women, men and children of colour.

These admirable political efforts in legal theory have, however, primarily approached the corporeal body as a simple substance, an object which is external to the law and which needs to be retrieved. As such, political legal theories share the ontological presuppositions of mainstream legal studies and jurisprudence and have unwittingly repeated the privileging of mind over body, thereby yielding other problems. For example, because the CLS critique of rights presupposes a determinate human existence outside power—unalienated relatedness or intersubjective zap—which is subseqently violated by the abstracting or reifying power of abstract rights, it has dismissed rights-talk as false consciousness and become open to the charge of elitist theoreticism. The recourse to embodied experience in both feminist jurisprudence and critical race theory has not fared better. Feminist jurisprudence has been largely unsuccessful in escaping the impasse of the sameness/difference debate. The affirmation of women's difference leads on the one hand, to the inability to claim legal equality through anti-discrimination legislation and on the other hand, to a privative definition of women's experience. The notion of minority experience in critical race theory is equally fraught.

In fact, the privileging of embodied experience as the repository of norms of justice has merely extended the empire of legal reason over bodily differences which are characterised as collective units whose autonomy must be safeguarded. These differences are seen as substantive qualifications to or modifications of the neutral and universal subject before the law. It is presupposed that these differences can be rationally determined and that they have to be taken into account so that the autonomy of different groups can be protected. The limitations of this approach and its ontological underpinnings become explicit when pregnancy has to be described in terms equivalent to hernia for women to get compensation, and when the recognition of Aboriginal customary law occurs through its incorporation into the general legal framework in subordination to Western common law.

It therefore seems important to begin to rethink embodiment and difference as a limit to the power of knowledge co-belonging with an autonomous self. Towards this end, previously neglected strands of modern Continental philosophy may offer fruitful alternatives to the rational-redemptive perspective implicit in contemporary legal studies. Rationalist legal theory underplays the mundane fact that in order for the law to function at all it must first and foremost have a hold over bodies. As Nietzsche reminds us in the *Genealogy of Morals*,[3] the alibi which we call justice functions by a mnemotechnics of pain: the permanent inscription and etching of the body in order to produce 'man' as a responsible subject.

The linking of embodiment, responsibility and obedience has two important consequences. First, it follows from this that the body plays a formative role in the securing of rational consensus. Corporeality therefore needs to be reconceptualised as active and productive, as preceding and possibly outstripping reason's power of knowledge. Spinoza and Nietzsche are the classical modern philosophers of active corporeality. Contemporary French philosophers such as Derrida, Deleuze and Foucault write in the wake of their influence. Hence, to a greater or lesser degree, each presupposes an intellectual framework where corporeality plays an important role in the critique of philosophies of consciousness or the subject. This is more obvious in the case of Foucault and Deleuze.[4] But any competent reading of Derrida[5] would also grasp that the notion of general textuality refers to the infinite cross-hatching that is the condition of possibility of being-in-the-world as an embodied being. Second, the fact that we are embodied beings should remind us that we exist originally with others and that the valued quality of autonomy may be secondary. This seems a fruitful path toward rethinking difference before law. Indeed, combined with contemporary French philosophy's equally strong interest in how difference or otherness constitutes identity,[6] the retheorising of corporeality poses challenging questions for political legal theories interested in issues of justice and the position of women, minorities and other oppressed groups vis-a-vis the law.[7]

It should, however, be noted that the reception of French philosophy as postmodern theories of discourse, interpretation and linguistic undecidability has obscured this interest in corporeality. Thus, the project of rethinking corporeality in law is not strictly identical to the various accounts of interpretive freedom espoused by postmodern legal theory.[8] These ultimately presuppose the primacy of a free consciousness as an interpretive subject who can recognise the fact that its interpretations and perspectives are limited and decide to be responsible to these limitations.

Theoretically speaking, the essays in this collection are motivated by the challenge of contemporary French philosophy and, in their different ways, attempt to rethink the role of the body in the founding, maintaining and regulation of social consensus and legal systems and to elaborate on its implications for issues of legal responsibility and justice. Yet, most of these essays also find their impetus from urgent historical and contemporary events and issues and are concerned about the adequacy and relevance of the theoretical approaches they deploy to analyse these events and issues. Two essays (Patton and Povinelli) are sustained analyses of *Eddie Mabo v State of Queensland* (*Mabo*), the landmark Australian case recognising land rights for Aboriginals. Other essays deal with the Holocaust, surrogacy, murder, the media and insanity, taxation and genetic engineering.

As a whole then, the collection attempts to interrogate the body of law itself. 'The body of the law' is an ambiguous phrase. Yet, only this ambiguity suffices to indicate the ubiquity of the law once it is theorised in terms of embodiment. Conventionally, 'the body of the law' designates positive law as a determinate corpus: legal codes, statutes and the rulings of common law. But it can also mean the subjected body that belongs to and is part of the law as the condition of possibility of the law, the various types of bodies as objects produced by legal regulation, and the diffusion of the law through the non-legal bodies and structures which support it. *Thinking Through the Body of the Law* attempts to track the relations between the law and its various bodies.

The three essays in the first section examine the ethical implications of the complex role of embodiment in the making of the body politic and the legal subject. Drawing on the work of Robert Cover and Nietzsche, Pheng Cheah and Elizabeth Grosz argue that an ineliminable violence occurs in the processes which give us body and that this violence is the condition of possibility of legal obedience or rational fidelity to law. They then suggest that an account of justice which acknowledges the link between law, violence and our corporeal being-with-others may be helpful in negotiating the impasses of the sameness/difference debate. Moira Gatens demonstrates the importance of Spinoza's philosophy for an alternative account of the responsibility of the civil body. Drawing a contrast between societies based on utility and capture and societies based on embodied rational self-understanding, she argues that our modern societies of a pluralist composition should shift from a model of law which stresses individual culpability. Instead, the civil body should begin to take responsibility for developing the powers and capacities of individual citizens as this will enhance its virtue. Paul Patton suggests that the *Mabo* decision is an implicit challenge to liberal approaches to society and justice that insist upon the uniform identity of the body politic and equal treatment of its citizens. Yet, he cautions us that the decision is also a failure on the part of the Australian body politic to affirm unassimilated cultural difference.

But the body of the law also creates more specific bodies, the regulation of which serves the substantive political and legal disciplinary function of maintaining a specific social order. On the one hand, this involves the projection of a regulative ideal, which is also the ontological and epistemological claim justifying legality, to be embodied in a regime of law consisting of legal subjects. These legal subjects are thus incorporated into a limited juridicial status which defines them, by inclusion, exclusion or extermination from the body politic. For example, the vision of social control found in penal policy defines the body of the criminal, excludes them from the body politic through the process of trial and imprisonment with the concomitant processes of popular culture; operates on the body of the prisoner through surveillance, torture, confinement; and, in the case of the condemned, eliminates them by physical extermination. This creative/regulatory function of the law over bodies is nowhere as violently visible as in instances of the founding or maintaining of national constitutional order. As Povinelli underlines in her chapter, the social order of the coloniser in contemporary Australia is maintained by the creation of the Aboriginal body as a legal subject in various ways even as a prima facie competing legal body attempts to create and maintain a more progressive social order through a different set of legal regulative functions. In his chapter on the Holocaust, Fraser demonstrates that the protection of the body politic through the creation of special bodies can easily and logically lead from exclusion to extermination since the regulative ideal of law itself is its own condition of possibility.

On the other hand, law and legal rules—the body of law in the narrow and literal traditional sense of the regulative instruments such as statutes, judge-made rules (case law) etc.—serve not just to produce generalised and to a certain extent abstract bodies of legal subjects, but also act more concretely to create specific body types in particularised ways. Thus the body of the taxpayer as legal subject (Grbich) or the life form object/subject of patent law (Vasseleu) are created and extinguished in the ontological/eschatological process and minutiae of legal rules and regulations. Rosalyn Diprose offers a detailed critique of this legal process in the context of the ways in which technologies and legal categories cooperate in the creation of sexed bodies as objects of legal and commercial exchange. Together, these three essays provide a complementary set of feminist readings of the body of the law and the law of the body.

The creation of the collectivised legal subject and the careful, often tedious incremental creation of legal subjects through the actions and interactions of various legal rule-making bodies can appear alienated and distant, abstract or deeply embedded in processes and mechanisms beyond our control. It is therefore important to remember that the regulative and disciplinary body is part of a more diffuse web of events and relations. When we begin to consider the production of law's corporeal images and realities as they are found in diverse and diffuse ways in the structures and images of our popular cultural images, we not only see the processes and effects of the creation and circulation of these bodies of law but also the possibilities for achieving transformative goals in the body and bodies of law. Threadgold and Kennedy argue that images and realities of legal embodied subjects are in fact created in our quotidian contacts with popular culture. By adopting a textual and political stance of embodied engagement with these bodies of law we can perhaps begin to explore the possibilities inherent in the claims of law itself to/over the creation of the legal subject for achieving different incorporations of the regulative ideal.

We suggested above that once it is theorised in terms of embodiment, the ubiquity of the law can only be captured by the ambiguity of the phrase, 'the body of the law'. Consequently, the essays in this collection are situated at the interstices of various disciplines and areas of specialised knowledge which they attempt to open up for further investigation and interpretation. They touch on issues that are drawn from, and bear on, disciplines including philosophy, law and legal studies, feminist studies, social and political theory, communication studies, critical theory and cultural studies. All in all, the injunction to think through the body of the law is an exhortation towards further dialogue from others in an ongoing participatory critique of the law. It is an exhortation that we should not treat the law as something distant and far removed from us, and hence, something which will remain oblivious to our critiques. Law structures our everyday lives and it is in turn penetrated by the everyday. It is part of us even as we are part of it. The possibility of ongoing legal transformation is inscribed here.

PART I

The making of the legal body: ethics and politics

1

The body of the law: notes toward a theory of corporeal justice

Pheng Cheah and Elizabeth Grosz

Political critiques of rationalist legal theory often begin by questioning the premise that the law embodies universal reason and truth. As such, these critiques are the counterpart in legal theory to the more general critique of post-Enlightenment philosophical concepts of rationality which have privileged mind over body. Analytical jurisprudence, the most institutionally-rooted theory of modern legal systems, is, after all, part of a larger philosophical history in which law, as *nomos*, has always been predicated as a function of the mind and therefore in a hierarchical opposition to materiality which law serves to order and govern. Thomas Aquinas, for instance, saw law as the rule and measure of acts, an exercise of reason in techniques of virtue.[1] The historical shift away from theories of natural law has sharpened the rationalist axiom that the law judges minds because it is an effect of reason. As the phrase 'positive law' reminds us, law is the product of the positional power of the mind.[2] Hart defines positive law as a series of rules that normatively bind a self-consciously critical and accepting subject.[3] Similarly, for Hegel, the self-conscious determination of right confers an objective reality to right as positive law.[4] In fact, most of our contemporary theories of the legal system are based on a mind/body dualism, where obedience to the law ultimately stems from the evidentness or self-presence of legal norms to the legal subject's power of reason.[5]

The mind/body dualism is fundamental to the ways in which human subjectivity has been understood since the earliest origins of our culture. The body is unruly and requires the direction of reason to regulate it. Since men and masculinity are most commonly characterised as creatures of reason, while women and femininity are commonly associated with 'irrational' corporeality,[6] the mind/body polarisation has historically functioned hand-in-hand with the ways in which the relations between the sexes are conceived and particularly, with the social, cultural and legal homogenisation of women's specificities into models produced by and functioning in the interests of a universalism that disguises its affinity with patriarchy. As Irigaray has convincingly argued,[7] it is patently unjust to talk of women's access to equal privileges, rights and responsibilities and to their equal access to the law in terms of disembodied, abstract or universal human or civil rights. These rights, and the laws formulated to ensure them, neutralise women's particular and differential social roles, reducing them to terms which have been formulated by and are relevant to men alone. This is perhaps most starkly represented in the law's inability to differentiate the position of the battered wife, who after a period of being terrorised, kills her husband, from the position of the male murderer who may well occupy the same broad social position as his victim. Thus far, the law cannot or has not been able to acknowledge the role of bodily specificity in the social positioning of (sex, race, class) subjects in different relations to legal institutions and practices.

Over the past two and a half decades, much critical legal theory has moved towards the promotion of equality which recognises sexual and racial diversity. These affirmations of corporeal specificity have sometimes explicitly endorsed a reversal of the mind/body opposition. This is especially so in the United States[8] where some theorists have suggested that the perfect embodiment of justice is to be found in a Law with a polymorphous body, capable of containing multitudinous differences.[9] Such a vision of law computes openness to difference as an aggregation of different, self-present identities, an endless series of 1+1+1+1.[10] Note however, that in the argument for diversity, the bodily specificity of different identities is taken to be self-evident in the experiences of the subjects themselves. The reversal of the mind/body opposition in most legal theories of difference thus remains within the conceptual parameters that articulate the opposition in the first place: self-evidence and self-presence. Effectively, the self-presence of the Cartesian *cogito* as universal mind has been relocated in the self-present body. This is the corollary to the sub-division of universal truth into partial truths. Consequently, in most legal theories of difference, violence is an external force which acts to distort and compromise bodily differences which exist in a state of wholeness and peace outside historical violence. Thus, legal violence is said to occur when the law fails to accommodate these embodied differences, and legal reason is urged to be more self-reflective about its own particularistic interests and more caring and understanding about specific 'others' in the name of justice. Effectively, legal reason is urged to incorporate the body into its self-evident norms.

However, theorising the body as a self-evident subject or object which legal reason should incorporate in order to be just, engenders its own unfortunate impasses. Consider, for instance, the curious status of the body in Zillah Eisenstein's exemplary solution to the sameness/difference debate. The argument that sex equality must recognise differences is, Eisenstein writes, as dangerous as it is ethically imperative because New Rightists and neo-conservatives can also use differences as a reason to reject the concept of equality.[11] In the dominant frame of legal discourse, Eisenstein continues, difference and equality are mutually exclusive concepts. On the one hand, a recourse to a notion of real differences in nature between the sexes can lead to legally sanctioned discriminatory treatment because 'discrimination . . . is only illegal or unconstitutional when the classes being compared are similarly situated'.[12] On the other hand, equal rights legislation or legislation for equal protection under the law is premised in a vision of equality which assumes that women are the same as men. Any invocation of the *Equal Rights Amendment* cannot, for instance, take into account the specific sex characteristics of pregnancy in relation to sex equality.[13]

Eisenstein's exemplary solution to the problem of how to think equality within difference is to think of sexual difference as pure heterogeneity. She posits a distinction between a merely oppositional difference and a truly heterogeneous difference which is now commonplace in feminist legal theory. This distinction hinges on an ambivalent separation of sex as a biological category from gender as the cultural interpretation of biological existence.[14] On the one hand, since phallocratic law reduces a woman's biological potential to her determined function, Eisenstein must refute the biological justification for sexual inequality. Hence, she argues that sex and gender exist in a relation of relative autonomy. However, Eisenstein also realises that she cannot consistently maintain the separation. For in order to mount an argument *for* the legal recognition of sexual specificity, she also needs to insist that, notwithstanding its violent effects, gender difference points towards a more heterogeneous difference.[15] Here, Eisenstein connects sex and gender through the intermediary of discourse. As an interplay between ideality and materiality, discourse interprets a pre-existing materiality and also constructs it through the frame of interpretation. Eisenstein suggests that legal discourse produces gender difference by interpreting a prior heterogeneous difference through a gender-hierarchical frame.

Eisenstein's political argument for specificity maintains the relation between sex and gender in such a way that while the two terms can be *factually independent*, they should be *normatively* linked in a continuous relation between a material ground and non-distortive ideational constructions of that ground. As such, her argument implies three inter-related axioms about the sexed body. First, the sexed body is, in the original instance, a simple self-identical substance. Second, this self-identical substance exists outside power. Third, this substance is an exterior origin of non-violence that can be grasped by reason as the goal for normative transformation.

Our reading of Eisenstein must seem strange given that she explicitly espouses the thesis that discourse produces or constitutes reality since this thesis does not allow for an exterior location of truthfulness which is independent of power. However, Eisenstein actually attenuates this thesis into the weaker version that discourse only partially constitutes the real. Even as she suggests that 'there is no such place as outside [society, history and language], even for the body',[16] she makes a normative distinction between existing reality as it is constituted by the categories of the human mind and an ungraspable ontological state prior to the structuring of human reality by value-laden categories. Sexual difference as opposition is true to the extent that it is a dominant discourse-universe. But it is also false because it is not the truth of sexual difference as heterogeneity in an ontological sense.[17] Implicitly, Eisenstein presumes a phenomenological access to an ontological plurality, a kind of original intuitive self-reflexive state of being-in-the-body that is precategorial, prelinguistic, and can therefore serve as a normative ground for the political retrieval of true difference before the law. She also implies that justice is achieved when embodied reason is coextensive with the law.

Eisenstein's solution is exemplary of the way in which legal theories of difference attempt to resolve the problem of opting for either difference in nature or equality/sameness in culture. The point we want to make is that such an argument remains marked by a residual philosophy of the free causality of embodied will. Indeed, as we suggested above, it is confined within the parameters of a reversed mind/body split because it conceives of justice in terms of a truth-grasping and self-reflective will that knows its own bodily limits.

The general weakness of such arguments is that the possibility of resistance and institutional change can only be explained dogmatically; in terms of the self-evidence of the norms of Justice (recognition of heterogeneity, respect for known differences etc.) which recriminate a repressive Law. Indeed, the dissociation of justice from power, force or violence, unintentionally replicates a fundamental feature of analytical jurisprudence: the coextensivity of normativity with reason. Hart's attempt to replace a coercive vertical relationship between commander and commanded with the idea of a rule of law hinges on a structural link which he posits between the normative force of a rule and rational activity as the critical process of justification. Similarly, despite his criticism of Hart for ignoring moral fidelity to law, Lon Fuller also characterises moral obligation in the same terms that Hart uses to describe legal obligation. For Fuller, the principles of critical morality are self-evident and self-justifying because they are internal to reason.[18]

This self-critical awareness—in Eisenstein's case, the awareness of one's bodily specificity—must be lodged, however provisionally, in some outside-of-power. The political hope is that its norms will become principles of the legal system. Yet, as Eisenstein realises, the problem is that this exterior location can only be a nebulous and naive fiction: 'if the body is already engendered in this way, how can we claim our bodies without reproducing the inequities of the gender-system? . . . [S]o we become involved in explicating patriarchal relations without knowing where patriarchy begins and ends in the definition of a woman's or a mother's body. What aspect of the body constitutes a woman's potential capacities, and what part articulates her oppression?'.[19]

Eisenstein's impasse indicates that we should think the violence of the law more broadly, as a constitutive and constituting violence that must be interminably negotiated instead of a contingent accident that self-critical reason can escape. Such a questioning of the rationalist paradigm for justice in arguments for bodily specificity before law need not lead to irrationalism, nihilism and the prison-house of power if we break the time-honoured link between justice and self-knowledge outside violence. We make the counter-proposition that justice and the law may be understood not as functions of the mind but as functions of the body. Alternatively, if we wish to maintain the link between law and the mind, we might see the mind itself as an effect of the social inscription of the body; where a psychical interiority is generated from the habitation of the body.[20] The law may be understood as an effect of contingent social configurations which inscribe the body and generate a rational force that will in turn legitimate these configurations in rational-teleological terms. The next section of this paper explores the internal conjunction between violence, law, bodies and subjectivity. In the concluding section, we revisit Foucault's thesis of productive power to suggest that the structural co-implication of our bodies with legal institutions and violence in general is the condition of possibility of justice.

The law, violence and the body

Any theory of substantive justice based on self-critical legal reason must come to terms with Robert Cover's provocative claim that the definitive characteristic of the act of legal interpretation is its necessary connection to physical violence. 'Legal interpretation', Cover writes in his opening sentence, 'takes place in a field of pain and death'.[21] In view of the standard definition of law as a justification for the use of collective power against individual citizens or groups,[22] we might be inclined to understand Cover as saying that an act of legal interpretation may result in the imposition of violence. Cover, however, suggests a more profound link wherein violence is constitutive of the meaning of law itself.

He argues that for law to be able to justify state coercion, it must first presuppose an institutional context which translates the linguistic act of legal interpretation into the physical actions of others in a predictable way. Analytical jurisprudence sees this translation as being effected by a self-conscious and rational acceptance of the grounds of law because of their rational or, in some cases, moral force. Rejecting this rationalist explanation, Cover argues that the chasm between legal thought and action can only be bridged by organised structures that overcome our socio-cultural and moral inhibitions against the infliction of violence on others. First, for a judge or official of the law, the meaning of an act of legal interpretation is generated by a context of domination instead of being immanent in the word of the law. Second, the rational acceptance of the interpretation as meaningful on the part of subjects before the law also takes place within distinct roles prescribed by effective social organisation or control. Cover describes this structure as a reciprocal bond:

> [N]either effective action nor coherent meaning can be maintained, separately or together, without an entire structure of social co-operation. Thus, legal interpretation is a form of bonded interpretation, bound at once to practical application (to the deeds it implies) and to the ecology of jurisdictional roles (the conditions of effective domination). The bonds are reciprocal. For the deeds of social violence as we know them also require that they be rendered intelligible—that they be both subject to interpretation and constrained forms of behaviour that are 'roles'. And the

behaviour within roles that we expect can neither exist without the interpretations which explain the otherwise meaningless patterns of strong action and inaction, nor be intelligible without understanding the deeds they are designed to effectuate.[23]

Consequently, law as a mechanism of state-organised social control exists in an irresolvable tension with the interpretive, meaning-generating side of law. This view of law explicitly refuses the equation between law and rational human freedom conceived as a state of non-violence. Instead, it suggests that in order for law to be an instrument of rationalised violence, it must first of all be a productive force which, operating through an effective institutional setting and social preconditions which it also produces, confers meaning upon each subsequent negative exercise of juridical violence.

However, Cover is not a legal nihilist who analyses law's violence as evidence of might being right. For Cover, the violence of law is not, in the original instance, a historical violence, it is ontological. The link between violence and the law is based on a philosophy of meaning and worldhood which emphasises the primacy of contingency. For Cover, the meaning-making aspect of law exists because law is a world-building activity, a response to the fact that we live in a contingent cosmos.[24] 'Law is the projection of an imagined future upon reality'.[25] Its 'institutions create the context for changing the contingent to the necessary'.[26]

While this thesis can also ground the most dogmatic of humanisms, Cover stresses its darker side: the bonds that hold together a shared normative universe or *nomos* are necessarily violent because they are established by a projective imposition of ideality onto materiality. Cover's most vivid synecdoche for law is the body of the martyr under torture. However, the figure of the body in pain does not suggest that legal violence is a species of repressive historical violence. On the contrary, the body under torture is a paradigmatic example which discloses the general structures of ontological violence:[27]

> Precisely because it is so extreme a phenomenon, martyrdom helps us see what is present in lesser degree whenever interpretation is joined with the practice of violent domination . . . Martyrdom . . . reminds us that the normative world-building which constitutes 'Law' is never just a mental or spiritual act. A legal world is built only to the extent that there are commitments that place bodies on the line. The torture of the martyr is an extreme and repulsive form of the organized violence of institutions. It reminds us that the interpretive commitments of officials are realized, indeed, in the flesh. As long as that is so, the interpretive commitments of a

community which resists official law must also be realized in the
flesh, even if it be the flesh of its own adherents.[28]

Cover urges us to remember that as *nomos*, law is a world-
building activity. However, in a contingent cosmos, the production
of communal meaning involves the risk of pain. In the first
instance, the violence of world-making occurs in the making of
the legal body. Insofar as Cover sees violence as the condition of
possibility of law in general, the very essence of law, his is a kind
of transcendental argument. It has two fundamental implications.
First, the violence of law is not a contingent accident that befalls
humanity from outside but inheres in all attempts for creating a
shared reality. The crucial point is that this violence cannot
subsequently be rationalised by communal norms because pain is
incommunicable and cannot be shared. This violence of the production of meaning circumscribes all claims to meaning.[29] The
organised violence of institutions opens up the space of historical
violence and non-violence because it is only within this organised
space that we have learnt to condemn acts of oppression. But this
opening also undercuts all forms of meaning-making or community because pain cannot be shared. We cannot not desire a world
of shared norms or rules of legitimation. Yet, the making of such
a world always already involves violence. Both domination *and*
resistance to domination, as types of world-building activity, are
founded on an ontological violence which tragically circumscribes
their success.
  Second, law in general as ontological violence is a constitutive
force which shapes the material processes of embodiment into the
body of a human individual capable of sociality and ethics. Since
this force is theoretically prior to both individuality and sociality,
we cannot see it as the causal effect of an agency external to the
body, for instance, reason or culture. This would beg the question
of how reason and meaning is produced in the first instance. There
is not, on the one hand, law, and on the other, bodies which are
objects to be disciplined. It would be more appropriate to speak
of law in general as an originary and inhuman violence operative
in embodiment and which is subsequently appropriated into
human action and explained in terms of social causes. Violence
in this sense is not the consequence of an instrumental force
unleashed by a human agent. Instead, a founding violence at the
level of the body stands at the origin and limit of the law. Cover
frames each legal decision of right and wrong in the radical
uncertainty of original violence.
  This alternative view of the relation between violence, the body
and the law is very different from the mind/body dualism

presupposed by rationalist legal theory. It has strong points of similarity with Nietzsche's view of the role of body in the creation of social organisation and systems of justice. For Nietzsche, the body is a major force in the production of knowledge and truth while at the same time, the object of social coercion and control required for the operations of a rational, religious or secular culture. Nietzsche's conception of the body is active and productive. Both at an organic or cellular level, and as a total, integrated organism, an animal, the body is the source and site for the will to power and the movement of active (as well as reactive) forces.[30] Knowledge and power are, for Nietzsche, the results of the body's activity, its self-expansion and self-overcoming. The will to power involves a struggle to survive, to grow, to overcome itself on the level of cells, tissues, organs, where the lower order bodily functions are subordinated to and harnessed by higher order bodily processes and activities (the brain being considered the highest).[31] The forces and energies comprising the body are made up of micro-wills which struggle amongst themselves for supremacy.[32]

Nietzsche suggests a parallelism between the organic and the subjective: just as the subject is a multiplicity of forces, so too, the organism is not singular and unified. It is a series of interacting and conflicting energies which struggle among themselves, gain dominion or become subordinated through the dominance of others. The unity (of either subject or body) is the result of the cruel suppression or subordination of the multiple conflicting forces. For Nietzsche, these organs, bodily processes, muscles and cells neither yield knowledge nor even error but generate and necessitate interpretations, perspectives, partial and incomplete acquaintance, which serve its needs in the world, and which may enhance its capacity and hunger for life. They enable the organism to function in the world. The will to power is the drive towards self-expansion, the movement of becoming, for it increases the body's quantity and quality of forces and energies, a drive towards 'vigorous, free, joyful activity'.[33]

Instead of seeing the body in terms of the mind/body distinction, or regarding it as a substance to which various attributes, like consciousness, can be added, Nietzsche sees it in terms of a political/social organisation in which there is a kind of chaos of whirling forces, defined in terms of their quantities and intensities more than in terms of distinct characteristics. These forces or energies (at both the levels of organic and inorganic matter) are divided into dominant or active, and subordinated or reactive forces. Active forces care for and concern themselves with only their own wellbeing and expansion; reactive forces, by contrast, give primacy to active forces, finding their principle of action outside themselves. The active forces, inside and outside the body, are noble and aristocratic, for they govern, they expand. Reactive forces are not weaker than active ones (on the contrary, they tend to overpower active forces and convert them into reactive forces); they are slavish insofar as they are adapted towards the active forces, reacting to their initiative and impetus.

Given the plasticity and mobility of active forces, and given that these forces are not governed by or directed towards pre-ordained objects, the body itself must be seen as a pliable and potentially infinitely diverse set of energies, whose capacities and advances can never be predicted. In this sense, Nietzsche's conception directly inherits the tradition propounded by Spinoza in his assertion that we do not know, cannot know, what the body is capable of doing or achieving. The body's capacity for becoming cannot be known in advance or charted, its limits cannot be definitively listed. The body itself, in its micro-forces is always in a position of self-overcoming, the expansion of its capacities. Out of the chaos of active and reactive forces comes a dominating force that commands, imposes perspective, or perspectives. Consciousness can be regarded as the direct product or effect of reactive forces in the governance of the body. Consciousness is a belief, an illusion, a convenient fiction, on the one hand useful for life; on the other hand, an effect of the inwardly inflected, thwarted will to power or force that, instead of subduing other bodies and other forces, has sought to subdue itself.[34] The subject's psychical interior or soul can be seen as nothing but the self-inversion of the body's forces, the displacement of the will to power's continual self-transformation back onto the body itself: in this sense, there is and has always only ever been body. Consciousness, soul or subjectivity are nothing but the play of the body's forces that have congealed into a unity and are endowed as an origin. The body's forces and instincts are not simply part of nature or essence, they are entirely plastic, fluid, capable of taking any direction and any kind of becoming:

> All instincts that do not discharge themselves outwardly *turn inward*—this is what I call the *internalization* of man: thus it was that man first developed what was later called his 'soul'. The entire inner world, originally as thin as if it were stretched between two membranes, expanded and extended itself, acquired depth, breadth and height, in the same measure as outward discharge was *inhibited*.[35]

Consciousness or the psyche is a consequence of the modulations and impulses of the body. It is for this reason Nietzsche suggests that looking inward, as is ordained by introspection or psychology, self-consciousness or self-reflection, is both illusory and misleading. Illusory, because the psychical interior is in fact a category, project or product of the body that, for various reasons (grammatical, cultural, habitual), has been mistaken for mind; and misleading, insofar as self-reflection, the goals of self-knowledge mistake an effect for a cause, mistake an instrument or tool with its producer. For Nietzsche, knowledges in general are drives for mastery—consequences of the will to power. Bodies construct systems of belief and knowledge as a consequence of the impulses of their organs and processes. Among the belief systems that are the most pervasive, long-lived and useful are those grand meta-physical categories—truth, subject, morality, logic—which can all be read as bodily strategies or resources which contribute to the will to power. For example, to posit a doer beyond the deed is a useful or enabling fiction, a fantasy that helps to explain the body's drives to expansion, to life, to joy.

By describing reason as a product-effect of bodily forces out-side the rational/irrational opposition, Nietzsche's idea of the will to power is similar to the original violence of law as *nomos* intimated by Cover. Nietzsche argues that to establish sociality, the active forces of the body need to be rendered reactive, turned back on themselves, to produce subjects which are obedient, civil and law-abiding beings. This occurs primarily through rendering the body obedient by the inscription of the law. *On the Genealogy of Morals* outlines the rudiments of an account of body-inscription as the cultural condition for establishing social order and obedi-ence. Nietzsche locates morality and the law in the mythical origins of culture in the ability to make promises, to keep one's word, to propel into the future an avowal made in the past or present. This ability is dependent on the constitution of an inte-riority, a moral sense, a will. The ability to make promises involves renouncing forgetfulness, at least in part and in spite of interven-ing events. It is the ability to put intention or commitment into action and this requires the institution of a counter-forgetfulness.

Nietzsche's insight is that pain is the element crucial to insti-tuting memory. Civilisation comes about only by branding the law on bodies through a *mnemonics of pain*, a memory fashioned out of the suffering and pain of the body:

> . . . 'If something is to stay in the memory it must be burned in: only that which never ceases to hurt stays in the memory'—this is a main clause of the oldest (unhappily also the most enduring) psychology on earth. One might even say that wherever on earth solemnity, seriousness, mystery and gloomy coloring still distinguish the life of man and a people, something of the terror that formerly attended all promises, pledges and vows on earth is *still effective*

> . . . Man could never do without blood, torture, and sacrifices
> when he felt the need to create a memory for himself; the most
> dreadful sacrifices and pledges (sacrifices of the first-born among
> them), the cruelest rites of all the religious cults and all religions
> are at the deepest level systems of cruelties—all this has its origin
> in the instinct that realized that pain is the most powerful aid to
> mnemonics.[36]

The degree of pain inflicted, Nietzsche suggests, is an index of
the poverty of memory: the worse memory is, the more cruel are
the techniques for branding the body. It is as if the skin itself
served as a notebook, a reminder of what was not allowed to be
forgotten. Where this procedure is internalised to form what is
known as conscience, the less pain or sacrifice is required. The
unforgettable is etched on the body itself:

> The worse man's memory has been, the more fearful has been the
> appearance of his customs; the severity of the penal code provides
> an especially significant measure of the degree of effort needed to
> overcome forgetfulness and to impose a few primitive demands of
> social existence as *present realities* upon the slaves of momentary
> affect and desire.[37]

The establishment of a memory is the key condition for the
creation of social organisation, economic and contractual relations
and systems of justice. Nietzsche suggests that economic and social
relations function only if the relation that bonds debtors to
creditors is founded on some sort of contractual guarantee which
ensures that debts, in some way or other, will always be paid.
The presumption founding economic, social and judicial relations
is that every debt and obligation has an equivalence, in the last
instance, between the debt owed and the pain the creditor can
extract from the debtor. The cost or price of an unkept promise,
an unpaid debt, an act of forgetfulness—is the debtor's pain. This
system of equivalences, which is very often carefully codified in
terms of the precise value of body organs and intensities of pain,
is, for Nietzsche, the foundation of legal systems. The explicit
means that law uses to achieve such an equivalence is punishment.
This equivalence ensures that, even in the case of economic
bankruptcy, the debt is still retrievable from the body of the
debtor; in some sense at least, the debt can always be repaid.
Nietzsche cites a number of examples from Roman law where
damages are not measured by equivalent, substitutable values, as
occurs in economic exchange, but by the extraction of organs,
parts, forces and energies from the debtor's body.[38]

This is clearly a system of recompense through socially and
juridically sanctioned cruelty. Contrary to legal idealisations which

based contractual connections on a prior system of justice, Nietzsche argues that both are founded on blood, suffering and sacrifice. The equivalence of the pain caused to the debtor and the amount owed on the debt is the formula of the social contract. Any contract is thus ultimately founded on a kind of bodily collateral. Contrary to Levi-Strauss, the social order is not founded on exchange but on credit: on the rule that, at bottom, the body can be made to pay, to guarantee. The injury caused by the failure to keep promises, to pay off debts, to remember to what one is committed, is rendered commensurate with the degree of pain extracted from the body. This equivalence is possible, and is founded on the prior equivalence of the degree of suffering (of the debtor) with the degree of pleasure in causing suffering (for the creditor)—a kind of primitive, aristocratic urge to sadism.[39] For Nietzsche, this debtor–creditor relation and its lust for cruelty is a figure for the basis of all other social relations, moral values and cultural production. Morality and law share a common genealogy in barter and cruelty: memory, social history, cultural cohesion are branded onto the flesh.[40]

Although a system of cruelty and coercion—the mechanics which institute trust, faith and a common bond between individuals who share a culture—stands at the (mythical) origins of civilisation, the advances of civilisation are themselves no less cruel or corporeal: there has been a kind of social sublimation, a desensualisation and a series of refinements to these processes of social engraving of the law on bodies but it remains more or less a requirement of the social capture of the will to power. The law today is no less corporeal, no more absolutely just or fair than it has ever been; nor is it necessarily any kinder or more humane. In Nietzsche's words:

> Perhaps the possibility may even be allowed that this joy in cruelty does not really have to have died out; if pain hurts more today, it simply requires a certain sublimation and subtilization, that is to say, it has to appear translated into the imaginative and psychical and adorned with such innocent names that even the tenderest and most hypocritical conscience is not suspicious of them.[41]

Cover's argument was that obedience to the law could not be understood outside of a context of historical domination. This context of domination which makes legal interpretation effective is a manifestation, at the level of history, of the ontological violence intrinsic to law as such. In a contingent cosmos, there is no shared meaning without the risk of pain, an experience which cannot be shared by its victim and its perpetrator. Hence, 'as long as people are committed to using or resisting the social

organisations of violence in making their interpretations real, there
will always be a tragic limit to the common meaning achieved'.[42]
Nietzsche provides a philosophical elaboration of ontological violence as the corporeal inscription which produces the social
individual. The Nietzschean model of corporeal inscription can be
read as describing the requisite moments of law in general as
world-building. The so-called rational force of law, the moment
of enlightenment or legitimation, is first of all the pain that passes
through and in-forms the materiality of the body. It is this
productive moment which incarnates the law through its iterability
in determinate bodies to constitute the consciousness of a subject
before the law. If we understand the processes of body-inscription
as literal and constitutive, then law is neither simply a coer-
cive/repressive force nor simply a rational force. Outside of and
making possible that opposition between coercion and reason, law
is a productive force which is exercised in a positive way to
produce bodies as the instruments of rational subjects or agents.

The law of the body: productive power, resistance and justice

We have suggested that the violence of law should be seen as an
original violence, a quasi-transcendental condition of possibility
of inhabiting a world. The obvious polemical contrast is with
rationalist accounts of legality and civil society which posit a
fictive contract affirmed by rational consent. In such accounts,
law is seen as an instrument of pre-existing rational beings and
the legal use of coercion is rationally justified. These rationalist
theories of legal obligation are not simply wrong since, when
pushed to be reflective, people constantly explain their everyday
relations to the law by such means. We have simply asked how
this state of affairs is possible. In other words, how is a determinate body which possesses rational agency and which can have
access to positive legality constituted? Hence, our quasi-transcendental argument should also be distinguished from accounts which
see violence as a consequence of the entry of the body into society,
a variety of the social construction thesis.

In his essay, 'Tools for Body-Writing', Michel de Certeau
argues that juridical inscriptions constitute the body as part of
social or collective order, regularising and normalising it, structuring the broad category of subjectivity required in particular
epochs.[43] Subjects are not preformed while legal and medical
institutions work upon them as separable entities: rather, subjects
are constituted as such through their necessary enmeshment in
these and other social institutions. Body-writing constitutes bodies

as networks of meaning and social significance, producing them as meaningful and functional 'subjects' within social ensembles. For de Certeau, flesh, a raw formless materiality is transformed through corporeal inscriptions (juridical, medical, punitive, disciplinary) into a distinctive body capable of acting in distinctive ways, performing specific tasks. Bodies are positioned by various (religious, familial, secular, educational, etc.) narratives and discourses to become emblems, tableaux of social laws and rights, illustrations and exemplifications of law, forming and rendering pliable flesh into determinate bodies. The subject is marked as a series of inscriptions from/of the social. Its flesh is transformed into a *body* organised and hierarchised according to the requirements of a particular social and familial nexus. The body can then be read as an agent, a labouring, exchanging being, a subject of social contracts, and thus of rights and responsibilities.

In de Certeau's model, the body, preconstituted in nature, is transcribed and marked by culture. He posits a carnality or flesh outside of or prior to inscription. Flesh is a point of departure and a locus of incision, a prior point of 'reality' or 'nature', the raw material of social practices. De Certeau conceives of this intextuation of bodies as the meeting of limits imposed from two directions. On the one hand, there must be a certain resistance of the flesh, a residue of its materiality left untouched by the body's textualisation; and on the other hand, the limit imposed by the inability of particular texts or particular languages to say or articulate everything. The non- or pre-inscribed corporeality of the flesh is an 'inarticulate, unthought suffering',[44] something which resists determinate production because it remains unthought.

This type of explanation is certainly more helpful than a theory of ideology because it explains the inculcation of social values and domination as a movement of the text into the body and the body outside of itself and into socio-cultural life. However, as resistant materiality, de Certeau's unthinkable carnal substance is a negative version of the recognisable corporeal differences invoked by the argument for specificity we saw in Zillah Eisenstein. It is inadequate for the same reasons. Both justice and resistance are seen in terms of the rational recuperation of a simple and full òutside-of-violence, a transcendent exteriority. Consequently, when figured into the location of justice, this transcendent substance outside violence is simply a relay of history-transcendent legal reason. It is forgotten that because we always already inhabit a normative world or desire to realise other normative worlds, all rational-normative grounds for legitimation and transformation which we posit are already product-effects of structures of violence. This point has important ramifications for the project of affirming

specificity in legal theory. In the sameness/difference debate, the
normative element of sexual specificity is asserted as obvious to
self-present reason. However, since bodies are always historically
sedimented, violence occurs in the very production of determinate
self-identical body-types. Bodily identity is never static, never in
self-possession but a gift; given by a relational field of value which
shifts in each and every situation. This means that the self-evidence
of specific embodied identities qua normative ground for legal
transformation can never be taken for granted. As the critique of
feminist legal theory by women of colour indicates, we can never
be sure that the body-types of 'woman' and 'person of colour',
as determinate categories for legal redress, do not in turn exclude
women of colour. As Nitya Duclos wisely writes, 'renegotiating
feminist identity starts by learning to accept some humbling truths:
namely that "everybody wants difference but nobody wants any-
body to really be different" and that we all have the capacity to
dominate as well as the capacity to be dominated'.[45]

But does our critique of rationalist legal theory, including legal
theories of difference, lead to irrationalism and nihilism? This
question appears to have two aspects. First, if we are already
constituted in ways which are implicated in structures of violence,
then how is resistance possible? Second, how can legal transformation be justified by normative criteria if normativity is
coextensive with violence? The first question leads us to Michel
Foucault's sustained critique of a juridical account of power and
resistance. The second question involves retheorising justice.

Foucault's critique of a juridical concept of power is most often
interpreted as a historicist argument about a shift from the right
over death to a power to actively foster life through a micro-
political regulation of the body.[46] He has sometimes been read as
a theoretician of the prison-house of power in disciplinary or
carceral society. We want to suggest, however, that it is misleading
to focus exclusively on the *oppressive* aspects of the capillary
coding of power in Foucault because this results in a diffusive
expansion of juridical power into a virtual prison-house that
infiltrates every level of social life. This interpretation, we suggest,
mistakenly conflates two separate levels of Foucault's argument.

For Foucault, a theory which primarily locates resistance in a
critical and oppositional consciousness struggling against an
oppression imposed from outside is inadequate for two reasons.
First, it is descriptively inadequate because the capacity for rational calculation and decision-making in political critique is already
a product of disciplinary power:

[T]he individual is no doubt the fictitious atom of an 'ideological' representation of society; but he is also a reality fabricated by this specific technology of power that I have called 'discipline'. We must cease once and for all to describe the effects of power in negative terms: it 'excludes', it 'represses', it 'censors', it 'abstracts', it 'masks', it 'conceals'. In fact, power produces, it produces reality; it produces domains of objects and rituals of truth. The individual and the knowledge that may be gained of him belong to this production.[47]

This aspect of Foucault's argument is generally used to support the prison-house of power thesis. However, Foucault's suggestion that 'disciplinary coercion establishes in the body the constricting link between an increased aptitude and an increased domination'[48] does not entail a state of absolute oppression or the loss of any capacity for struggle and resistance. To the contrary. The new economic formation of capitalism requires an increased aptitude in the populace at large, prior to and alongside of, the extraction of this aptitude as labour-power through subjection. As a result, power-structures become tangibly relational because they always already invest the body to constitute it as productive.

Indeed, Foucault's second point is that a relational mode of power actually allows more room for resistance. This is because the micro-structures which subtend and produce *economic* oppression pass through the bodies of the subjected in ways that cannot be fully accounted for. In an interview-response to the suggestion that he tries to make power all-seeing, Foucault states this point succinctly:

> Power is not omnipotent or omniscient—quite the contrary! If power relationships have produced forms of investigation, of analysis, of models of knowledge, etc., it is precisely not because power was omniscient, but because it was blind, because it was in a state of impasse. If it is true that so many power relationships have been developed, so many systems of control, so many forms of surveillance, it is precisely because power was always impotent . . . In other words, I was putting forth the hypothesis that there was a specificity to power relationships, a density, an inertia, a viscosity, a course of development and an inventiveness which belonged to these relationships and which it was necessary to analyze.[49]

Foucault's objections to a juridical view of power are simultaneously hopeful and sobering. An analysis of power which stresses relationality makes visible the prolific sites of possible resistance. Our bodies are the medium through which power functions. By virtue of their location within power, our bodies are also effective sites of resistance to power's capillary alignments. Since law is an effect of a stasis of power-relations, the structural co-implication of power and the body in the securing of legal obligation and obedience is the source for persistent and hopefully thorough-going legal transformation.

But by the same token, the focus on relationality also warns us that our critical strategies of emancipation are constituted and inscribed within power and are hence always of limited value, always in a certain way, blind. Because power-knowledge frames doing/knowing in radical undecidability, resistance needs to be rethought as an interminable practice. We can only ever know (how to) act/do within a pre-given but ungraspable field of power-knowledge relations. This field of forces constitutes 'us' as well as 'them' against whom we resist. In the final analysis, power-knowledge as a field of immanent and shifting force-relations is unmotivated. It is inaccessible to both cognitive mastery and practical intentional control. By virtue of this uncon-trollability, power is also the origin of resistance to oppression, the paradigmatic case of absolute control at an institutional level. In the first volume of *The History of Sexuality*, power as a field of forces is something which can only be named catachrestically because it can only be descriptively isolated in its dissimulation. Power can only be objectified through its inert states or codings, the institutional forms which are its mere effects.[50]

By suggesting that disciplinary power produces an individual body which is 'natural and organic',[51] Foucault clearly rejects the philosophical presuppositions of arguments of embodied specific-ity in much political legal theory. To claim an embodied givenness outside of law and violence as a site from which to reproach the law in the name of a more sensitive justice is to disavow the investment of the body by networks of power-knowledge, even as the stuff of one's embodiment is constitutively enabled by it. Foucault explicitly urges us to abandon 'the opposition between what is interested and disinterested, the model of knowledge and the primacy of the subject'.[52] However, abandoning the philo-sophical premise of a self-reflective embodied will does not entail rejecting its validity or urgency as a product-effect with a capacity to calculate legal norms which are more tolerable in a given situation. Foucault does not reject the necessity of political calcu-lation. Calculation inevitably takes place with reference to self-present criteria that pertain to the states of power inevitably engendered by the unequal nature of force-relations. Instead, his caution is against the dogmatic assertion that such criteria can be absolutely self-justifying because they escape the non-egalitarian force-relations which constitute them in the first place.

The capacity for resistant political calculation is also intermi-nably framed by the incalculable force-field of power-knowledge.

Like the aims and objectives of power, the goals of resistance do not arise in the first instance 'from the choice or decision of an individual subject'.[53] They are given or immanent in the complex strategical situation of a specific socio-historical moment. At a subsequent level, these goals are rationally formulated, seized and acted upon by social agents, subjective unities which are themselves the effects of power.[54] Foucault's thesis of productive power explains the inevitable failure of resistant political reason, where failure is not perjorative since it is also resistance to political totalisation. It tells us that instead of fossilising specificity into determinate body-types, we need to examine how different (sexed, raced, classed) identities are determined by and within each given power-situation and what mechanisms enable them to step into a court of claims.

But if Foucault elaborates the capacity or 'how' of systemic political change, his analytical focus obscures the normative aspect of legal transformation from the standpoint of legal institutions and bodies before the law. Foucault seems to have overstated his case against 'the system of Law-and-Sovereign' with the consequence of de-emphasising the productive role of law's legitimating function. He seems not to have explored the vulnerability of the law qua norm-generating mechanism in terms of why legal transformation is possible. He seems to be evading the possibility that the contamination of law and power is bi-directional, that the coding of power by the law also transforms the field of power. Our point is that although law is only a provisional localisation of the network of power-knowledge, the passage of power-relations through its institutions and apparatuses will also alter the field of power and this will lead to a transformation of the strategic power-body nexus.

Indeed, because political calculation always takes place within a given situation, it must negotiate with the normative criteria that invest the force field of knowing-doing. For example, the concept of individual human rights is a legal principle that informs the way we think about and deploy our bodies. Such concepts are not teleological ideals which have an absolute validity because they are produced within the strategic field of power relations which we inhabit. Nonetheless, the point is not to simply condemn these legal principles as essentialising fictions by an act of willed choice but to acknowledge the usefulness of their conditioning power on our ability to act/know, even as we admit that these concepts are themselves limited and conditioned. Hence, we might argue that because legality is concerned with legitimation and the production of rational meaning through the body, the empire of legal reason must try to accommodate all types of bodies. Anti-discrimination and equal rights legislation and case law, as well as essays in critical legal studies, feminist legal discourse and critical race theory which have made their way into prestigious law journals, are all indices of this.

In any event, we began with the question of how an ethical affirmation of specificity was possible that was not just a dogmatic assertion of the need for specificity which characterises the sameness/difference debate. How, in other words, can we retheorise responsibility to specificity if bodily identity is itself produced by structures of violence? The issue of normativity is crucial here. Touching on the Hart-Fuller debate, we suggested earlier that regardless of whether it is theorised as immanent or transcendent, normativity has always been posed in terms of self-present reason. From this perspective, Foucault's failure to consider the normative aspect of law is analogous to Cover's argument that ontological violence is an unerasable 'tragic limit to the common meaning that can be achieved'.[55] Cover founders on the question of normativity because he subscribes to a theory of justice where normativity is intimately tied to rational understanding between subjects. For Cover, the violence intrinsic to the making of the legal body is antipathetic to normativity because pain cannot be shared with or made significant to the other, and hence, disrupts the norm- or community-generating aspect of law. Such a theory of justice is rationalist because it presupposes that the normativity of law cannot be thought outside a coextensive relation with self-present reason.[56] As Austin Sarat and Thomas Kearns put it, 'violence and law can never adequately and satisfactorily be reconciled. They are social facts in opposition that no amount of theoretical ingenuity can harmonize'.[57] Similarly, Foucault's justification of his failure to consider the normativity of law in terms of his critique of juridical concepts of power also indicates an equation of normativity with rational understanding or a realm of truth outside of power.

The violence of embodiment can, however, have an ethical significance if we shift ground and rethink the limit of violence in terms which exceed the illusory search for self-presence outside violence. In her response to Robert Cover, Drucilla Cornell suggests that the important question 'is not whether or not there is intelligibility, but rather what figure the Good can take on after the deconstruction of foundationalist philosophy'.[58] It is interesting to observe that Cornell also responds to feminist critical legal theory with a friendly criticism. She argues that a feminist jurisprudence whose ideal judge should recognise their own perspective and the differences of others engages in a violation of justice. This is because such a position precomprehends a self-present idea of justice by assuming that we can fully realise the ethical relation in the sphere of law.

By way of contrast, the deconstructive idea of justice begins from a critique of ethical and legal philosophy which takes the subjective will and self-presence as its fundamental premises. It begins from the ineliminable fact that the otherness of the other is violated in its very appearance or presentation. The early Derrida speaks of this irreducible violence as the non-ethical opening of ethics, the relation with the other that violates the other in order to allow us to relate to it ethically.[59] The ethical or just relationship to the other, insofar as it must maintain the absolute singularity of the other in my relation to it, becomes an impossible relationship since relating to the other as an other present to and for me deprives it of its singularity. In the register of legal-juridical discourse, the relation to the Other passes through the universality of the law which interrupts the singularity of the face-to-face.

Consequently, Derrida thinks of justice as the ever-receding source of normativity, where normativity is an infinite responsibility to the absolutely other.[60] The crucial point here is that the otherness or exteriority to which such a limitless responsibility is owed is not a simple outside which is determinable by the intentional subject. It is an absolute exteriority that grounds the juridical subject which comes to be in response to this call from outside. However, the exteriority of the other is also not a simple and full outside which has no relation to the world of presence. Instead, it is a quasi-transcendental which is implied within the world of presence in its very effacement.

Given his interest in a deconstruction of the philosophy of the subject, the later Derrida figures this limit to self-presence as the aporetic discontinuity-in-continuity between justice and law. Justice is the impossible experience of absolute alterity, the normative source of persistent legal transformation which gives itself to us in its own violation as the law.[61] Given our interest in the need to rethink embodiment in view of the impasses of the sameness/difference debate, we want to suggest that this quasi-transcendental exteriority or otherness which constitutes the legal subject might just as well be the shifting processes which give us body and hence, embodied identity.

How might this be reformulated into an outline for a theory of corporeal justice? First, embodiment incarnates the ontological violence which characterises our relationship with the absolutely other. As such, embodiment is the site of the co-implication between normativity and violence. Cover intimated as much by locating ontological violence in the making of the legal body. My

body is therefore the way in which I exist in myself, only by being
at the same time, outside myself, because it is given by the other.
The space of my bodily finitude is how the infinite other places
me and is the place of my response. Hence, before and after
making possible the opposition between self and determinate
other, sameness and determinate difference, embodiment would be
the prepropriative site of difference as such. When we think of
ourselves as determinate subjects or bodies possessing rights
before the law, we cut ourselves off from the ongoing relations
which constitute us in the first place. Consequently, the normative
legal criteria we prescribe on such a basis must perforce fail to
take into account the changing nature of these relations which
might constitute us as determinate selves and others in a multiplicity of different ways which we cannot fully predict.

This violence is precisely the tragic limit of the *nomos* which
Cover described. However, the crucial difference is that for
Derrida, the relation to the Other which passes through universality is not in a simple antagonism with the relation which
protects the otherness of the other. Both are in an aporetic
embrace. We can only relate ethically to the other by violating its
otherness and the call to be ethical demands this risk:

> Do not these two relations imply each other at the moment they
> seem to exclude each other? Does not my relation to the
> singularity of the Other as Other pass through the law? Does not
> the law command me to recognize the transcendent alterity of the
> Other who can only ever be heterogenous and singular, hence
> resistant to the very generality of the law?[62]

Hence, for Derrida, the blindness of the universal law to the
singularity of difference as such, the irreducibility of ontological
violence in the founding of the law, constitutes the normative
source of persistent legal transformation, the locus of a justice
that is always yet to come. Posed in this way, transformation is
neither the recovery of a state of peace outside social, cultural or
institutional violence nor the development of our social and
political institutions towards the regulative ideal of perpetual
peace. Instead, transformation involves a limitless responsibility
towards the ineliminable ontological violence which inheres in our
corporeal being-with-others.

On the other hand, justice also requires us to think of the
other as a determinate other, or other self in order for us to relate
to it justly. In Drucilla Cornell's succinct words, 'Derrida
demonstrates that ethical asymmetry must be based on a phenomenological symmetry if it is not to be reduced to another excuse
for domination and, thus, for violation of the Other'.[63] Here,

THE BODY OF THE LAW

embodiment is the site of the relationship between ethical asymmetry and phenomenological symmetry because in the mundane everyday of embodiment, each body is constituted and valued relationally with respect to other bodies. The specificities of each body, the particularities or singularities that subjects in their social constellations are, need to be accounted for if the law is to adequately address the major social differences that still divide culture according to male and female, black and white, indigenous and emigrant, and bourgeois and working class categories. A theory of corporeal justice would demand that we account for differences in the bodily make-up of subjects before the law, even as and because the *a venir* of our embodiment strains the limits of empirical knowledge.

The double gesture of corporeal justice which we have described in the most general terms needs to be fleshed out in each and every situation before-the-law. Theoretically speaking, however, it involves, in some measure and with appropriate caution, an interchanging of difference in Derrida and power in Foucault, a supplementing of one philosopher with the other so that we can account for both the 'ought'/'should' and 'can' aspects of political and legal transformation. On the side of Foucault, a deconstructive thinking of justice helps us understand why resistance leads to transformation and why this transformation must be interminable. On the side of Derrida, the deconstructive arguments about justice can be analysed more empirically in terms of the networks of power/resistance that traverse the politico-legal subject and enable it to calculate in a specific strategical situation. Placing the body, rather than consciousness, intention or interiority in the centre of legal focus as we have done may help account for and perhaps even transform the existing social inequities which make an abstract system of law participate in and reproduce these inequities.

It has been suggested that the conventional icon of blindfolded Justice indicates perfect impartiality to both litigants, an attitude of separation and distance which does not regard potentially prejudicial phenomenal differences between subjects before the law.[64] The affirmation of specificity and diversity in contemporary legal theory attempts to lift the blindfold, to be sensitive to phenomenal differences and to recognise varying embodied needs. We have suggested why this might be inadequate. For us, embodied justice is blind because it never inhabits the self-present identity of legal reason but subsists in the ever-shifting relation to indeterminable alterity which characterises a legal reason that is corporeal.

2   Spinoza, law and responsibility
Moira Gatens *

... it is a question of knowing whether relations (and which
ones?) can compound directly to form a new, more 'extensive'
relation, or whether capacities can compound directly to constitute
a more 'intense' capacity or power. *It is no longer a matter of
utilisations or captures but of sociabilities and communities.* How
do individuals enter into composition with one another in order to
form a higher individual, ad infinitum? How can a being take
another being into its world, but while preserving or respecting the
other's own relations and world? And in this regard, *what are the
different types of sociabilities,* for example? *What is the difference
between the society of human beings and the community of
rational beings?*[1]

What would be involved in thinking, with Spinoza, through the
body of the law? One could think through the *human* body
understood as the object of the law. Then again, one could
understand law as the means through which the *civil* body
expresses its own self-understanding, or in Spinoza's terms, its
own endeavour to preserve itself. In any case, when one thinks
with Spinoza one cannot approach questions of 'the body' or 'the
law' without first distinguishing types of body and types of law.
Deleuze's comments, above, concerning types of sociability will
provide the *leit motiv* of this chapter: Spinoza is worth considering
in this context because of the manner in which he contrasts the
sociability of compatible bodies with other forms of association,
for example, those built on *utility* or *capture.* Traditional accounts
of the formation of societies tend to focus on the utility of persons

for one another and the capture (of the powers and abilities) of persons by others. Moreover, such accounts typically conceive of law as a coercive instrument of social control.

Spinoza 'writes' the body and the law on an immanent register which accommodates, without contradiction, multiple forms of sociability: associations built on superstition, tyrannies grounded in fear and hope, communities of rational individuals, societies bound by the ties of friendship. None of these forms of sociability contradict the deceptively simple claim that the right 'of every individual thing, [including its right of existing] extends as far as its power'.[2] This seems an unlikely starting point for a philosopher whose major work is titled *Ethics*. It will be necessary to offer some account of his understanding of bodies, rights and powers before considering his thoughts on law and ethics. The first two sections of this chapter will consider Spinoza's notions of the body and law, respectively. The third and final section will present an understanding of the civil body as a locus of responsibility.

What is a body?

The originality of Spinoza's account of the manner in which bodies are composed and decomposed can be thrown into stark relief by recalling Descartes' explanation of the distinction between death and life:

> . . . the body of a living man differs from that of a dead man just as does a watch or other automaton . . . when it is wound up . . . from the same watch or other machine when it is broken . . .[3]

This thoroughly mechanistic conception of the body has led to insoluble problems at the level of accounting for that strange hybrid which is human being. According to Descartes, all that exists does so under one of two radically distinct substances, thought and extension. Human being, thus radically divided within itself, is composed of a free soul whose essence is to think and a determined body whose essence is to be extended. The unity of mind and body cannot be rationally demonstrated but rather is 'experienced'.[4] Such 'experience' involves the soul's suffering the actions of the body and the body suffering the actions of the soul. Action in one equals passion in the other with soul and body incapable of acting or suffering in concert. It is not difficult to see the compatibility between Cartesian dualism and the legal notion of *mens rea*, along with exceptions to this rule. That soul (mind) that freely forms an intention to perform an evil act is deemed guilty of, that is, responsible for, that act. Exceptions to

this law include insanity and diminished responsibility. Such con-
ceptualisations of responsibility or guilt rely heavily on a Cartesian
view of the subject.

By contrast, Spinoza argues that there is only one substance,
which is single and indivisible; body and mind enjoy only a modal
existence and may be understood as 'expressions' or modifications
of the *attributes* of substance, that is, extension and thought,
respectively. Human being is conceived as part of a dynamic and
interconnected whole:

> . . . we have conceived an individual which is composed only of
> bodies which are distinguished from one another only by motion
> and rest, speed and slowness, ie., which is composed of the
> simplest bodies. But if we should now conceive of another,
> composed of a number of individuals of a different nature, we
> shall find that it can be affected in a great many other ways, and
> still preserve its nature. For since each part of it is composed of a
> number of bodies, each part will therefore (by L7), be able,
> without any change of its nature, to move now more slowly, now
> more quickly, and consequently communicate its motion more
> quickly or more slowly to the others. But if we should further
> conceive a third kind of individual composed of this second kind,
> we shall find that it can be affected in many other ways, without
> any change of its form. And if we proceed in this way to infinity,
> we shall easily conceive that the whole of nature is one individual,
> whose parts, ie., all bodies, vary in infinite ways without any
> change of the whole individual.[5]

The human body is understood by Spinoza to be a relatively
complex individual, made up of a number of other bodies. Its
identity can never be viewed as a final or finished product as in
the case of the Cartesian automaton, since it is a body that is in
constant interchange with its environment. The human body is
radically open to its surroundings and can be composed, recom-
posed and decomposed by other bodies. Its openness is both a
condition of its life, that is, its continuance in nature as the same
individual: '[t]he human body, to be preserved, requires a great
many other bodies, by which it is, as it were, continually regen-
erated';[6] and of its death, since it is bound to encounter bodies
more powerful than it which will, eventually, destroy its integrity
as an individual—though such destruction always and necessarily
implies further compositions, distinct from the first. Such encounters with other bodies are good or bad depending on whether they
aid or harm our characteristic constitution.

The human body, like every other animate body, does not owe
its power of movement to either an inbuilt automatic mechanism
or a mysterious soul-substance which can will movement in the

body. Rather, the human mind expresses under the attribute of thought '. . . the idea of a singular thing which actually exists', that is, '[t]he object of the idea constituting the human mind is the body, or a certain mode of extension which actually exists, and nothing else'.[7] The complexity of any particular mind—and Spinoza does not deny that animals have minds—depends on the complexity of the body of which it is the idea.

As Hans Jonas has observed, Spinoza's account of the mind and body offers, for the first time in modern theory, 'a speculative means . . . for relating the degree of organization of a body to the degree of awareness belonging to it'.[8] Reason is thus not seen as a transcendent or disembodied quality of the soul but rather reason, desire and knowledge are embodied and dependent, at least in the first instance, on the quality and complexity of the corporeal affects. There is no question of mind/body interaction here since '[t]he body cannot determine the mind to thinking, and the mind cannot determine the body to motion, to rest or to anything else'.[9]

Descartes' attempt to account for mind/body interaction through the 'occult hypothesis'[10] of the pineal gland is not the only casualty of this monistic conception of human being. Spinoza also rejects outright that which this hypothesis assumes: a soul possessed of free will. The will and the intellect are not considered by Spinoza to be separate faculties, rather '. . . there is no volition, or affirmation and negation, except that which the idea involves insofar as it is an idea'.[11] Nature in all its aspects is governed by necessary laws and human being, no less than the rest of nature, is determined in all its actions and passions, contrary to those who conceive of it as 'a dominion within a dominion'.[12] The fundamental and determined desire of any existing body is its endeavour to persevere in its existence. Such endeavour or striving, Spinoza names *conatus*. Deleuze indicates the complexity of this notion in the following terms:

> . . . the *conatus* defines the *right* (*droit*) of the existing mode. All that I am determined *to do* in order to continue existing ,(destroy what doesn't agree with me, what harms me, preserve what is useful to me or suits me) *by means of* given affections (ideas of objects), *under* determinate affects (joy and sadness, love and hate . . .)—all this is my natural right. This right is strictly identical with my power and is independent of any other ends, of any consideration of duties, since the *conatus* is the first foundation, the *primum movens*, the efficient and not the final cause . . . The rational man and the foolish man differ in their affections and their affects but both strive to persevere in existing according to

these affections and affects; from this standpoint, their only
difference is one of power.[13]

This passage makes clear the gulf which separates Descartes and
Spinoza. For Spinoza, body and mind *necessarily* suffer or act in
concert. For, '. . . in proportion as a body is more capable of
doing many things at once, or being acted on in many ways at
once, so its mind is more capable than others of perceiving many
things at once'.[14] An increase of power in the body, has as its
necessary correlation, an increase in the power of the mind, and
vice versa. Nor does an individual who thrives indicate a will that
is both free and enlightened, but rather indicates the determinate
power of that particular thing to maintain itself in existence and
to combine with those things that agree with and enhance its
power. Human freedom, though not free will, amounts to the
power that one possesses to assert and extend oneself in the face
of other (human and non-human) bodies that strive to do likewise.
On this ethical stance, virtue cannot be reduced to the cultivation
of good habits, but rather concerns the power of any particular
individual to continue in its existence. All bodies (including non-
human bodies) possess this virtue, though to varying degrees.
Human virtue is qualitatively distinct from the virtue of other
things insofar as it concerns the endeavour to increase one's power
of existing in accordance with reason, which is a specifically
human power. For Spinoza, human being is determined by the
exercise of such reason in pursuit of that which it understands to
increase its power.

Where does this leave legal and moral responsibility? If all our
actions are determined, then how can we be held responsible for
them? It is this issue, more than any other, that earned Spinoza
the titles of immoralist and atheist. Spinoza maintains that the
notions of right and wrong, just and unjust can arise only in a
polity. Hence, any notion of responsibility for particular actions
can arise only in the context of a complex civil body.

If one examined Spinoza's view of the human individual in
isolation one would be confronted by an individualistic ethical
theory of extreme egocentrism. However, one cannot make sense
of Spinoza's philosophy—which is deeply opposed to all forms of
anthropocentricism—if one privileges the human body. Since a
large component of the striving of any body is its necessary
relations with other bodies, human striving, like all striving, seeks
to join itself with that which increases its power (hence Spinoza's
definition of joy)[15] and destroy those bodies that decrease its
power of acting (hence Spinoza's definition of sadness).[16] This is
why Deleuze understands Spinozistic reason, at its most funda-

mental level, as '. . . the effort to organize encounters on the basis of perceived agreements and disagreements' between one body and the next.[17] This effort to select or organise our encounters leads to the formation of associations or sociabilities between bodies of similar or compatible powers and capacities: that is, it leads human beings to society. As will be argued at the close of the section on Law as command versus law as knowledge, Spinoza's account of the formation of *types* of sociability implies historically and culturally variable conceptions of reason. This view of reason is another important departure from Descartes, who applied the same method in the ethico-political realm that he elsewhere applied to optics and science: 'there cannot be more than one opinion which is true' and in relation to civil life he further remarks that '. . . the single fact of diversity among states suffices to assure us that some states are imperfect'.[18] Diversity in legal and moral codes, from this perspective, is inevitably a sign of error. Spinoza, on the contrary, offers a perspective from which to think through difference and embodiment in terms other than error or notions of cultural superiority and inferiority.

Spinoza does not define human being as essentially *homo socius*. He claims, on the contrary that '. . . men are not born fit for citizenship, but must be made so'.[19] Human beings come to form associations not because of an inherent sociability but rather because in pursuing their own preservation and their own increase in power they come to see that by joining with or conquering other human bodies they increase their power and hence their right, since 'each has as much right as he has power'.[20] Such associations, in other words, are formed indirectly (through the pursuit of something which is perceived as good) rather than directly. It is only within such associations that human beings may develop their power of reason and justice. This is because '. . . nothing is forbidden by the law of nature, except what is beyond everyone's power'.[21] Hence, '[w]rong is conceivable only in an organized community . . .'[22] and '. . . justice and injustice cannot be conceived of, except under dominion'.[23] It is only in civil society that human being can strive effectively and directly to increase its peculiar power: understanding, or reason, which entails a power of *selecting* encounters with others. And it is in civil society only that human freedom—conceived as an increase in one's power to act rather than be acted upon—is possible.

However, insofar as Spinoza's account of the emergence of civil society is based on hope and fear and threats, it is not markedly different from the better known accounts of social contract theory, for example, Hobbes. In order to see what the Spinozistic view contributes to the notion of responsibility and the manner in which that notion is tied to his notion of civil society, attention needs to be paid both to his peculiar conception of law and its relation to bodies and powers.

Law as command versus law as knowledge

In *A Theologico-Political Treatise*, Spinoza treats divine (or natural) law, ceremonial law, and civil (or human) law.[24] Each of these occupies a special role with reference to his epistemology. The three kinds of knowledge (corresponding to imagination, reason, and intuition) outlined in the *Ethics*,[25] find their analogues, though not in a one-to-one relation, in his typology of law.

Spinoza understood it to be a source of great confusion, and the cause of considerable human misery, that natural law is so frequently understood on the model of law as command or decree. He insists that natural laws, whereby 'all things exist and are determined' are impossible to break, change or disobey, since they 'always involve eternal truth and necessity'.[26] It is the imagination only which grasps god as a lawgiver and punisher.[27] As one commentator explains:

> there is no law intrinsic to nature that is not the law of god, since god is taken as coextensive with nature . . . it is impossible to speak of events or behaviour as obeying or not obeying the natural law. Rather this law is the actual nature of the entity itself, the actual order of the occasion, which entity and occasion are manifestations of god's nature.[28]

This adequate understanding of natural law concerns knowledge of the second kind, or reason, and far from such necessity representing a limit on our freedom, it is, according to Spinoza, the very condition of such liberty.[29] It is the illusion of free will, which is then projected onto an anthropomorphised nature, which obscures the freedom that we do possess: that is, the freedom to understand our situation and, on the basis of such understanding, act to maximise our power and our joy.

Civil law concerns '. . . a plan of life laid down by man for himself or others with a certain object', that is, '. . . to render life and the state secure'.[30] Such laws will not be universal and will both reflect and contribute to the reproduction of the particular historical, religious or national character of different peoples. Above all, the laws of any given civil body will reveal the historical and continuing basis of such complex associations. In contrast to natural law, human or civil law is able to be understood as command or decree but in a limited sense only. This sense concerns both the virtue or power of the state and Spinoza's conception of volition as inseparable from particular modes of understanding.

Civil law may be understood as command, though not in the sense often assumed by philosophers of jurisprudence. A sovereign or a state cannot command or decree anything at all, without qualification.[31] There is for Spinoza no absolute right of rule. This has some very interesting consequences for determining whether or not the state is exercising its power responsibly. As Cairns has pointed out, 'Spinoza shows that there is an inescapable connection between power and its proper exercise'.[32] Spinoza conceives of the state as a complex body that must possess a degree of self-knowledge if it is to persevere in its own existence.[33] The sense in which the state can exceed the proper exercise of its power is tied, precisely, to its continuing existence as a state. As Belaief argues: '[i]f anything lacks the power to function according to its essential nature, it can no longer be said to participate as the SAME thing in reality. This is as true for an individual law as it is for an entire legal system, as true for an individual man as it is for the state'.[34]

From this basis, one could argue that a state that exercises its power to enslave, oppress or exploit its population will be inferior in kind to a state that exercises its power in order to expand the capacities of its citizens. In this connection consider the distinction Belaief draws between Hobbes and Spinoza: 'In Hobbes' view there is no distinction between force and power with respect to the sovereign; in Spinoza's view force must be guided by reason if it is to become power.'[35] It is important to recall here that power *is* virtue for Spinoza. He writes '. . . civil jurisprudence depends on the mere decree of commonwealth, which is not bound to please any but itself, nor to hold anything to be good or bad, but what it judges to be such for itself'.[36] The ambiguity in the last phrase—'nor to hold anything to be good or bad, but what it judges to be such *for itself*'—is a telling one. If something is bad for it then the virtue of the state dictates its avoidance, just as every individual strives to seek that which it thinks is good for it and avoid that which is harmful. This understanding of the state entails an inherent, if self-imposed, curb on state power: the avoidance of those decrees, commands or enactments that will certainly lead to its harm or ruin. Thus, Spinoza is entitled to assert that '. . . he who holds dominion is not bound to observe the terms of the contract by any other cause than that, which bids a man in the state of nature to beware of being his own enemy, lest he should destroy himself'.[37]

The second sense in which the power of the state is limited

concerns Spinoza's particular understanding of volition, that is, he denies that the intellect and the will are separate faculties. He could not then be a proponent of the command theory of law in the same sense as, say, Hobbes or Austin.[38] Again, this feature of Spinoza's jurisprudence offers a means of determining the excellence, or otherwise, of any particular state, since its particular decrees or commands are manifestations of its own self-understanding. The will of the state, for Spinoza, can be no more arbitrary than the will of the individual; in both cases that which the body wills is determined by its relative virtue or ignorance. Again, Belaief makes this point succinctly:

> . . . since [on Spinoza's account] law is held to be a product of will this is tantamount to having it as a product of thinking and judging . . . the will of the sovereign, that is, laws, are not consecrations of the sovereign's desires but rather the ideas which he affirms. The goodness or badness of the laws will depend on whether these affirmed ideas are adequate or inadequate, true or false.[39]

These checks on sovereign power are interesting for two reasons. First, the notion that bad governments are responsible for their own ruin, common in political and legal theory, takes on an extra dimension in the context of Spinoza's philosophy. Bad government is also responsible for bad citizens. Spinoza argues that the raison d'etre for civil society and the laws it institutes concern the establishment of peace and security *in order that* both the minds and the bodies of citizens may be developed to their highest degree. On this basis Belaief argues that one may distinguish between a good law and a bad law in terms of its tendency either to aid '. . . an individual in the fullest development of his powers or virtues'[40] or to fail to '. . . aim towards aiding the development of men's powers'.[41]

Those who would claim Spinoza as an early proponent of liberal political philosophy must turn a blind eye to a crucial difference between him and liberalism. Spinoza does not allow the existence of any special rights to property or the person prior to civil life. The sovereign, on Spinoza's view, does not exist to enforce pre-civil moral, personal or property rights. Consequently, Spinoza's sovereign has a much greater responsibility to, and for, its citizens than on the liberal view. Spinoza's rejection of the existence of a priori rights or justice, places responsibilities on the civil body which go much further than its acts of omission, for example, the failure to provide protection for its citizens. Such a rejection places the onus of responsibility on the civil body for acts of commission also, that is, the actual behaviour and values of the citizens, since their morality is largely derived from and dependent on the particular laws of that state.

Second, because of the profound effect that laws have on the character of a people,[42] the ideas which the sovereign affirms become embodied in the population and perpetuated by social institutions. Further, if the social understanding of law as command is promulgated, it will have an inhibiting effect on the development of the capacities of citizens since obedience is not knowledge and can, at best, only imitate knowledge.[43] For Spinoza, it is the distinction between grasping law as arbitrary command and law as knowledge that marks the difference between human freedom and human bondage. If one understands the law as those ideas affirmed by the sovereign body for its preservation, and if one obeys the law, not to avoid punishment but because one understands and pursues the preservation of civil society then one acts *directly*.[44] If, however, one obeys the law from fear of punishment or hope of reward then one is under the external control of another and so in bondage. One acts only *indirectly*, in order to avoid some evil. Nothing follows from the second sort of acting, which is, strictly speaking, not an action at all but a passive reaction to an outside authority which is recognised as being more powerful than oneself. Hence, a state that encourages obedience without understanding will be one whose citizens are incapable of either acting or expanding their powers of acting. By Belaief's reasoning, this would be a bad government with bad laws. Those who act in the first manner, that is, directly, would constitute a community of rational beings, those who (re)act in the second manner, that is, indirectly, can easily become a society of slaves.[45] (This view of the law and civil society obviously begs the question in relation to those who are disadvantaged by civil arrangements, for example, indigenous peoples, women, and others. Some consideration will be given to this question in the next section, Toward a concept of embodied responsibility.)[46]

Such an analysis offers grounds for understanding, in its strongest possible sense, Spinoza's claim that the state has a duty to develop the minds and bodies of its citizens. As he says, in the section on freedom of thought and speech, in A *Theologico-Political Treatise*:

> . . . the ultimate aim of government is not to rule, or restrain, by fear, nor to exact obedience, but contrariwise, to free every man from fear, that he may live in all possible security; in other words, to strengthen his natural right to exist and work without injury to himself or others. . . . the object of government is not to change men from rational beings into beasts or puppets, but to enable them to develop their minds and bodies in security, and to employ

their reason unshackled . . . In fact, the true aim of government is liberty.[47]

This contrast between obedience and knowledge is certainly one way in which we could distinguish between an association of human beings founded upon fear and a community of rational beings. What would be the differences in the civil bodies and laws of each type of sociability? A state whose peace depends entirely on punishment will produce a particular type of sociability—a weak sociability that is built on sad passions, in particular, upon fear. However, a state that conceives and enacts punishment as 'just dessert' is arguably even more harmful than one that concerns itself with utility, since such a state validates and gives free reign to the most malignant passions by encouraging the worst excesses of revenge, hatred and cruelty. Such a state is arguably not performing its ultimate function as Spinoza conceived it: the increase of the capacity of its citizens to act, that is, freedom. Here we must disagree with Yovel and others who maintain that Spinoza lacks a dynamic or historical account of reason.[48] Moreover, Spinoza's historical appreciation of the dynamic nature of human capacities must be both extensive and intensive in the sense Deleuze implies in his comments cited at the beginning of this chapter. On Spinoza's view, the democratisation of sovereignty would inevitably bring about both an extensive and an intensive development of the capacities and powers of its citizens. However, the democratisation of sovereignty will inevitably alter the material composition of the sovereign body, along with the ideas which it affirms. Present notions of justice and fairness will sit less and less comfortably with ideas of the past that have become institutionalised in law and other social practices. The civil body becomes ill-at-ease with itself as institutionally embodied traditions and orthodoxy clash with the desire for change in various domains of social life, for example, relations between women and men, the treatment of minorities, and so on.

Upon what can a philosophy of immanence call in the task of evaluating its values? Evidently, one cannot go beyond the present and actual world—including its possibilities, its contradictions and tensions. As Yovel says:

> . . . human life is neither static nor repetitive, the ethical universe, too, assumes various faces and is open to change . . . The vehicle of these changes is human desire, embodied in actual life and practice and structured by social habits and institutions in which tradition and change, orthodoxy and revolt both play their respective parts.[49]

In the following section it will be argued that Spinoza's conception of human and civil bodies offers the rudiments for a new way of evaluating social habits, institutions and ethical responsibility.

Toward a conception of embodied responsibility

There are many senses in which a notion of embodied responsibility could be understood. Two disclaimers may assist to distinguish the Spinozistic position from others. First, Spinoza should be distinguished from contemporary versions of communitarianism. Community attitudes, for all their diversity, tend toward conservativism when it comes to the place, status and capacities of women and other so-called minority groups. Recent philosophical attempts to return to traditional notions of community-based virtue ethics are at their weakest on the question of women.[50] Second, Spinoza's position should not be conflated with a noblame individualistic determinism, such as that practised by the American attorney Clarence Darrow in the 1920s and 1930s. Individualistic determinism cannot explain, for example, men's disproportionate representation as the perpetrators of violent crimes and women's disproportionate representation as victims of violent crimes.[51]

How does a deterministic view such as Spinoza's treat the issue of individual responsibility? This is an issue which worried several of Spinoza's correspondents, including Blijenbergh, Oldenburg and Tschirnhausen. The latter two questioned both Spinoza's notion of necessity and his dismissal of free will, claiming that such notions 'excuse wickedness' and render 'rewards and punishments ineffectual'. Spinoza's responses are brief and to the point: '[h]e who goes mad from the bite of a dog is excusable, yet he is rightly suffocated'[52] and '[w]icked men are not less to be feared, and are not less harmful, when they are wicked from necessity'.[53] What more, then, can this view offer us here? I do not believe that it has very much to offer at the level of the individual. An analysis that limits itself to the individual and her or his affects cannot be any more coherent on Spinoza's view than the notion of just dessert. He does not accept the immortality of the soul nor the absolute existence of good and evil, or right and wrong. Civilly sanctioned moralities will be historically and culturally variable. This is simply to say that the meaning of human actions as well as the moralities of individuals are not *sui generis* but rather are developed in particular historical and political contexts. This, of course, creates great difficulty for those who would wish for a single locus of responsibility. If the reading of Spinoza offered here has any value then it lies in the claim that a community of rational beings would assume some responsibilty for its particular constitution. Such an assumption would draw attention away from the punishment of individuals and toward the social and structural causes of such behaviour.

If one accepts the reading of Spinoza offered here then one must also accept the notion that a rational civil body should take some responsibility for the acts committed by its citizens. Criminal acts are wrong or unjust, according to Spinoza, because they break the laws instituted to ensure civil peace. The breaking of such laws also breaks up the coherence, or the integrity, of the civil body. As this chapter was being written two cases of domestic murder were reported in a local Sydney paper on the same day. In each case a notion of embodied responsibility, incipient in Spinoza's philosophy of law, will be shown to be crucial to an adequate understanding of the actions of the individuals involved.

In the first case, Brian Maxwell killed his former wife, Marilyn Maxwell. He was in 'violation of a restraining order' as he waited outside the child-care centre where she worked, and he forced her into her car where he shot her three times. Outside the court which was hearing Maxwell's case, the dead woman's sister responded to a reporter's question concerning Maxwell's manslaughter plea by saying that if such a plea were accepted then '. . . it's going to give men . . . like Brian Maxwell a licence to kill their wives. Everybody who commits a crime could say at the time that they were in the wrong state of mind. Everybody could say that, surely.'[54]

In the second case, Steven Helsby killed his stepfather, David Helsby, by stabbing him through the throat with a carving knife while he slept. During Steven Helsby's trial the jury heard evidence from his mother, Mrs Helsby, that her husband '. . . had beaten her with brooms and metal rods, chained her up under the house in winter, punched her, sexually abused her, burnt her and choked her until she was unconscious'. Despite taking out a domestic violence restraining order several months before the stabbing and despite an attempt to leave her husband and go to a refuge, he had violated the restraining order, traced her to the refuge and brought her back home where the abuse had continued.[55]

These are particular cases which undoubtedly would have their own peculiar histories, nevertheless they share features in common with similar cases which one can read about reasonably frequently in the newspapers. The pertinent question here concerns the nature of the civil body from which such acts arise. Historical and present attitudes toward relations between men and women, husbands and wives, parents and children are writ so large in these cases as to be initially indecipherable. The history of women's tentative association with the civil body is, I suggest, germane to these incidents. In Australia it is not yet twenty years since the Family Law Act was amended to allow so-called 'no-fault' divorce and it is overwhelmingly women who are now filing for divorce. The relatively new powers of the Family Court are clearly resented in some sectors of the community. In the early 1980s the court was bombed and one Family Court judge was shot and killed at his home. Large sections of the community do not support recent family law legislation that recognises women's civil right to live as they see fit and to be protected from violence and rape in the domestic as well as the public sphere. It is important to note that both husbands, in the cases cited above, acted in defiance of the Family Court. In each case the existence of restraining orders were completely ineffective in protecting the women involved. Both husbands could be seen as grotesque caricatures straining against the changing civil status of women by attempting to uphold the law of coverture. Like all caricatures they capture a truth in and through their very distortion.

What would it mean to argue that these 'caricatures' capture a truth concerning dominant social habits, practices and beliefs— in short, that they capture something about social attitudes to marriage that are embodied in our civil existences? Women have not historically been entitled to protection from the civil body. Rather, the civil body had extended protection to its citizens, who as (male) heads of households were expected to provide protection for their wives in return for service and obedience. Marilyn Maxwell's sister's comment, above, captures something of the unease many feel in these sorts of cases. Her comment prods at the question I would like to raise here: what do these cases tell about the civil and private structures which underpin these incidents? Why does Marilyn Maxwell's sister think that to accept Maxwell's plea of manslaughter would give 'men . . . like Brian Maxwell a *licence* to kill their wives'? Unlike the judge in Maxwell's case (who appeared to agree with the sister), the court had no hesitation in accepting David Helsby's plea of manslaughter. Presumably this is partly because his act was construed as protecting his mother—something the civil body was patently unable to do—in the only manner that seemed possible: to destroy the cause of her suffering.

Punishing individual offenders in these cases does not address the underlying causes of such behaviour. An understanding of these underlying causes would need to confront the type of sociability in which we participate. This would involve, in turn, some recognition of the manner in which the history of our civil body has become embodied in our laws and other institutional practices. With reference to Deleuze's comment at the beginning of this chapter, it would mean recognising that the modern civil body was instituted by and for a particular politico-economic group of men and explicitly excluded women (and others). The relation of that body to women's powers and capacities was one of capture and utility rather than one of combining to form a sociability or ethical community *between* men and women. Of course, similar points could, and should, be made concerning indigenous peoples, working class men, and others.

What would a civil body have to be like in order to be capable of accepting responsibility for its embodied history and the affects of its citizens? A civil body whose principle of sociability is based in reason should be capable of undertaking an analysis of the history of its traditions and its institutions—an analysis, that is, of how we became what we are. Such analysis needs to face and acknowledge the brutality of some of our past laws as well as past treatment meted out to women and other non-enfranchised groups. So long as the law continues to treat the criminal as an aberrant individual or a monster and as the sole locus of responsibility, our civil body will continue to structure human relations in ways which systematically encourage violence. What is required is an analysis of women's historical and present relationship to citizenship, that is, a study of the specific conditions of women's civil existence. This would have to include attention to the marriage contract,[56] social arrangements for child rearing, women's economic status, as well as the connections between these. In short, the structural problem concerns how to bring women *fully* into civil society. Again, Spinoza makes a pertinent point here. If a democratic civil body is to provide all its citizens with safety and security then it must ensure a concordance, or harmony, among its various members [57] Harmony depends, above all, on an agreement in power, which in this context means civil power (or right).

Spinoza's largely neglected political and juridical theory offers a novel perspective from which to begin to think through the body of the law. This perspective should be of interest to those concerned to discriminate between different sorts of sociability without appeal to transcendent moral or crypto-theological categories. It offers an ethical stance without reducing ethics to a universal system of moral rules and so does not have pretensions to universalism. It provides a means by which one may value a sociability which has its basis in a community of rational beings, over one based on capture and utility, at the same time as showing the difference in attitude of each type of sociability toward notions of ethical and legal responsibility. A community of rational beings would look to the structural, as well as to the immediate, causes of violent behaviour and assume responsibility for such causes where appropriate—for example, attitudes to women that are embedded in the customs and laws of the civil body. Perhaps then, the construction of men as essentially violent, or of the criminal offender as a distinct species, would be understood as symptomatic of our ignorance concerning the type of body complex of which we are a part. Such an understanding would, in turn, be the harbinger of the death of a type: the intrinsically and wilfully evil criminal.

By contrast, societies which are predominantly governed by sad affects are those which expiate 'the sins of the people' by sacrificing the proverbial scapegoat. One of Freud's favourite anecdotes illustrates that the retributive urge is not only vengeful but neurotic. He liked to tell the '. . . comic story of the three village tailors, one of whom had to be hanged because the only village blacksmith had committed a capital offence'. The point of the story being that '[p]unishment must be exacted even if it does not fall upon the guilty'.[58] This response involves a certain *mésalliance* between the affect and its cause, that is, we are dealing with a response that is, in Spinozistic terms, based on the imagination or the first kind of knowledge. Again, it is Freud who offers a rather Spinozistic account of this phenomenon:

> We are not used to feeling strong affects without their having any ideational content, and therefore, if the content is missing, we seize as substitute upon some other content which is in some way or other suitable, much as our police, when they cannot catch the right murderer, arrest a wrong one instead.[59]

This approach suggests an interesting understanding of certain sorts of 'mob' sentiments and attitudes toward those accused of violent and disturbing crimes. There is no dearth of such examples in the present: Australia, England and the United States have all recently experienced instances of angry mobs gathering outside courthouses and police stations carrying primitive rope nooses and calling for the death penalty. These are affective responses to alarmingly violent incidents of child murder, rape, and so on. Presumably the specific causes of the affects of the individuals which make up the crowd are diverse (fear, guilt, shame, horror, envy). It is likely, for example, that men and women would have quite different underlying causes for their angry responses to rapists or sex-specific murderers. However, the focus here is on the affect of the mob. Whatever the particular individuals concerned may feel, the group affect is hatred toward that which they perceive to be the cause of their sadness or pain.

The irony of this hatred shown by mobs, often to those merely accused as well as to those convicted of violent or shocking crimes, is that it mirrors the very affects which gave rise to the crime itself: hatred and frustration arising from lack of power. To be consumed by the force of such affects entails that one need not consider the causes of the behaviour that result in rape, murder, violence. Since the guilty one is separated out from the rest of the community—exiled—he or she is no longer considered a part of the body that condemns him or her. This is one way in which the social body can absolve itself of responsibility for the acts committed, since between the criminal and us a distance and a difference has been created. It is this fabricated difference that contributes to the marked fascination/repulsion that so many, encouraged by the media, appear to have for serial killers or those convicted of particularly violent or shocking crimes. The frequent finding of such media exposés is that, according to neighbours and acquaintances, the so-called 'monster' was a quiet, polite 'ordinary sort of guy'. This ordinariness adds to rather than undermines his 'monstrosity'.[60] The spectacular cruelty of such crimes only serves to mask the underlying banality of a largely unchallenged *structural* cruelty in many of our social relations.

3 Mabo, difference and the body of the law

Paul Patton*

In *Mabo and Others v State of Queensland* (1992),[1] the High
Court of Australia affirmed the existence of a common law native
title which survived colonial settlement. For the first time, Australian law recognised a right to land—the ultimate source of
which lay in traditional ownership by indigenous peoples. By a
majority of six to one, the Court held that the plaintiffs, natives
of the Murray Islands off Cape York in the Torres Strait, were
'entitled as against the whole world to possession, occupation, use
and enjoyment of the lands of the Murray Islands', subject to the
overriding power of the sovereign State of Queensland to extinguish their title. The majority judges expressly refused to limit
their decision to the particular circumstances of the Murray
Islands, where the ownership of lands on which cultivation was
practised could be traced back through successive generations
prior to colonisation. Instead, they affirmed the survival of native
title as a general principle of Australian common law and suggested that its existence and extent should be ascertained by
reference to the laws and customs of the relevant indigenous
peoples, thereby rejecting the earlier view of mainland Aborigines
as nomadic people without proprietary relations to the land on
which they lived.

The Court also affirmed the power of the Crown to extinguish
native title by making grants of land. As a result, most property
rights will not be affected. The areas of Australia in which native
title might still exist are likely to be in remote and desert
regions, where the interests affected would be primarily those of

pastoralists and miners. Even so, the decision overturned what
had been the legal status quo with respect to the foundations of
Australian property law. It amounted to a judicial revolution in
respect of Aboriginal and Islander land rights. The *Mabo* case
raises a number of philosophical questions about the law, society
and justice. In particular, it raises questions about the role of
differences in social and political life, many of which have elsewhere been explored by feminist and post-structuralist theorists.
In what follows, I propose to pursue the question of the nature
and limits of the recognition of difference in this case. My aim is
twofold: first, to suggest that some aspects of post-structuralist
treatments of difference may help to clarify the *Mabo* debate.
Second, to suggest that *Mabo* provides a compelling test case for
such philosophical approaches to difference. After outlining the
grounds on which the *Mabo* decision recognises native title, I will
discuss difference in relation to the body of the law, and in relation
to the Australian body politic.

Intruders in their own homes

In its decision, the Court effectively overturned two principles
which, in the words of Justices Deane and Gaudron, 'provided a
legal basis for and justification of the dispossession' of the Aboriginal inhabitants of their traditional lands.[2] These included the
principle which underpins the application of English common law
to the colony of New South Wales, namely that the country was
effectively uninhabited prior to European settlement since the
indigenous inhabitants were a barbarous or unsettled people,
lacking any system of government or law. This was not, strictly
speaking, the legal doctrine of *terra nullius*. That term referred to
a doctrine in international law which provided one of the bases
for acquisition of sovereignty over a given territory. Under 18th
century international law, sovereignty could be acquired by conquest, cession or settlement, and while settlement had initially only
been justified in cases of truly uninhabited land, European practice
had extended the doctrine to allow 'settlement' of lands otherwise
occupied only by 'backward peoples'. Correspondingly, the view
became accepted in common law that when sovereignty was
acquired under this 'enlarged' notion of *terra nullius*, English law
became the domestic law of the colony since, by hypothesis, there
was no prior settled law in existence.

New South Wales has always been regarded as a settled colony.
Accordingly, this 'absence of law' or 'barbarian' principle became
the accepted legal basis for the importation of the common law

of England, and an implicit justification for the denial of Aboriginal ownership of land. Thus, a Select Committee of the British House of Commons on Aborigines reported in 1837 that their condition was 'barbarous' and 'so entirely destitute . . . of the rudest forms of civil polity, that their claims, whether as sovereigns or proprietors of the soil, have been utterly disregarded'.[3] This principle was given legal effect in a series of NSW judgements, beginning with the influential 1847 case of *Attorney-General v Brown* in which Stephen CJ asserted that 'the waste lands of this colony are, and ever have been, from the time of its first settlement in 1788, in the Crown', for the simple reason that there was 'no other proprietor of such lands'.[4] The principle was later endorsed by the Privy Council in *Cooper v Stuart* (1889). The apparent consequence of the failure to recognise Aboriginals as a people living in society and subject to law was that British settlement immediately extinguished their rights to land. In the words of Justice Brennan:

> According to the cases, the common law itself took from
> indigenous inhabitants any right to occupy their traditional land,
> exposed them to deprivation of the religious, cultural and
> economic sustenance which the land provides, vested the land
> effectively in the control of the Imperial authorities without any
> right to compensation and made the indigenous inhabitants
> intruders in their own homes and mendicants for a place to live.[5]

The absence of prior law principle is overturned by the High Court in *Mabo* on both empirical and jurisprudential grounds. It is rejected firstly as being based upon false assumptions about the nature of Aboriginal society at the time of colonisation. On this point, the Court followed the finding of fact by Blackburn J in *Milirrpum v Nabalco Pty Ltd* (1971), which established in law what had long been recognised by anthropologists and others, namely that Aboriginal societies did possess a system of laws.[6] Secondly, the principle is rejected as unjust 'by any civilised standard'. Justice Brennan speaks for the majority in suggesting that 'the common law of this country would perpetuate injustice if it were to continue to embrace the enlarged notion of *terra nullius* and to persist in characterising the indigenous inhabitants of the Australian colonies as people too low in the scale of social organisation to be acknowledged as possessing rights and interests in land'.[7]

The second principle which had hitherto sustained the non-recognition of any indigenous land rights in Australian law asserted that the acquisition of sovereignty carried with it the assumption by the Crown of absolute beneficial title to all land in the colony.

This was the prevailing interpretation placed upon Stephen CJ's statement in *Attorney-General v Brown* that the waste lands of the Colony are 'in the Crown'. It amounted to the view that, upon settlement, the Crown became more than just the source of all title to land in the colony, it became the owner of all land. As Brennan J points out, this view depended in part upon the preceding principle, which licensed the belief that there was in effect no other proprietor in occupation of the lands.[8] However, it also depended upon a failure to observe a distinction, drawn widely in both international and common law, between the Crown's title to a colony and the Crown's ownership of land within a colony. The majority judges drew attention to this distinction in order to separate common law real property rights from what is called the radical title to land assumed by the Crown upon settlement. Radical title is the underlying principle of the English system of real property law, ultimately derived from the system of feudal tenure. It is the basis of the Crown's power to grant property in land, and the foundation of Australian property law: 'a postulate of the doctrine of tenure and a concomitant of sovereignty'.[9] In rejecting the conflation of radical title and ownership, Brennan J affirms that 'it is not a corollary of the Crown's acquisition of a radical title to land in an occupied territory that the Crown acquired absolute beneficial ownership of that land to the exclusion of the indigenous inhabitants'.[10] As a consequence, he argues, the importation of English property law is of itself no obstacle to the recognition of indigenous people's interests in land.

The High Court decision in *Mabo* brings Australian law into line with the recognition of indigenous land rights in other common law countries such as New Zealand, Canada and the United States. In many respects, it remains a cautious accommodation between the rights of indigenous people and the interests of other land users. While it allows that native title may have survived in certain circumstances, it also reaffirms the right of the Crown to extinguish native title, thereby ensuring the continuity and stability of the system of land ownership which has evolved during the 200 years of European occupation. Indeed, only the existence of the *Racial Discrimination Act* 1975 prevents Crown authorities from continuing the past practice of expropriation without adequate compensation. Despite these limitations, the *Mabo* decision is an historic legal event. It overturns what had been assumed to be the law with respect to native title for over a century. It has radically altered the legal context of any future legislation or negotiation over Aboriginal and Islander land rights. It effectively changes the legal story of the dispossession of indigenous people. The fiction according to which settlement effected the instantaneous transformation of largely unoccupied and unowned land into English Crown property is now replaced by a story of piecemeal dispossession, as the Crown successively exercised its paramount power to grant parcels of land, thereby extinguishing native title. While the Court rejects the view that consent or compensation is necessary to ensure the legality of past expropriation of land, several of the judges refer to the injustice of the colonial dispossession of indigenous inhabitants. Such comments can only strengthen the political and moral case for compensation.[11]

For these reasons, and because of the subsequent year-long debate over the Federal Government's native title legislation (the *Native Title Act 1993*), *Mabo* has contributed to a widespread collective re-evaluation of the past treatment of indigenous peoples. It has given significant impetus to the political process of bringing about reconciliation between indigenous and non-indigenous Australians. Although not unrelated to the recent history of the land rights movement, the *Mabo* decision itself has greatly assisted the opening up of new legal and political possibilities. While not unaffected by recent developments in the law, international jurisprudence and Australian historiography,[12] the legal decision is one which, in principle, could have been taken at any time during the period of European settlement. As such, *Mabo* is an untimely event in Nietzsche's precise sense of that term: an event that involves 'acting counter to our time and thereby acting on our time and, let us hope, for the benefit of a time to come'.[13] It is one of those events in the history of a country after which, while many institutions remain unchanged, nothing is the same as before.

A fundamental problem upon which colonial societies such as Australia are founded is the relationship between colonists and indigenous inhabitants.[14] The precise nature of this problem depends upon the significant differences between their respective relationships to and use of the land. Different solutions have been adopted in different colonial regimes, not all of them involving complete dispossession and denial of native title. In Australia, the initial incapacity to perceive Aboriginal relations to the land in terms other than the absence of anything resembling property relations has only now shifted towards a positive recognition of the differences between Aboriginal and European sociality. In these terms, *Mabo* represents a transition from one solution to this fundamental problem to another, and a step towards the recognition of indigenous societies as different but not inferior. Nevertheless, by its very nature as a legal event, there are limits to this recognition of difference.

Difference and the body of the law

Responses to the *Mabo* judgement tend to polarise around the issue of difference versus equality. Conservative critics claim that it is divisive, arguing that the High Court's decision introduces an unacceptable difference into Australian society. In effect, the decision recognises a common law native title to land, the existence and extent of which is to be determined by reference to traditional laws and customs. It follows that only indigenous people can be bearers of native title, and that the common law thereby does recognise a property right which is not available to all citizens. The *Mabo* decision thus contains an implicit challenge to those classical liberal approaches to society and justice which insist upon the uniform identity of the body politic and the equal treatment of its citizens. To this extent, the critics are correct. However, contrary to what they claim, *Mabo* does not so much introduce division as recognise in the law of property the fundamental division upon which Australian society is founded. It thereby disrupts the benign pluralism implicit in the concept of multicultural society, and draws attention to the history and circumstances of the European occupation of this continent.

Race and difference

Defenders of *Mabo*, and indeed some of the judges involved, claim that it removes the stain of racism from Australian common law, and establishes racial equality before the law. Thus, Brennan J asserts that to maintain the authority of those earlier cases which denied the existence of any common law native title would 'destroy the equality of all Australian citizens before the law'.[15] In a sense, this argument is also correct. For while the decision introduces into the body of the common law a property right which is not the same as those available to non-indigenous citizens, it does extend to indigenous citizens the same rights to protection of their property as those enjoyed by non-indigenous citizens. The paradox, if it can be considered such, is that this equality before the law is only possible on the basis of an explicit recognition of difference, namely the differences between indigenous societies, their laws and patterns of land use on the one hand, and European conceptions of property on the other. It was precisely the failure to recognise these differences, except in negative terms, which lay behind Blackburn J's inability to find a property right in the laws and customs of the Yolngu plaintiffs in *Milirrpum v Nabalco Pty Ltd* (1971). Judged by reference to the European conception of property as involving a right to use and enjoy, a right to exclude others, and a right to alienate, the relationship of the Yolgnu people to their land could only be seen as the absence of any such proprietary relation.[16]

Here, as in other arenas in which questions of equality and difference arise, the issue is not simply the recognition of difference, but what differences are recognised and what normative structure is applied to such recognition. Earlier decisions in the colonial jurisdictions of English common law often recognised differences between European and indigenous sociality, but understood these in hierarchical terms as ordered along a natural scale of 'civilisation'. The supposed inferiority of Aboriginal societies in Australia served to justify forms of differential treatment which were at best paternalistic, at worst genocidal. In *Mabo*, the High Court takes the view that the differences between European and Aboriginal relations to and use of the land are not such as to preclude the recognition of native title under the common law. The extension of common law protection to indigenous property rights thus depends upon the recognition of the different basis for such rights. Conversely, the protection of native title depends upon treating indigenous property rights no differently than any other such rights recognised in common law. This latter requirement is clearly illustrated by the manner in which protection against further extinguishment of native title without compensation is afforded by the Racial Discrimination Act.

Mabo thus offers similar lessons for liberal political theory to those which many have drawn from recent feminist politics. On the one hand, political equality is essentially negative in the sense that it refuses to allow differences such as race, sex or wealth to count for the purpose of the rights and obligations which attach to citizenship. As Joan W Scott argues: 'equality, in the political theory of rights that lies behind the claims of excluded groups for justice, means the ignoring of differences between individuals for a particular purpose or in a particular context'.[17] On the other hand, such negative equality may perpetuate inequality in some situations unless it is supplemented by the positive recognition of differences: maternity rights, laws against vilification of certain minority groups and native title are all examples of such group-specific rights.[18] Mere legal recognition of title to land, however, may not be sufficient to establish positive equality between indigenous and non-indigenous citizens, particularly if it fails to take into account the spiritual and cultural dimensions of indigenous people's relationship to land. In view of the importance of traditional hunting and harvesting activities for the enjoyment and perpetuation of indigenous cultures, the question remains to what degree the recognition of native title in common law is a sufficient measure of positive equality?

Difference and equality

It is appropriate that the issue of difference and its relation to equality should be so sharply posed by a decision which concerns the common law. According to Professor Detmold, the recognition of difference is the very basis of law and community, and it is the common law which is 'the law of difference'. Accordingly, he argues, if there is a chance of understanding the nature of law, it will be found in the common law.[19] However, there are at least two distinct issues involved in this claim that the common law is essentially concerned with difference: first, how does the common law accommodate difference within the body of its own precepts and concepts? What drives it to draw distinctions and establish internal differences? According to what principles does the common law differentiate itself from itself? Second, how does the common law come to terms with the external difference created by the existence of other bodies of law? By what means does the common law recognise rights, entitlements and principles of law derived from outside itself? Both issues arise with regard to the recognition of native title in *Mabo*. In both cases, there are significant limits to the recognition of difference by the common law.

The question of difference within the body of the law arises in the context of the debate over the role of the High Court. *Mabo* has been simultaneously hailed as 'another triumph for the common law',[20] and denounced as the expression of an unacceptably high level of judicial activism. Some critics have accused the majority judges of overstepping the proper bounds of judicial reasoning and making a political decision.[21] No-one denies that the common law should evolve in response to changing practices and community attitudes. The issue in this case is whether or not the High Court has moved so quickly that its decision goes beyond what might reasonably be taken to be the values and aspirations of 'the Australian people', and whether it has the potential to upset expectations and render unlawful actions predicated upon the reasonable belief that all native rights to land had been extinguished. However, as the subsequent discussion has shown, 'the Australian people' remain sharply divided in the values they bring to the question of Aboriginal land title, while legal opinion remains no less divided over the proper limits to judicial law-making.

Over and above this public debate about the proper limits of judicial law-making, there remains the question of the common law's ambivalent relation to internal difference. In so far as the body of the law develops by differentiating itself (in the present) from itself (in the past), and to the extent that this process is led by forces outside the law, then it may be argued that the law is a body of the kind that has been of particular interest to post-structuralist philosophies, namely a differential body whose identity depends in whole or in part on relations with what is outside or beyond it. The Saussurean sign is one example of such a body, the kinds of rhizomatic multiplicity discussed by Deleuze and Guattari provide a further example: multiplicities, in the special sense they give to this term, 'are defined by the outside; by the abstract line, the line of flight or deterritorialization according to which they change in nature and connect with other multiplicities'.[22]

On the one hand, the common law is supposed to be by nature pragmatic, embodying the distilled wisdom of human experience and essentially oriented towards the practical functioning of society.[23] As such, the common law necessarily has one face turned towards its outside: social, economic, moral and political consequences may properly be taken into account in its deliberations. Thus, the majority judges in *Mabo* referred to contemporary attitudes towards the past treatment of indigenous peoples, and expressed the view that the law should be altered to conform with current conceptions of justice in this regard. Brennan J asserted that 'it is imperative in today's world that the common law should neither be nor be seen to be frozen in an age of racial discrimination'.[24] On the other hand, the utility of the common law and its very nature as a body of law require stability and consistency in the principles upon which decisions are made. In Justice Brennan's judgement, this requirement finds expression in the concept of a skeleton of principle embedded within the body of the law. He enunciates a general principle according to which rules of law may not be adopted if 'their adoption would fracture the skeleton of principle which gives the body of our law its shape and internal consistency'.[25]

How are these conflicting demands to be reconciled? There are no *a priori* grounds upon which to decide whether or not a given principle is skeletal. In his *Mabo* judgement, Brennan J emphasises the pragmatic basis for such decisions, pointing to the need to consider 'whether, if the rule were to be broken, the disturbance to be apprehended would be disproportionate to the benefit flowing from the overturning'.[26] In a judgement handed down five months after *Mabo*, this pragmatism is tempered by an appeal to 'the traditional methods of judicial reasoning which ensure that judicial developments remain consonant not only with contemporary values

but also with . . . "the skeleton of principle" . . . The law must be
kept in logical order and form, for an aspect of justice is consistency
in decisions affecting like cases and discrimination between unlike
cases on bases that can be logically explained . . . The tension
between legal development and legal certainty is continuous and it
has to be resolved from case to case by a prudence derived from
experience and governed by judicial methods of reasoning'.[27] In
other words, the common law is not an entirely differential body,
defined solely by its relations to things outside itself in the manner
of the Saussurean sign. It possesses its own internal consistency in
the form of a skeleton of legal principles whose mutual relations
are subject to the constraints of logical order and form. Nevertheless, as Justice Brennan's remarks suggest, the skeleton of the
common law is unlike that found in the bodies of higher animals:
it can be modified, extended or developed in any manner so long
as its overall shape and internal consistency are maintained. It is
more like the skeleton of certain forms of plant life, such as
rhizomes, where indefinite proliferation is permitted so long as
certain structural constraints are respected.

In the present case, the doctrine of tenure is an example of
one such skeletal principle. It is a fundamental principle of the
law of real property in Australia, ultimately derived from the
feudal principle of English law according to which all land is held
by grant from the Crown. Given that the entire system of land
title has grown up since 1788 on the basis of this principle, it is
in Brennan J's words 'far too late in the day to contemplate an
allodial or other system of land title'.[28] There appears to be no
logical reason why a colonial system of land law could not have
been developed upon bases other than that of the doctrine of
tenure. Brennan J points out that the centrality of this doctrine
to English law is merely a contingent feature of English legal
history.[29] It is therefore for pragmatic reasons that the Crown's
right to make grants of title to land is an essential postulate of
the system of property law and thus a skeletal principle which
ought not be broken.

The specific point of law on which the High Court rejects
previous authorities, colonial as well as imperial, is the identification of the radical title assumed by the Crown when it acquires
sovereignty with full beneficial ownership. The rejection of this
equation is the specific difference which *Mabo* establishes within
the law, and upon which it manages to reconcile the demands of
justice and contemporary anti-racism with those of consistency
and continuity. Grounds for the distinction between radical and
beneficial title are found in a series of common law cases reaching
back as far as the conquests of Ireland and Wales in the 17th

century, while the distinction itself may be traced to decisions of the United States Supreme Court beginning with *Johnson v McIntosh* in 1823.[30] In these cases, Marshall CJ introduced the concept of native title as an explicit compromise between the rights of indigenous people and those of the settlers who had taken up land after the conquest of Indian territories. The basis for this compromise was pragmatism pure and simple. Marshall CJ described native title as a 'new and different rule, better adapted to the actual state of things'.[31]

The common law is thus precisely the kind of differential body that Deleuze and Guattari call a multiplicity or rhizome. It is a differential body which exists simultaneously on two dimensions or planes: on the plane of logical order and form, it strives to preserve its internal consistency and to maintain continuity in its principles over time, while on the pragmatic plane it strives to accommodate the changes in practice, attitudes and values which sweep through the larger social body of which it is a part. If the fundamental principles upon which subsequent layers of legal opinion are deposited may be considered strata, then the external pressures acting upon the body of the law must be regarded as forces of de-stratification which occasionally produce sudden shifts in the weight of legal opinion and cause the collapse of apparently settled areas of law and the formation of new strata.[32] The affirmation of the doctrine that native title survives the establishment of sovereignty by settlement is just such a movement. It is a legal event which expresses a movement for change within Australian society, or what Deleuze and Guattari would call a line of flight. The explicit pragmatism of the *Mabo* judgement shows that while the process of judicial development may be 'governed' by the methods of judicial reasoning, the crucial determinant of its internal movements lies in the relation to forces outside the law.

Indigenous people, difference and law

To return to the issue of external difference: how does the common law take cognisance of prior indigenous interests in land? Once it is accepted that some form of native title survives annexation, there remains the question of what rights and interests are recognised under this heading. There appears to be a choice of strategies available. Either the Court translates the indigenous interests into some existing category of the common law, or it enlarges the system of common law categories by the incorporation of some new category derived from indigenous law. Deane and Gaudron JJ present this choice in the following terms: 'where the pre-existing native interest was "of a kind unknown to English law", its recognition and protection under the law of a newly settled British Colony would require an adjustment either of the interest itself or of the common law: either a transformation of the interest into a kind known to the common law or a modification of the common law to accommodate the new kind of interest'.[33] Precedent for both strategies may be found in cases decided earlier in this century. In *Re Southern Rhodesia* (1919), the Privy Council asserted that there was a need to establish that any indigenous rights which survived 'belonged to the category of rights of private property'.[34] Blackburn J followed this approach in *Milirrpum v Nabalco*, above, only to find that the Yolgnu people's relationship to their land did not conform to the essential elements of a proprietary relation as defined in British law.

By contrast, in *Amodu Tijani v Secretary, Southern Nigeria* (1921) and subsequent cases,[35] the Privy Council recognised interests in land such as communal title even when these departed from the kinds of interest known to British common law. The judges in this case spoke of the need to resist 'a tendency, operating at times unconsciously, to render [native title to land] conceptually in terms which are appropriate only to systems which have grown up under English law'.[36] The end result of pursuing this strategy is to render common law native title *sui generis* and distinct from all existing common law interests in land. This was the approach adopted by the majority in *Mabo*. The nature and extent of native title are to be determined 'by reference to the laws and customs of the indigenous people who, by those laws and customs, have a connection with the land'.[37] Native title is thus recognised and protected by the common law. However, its status remains marginal. The concept straddles the border which separates the common law from systems of customary law external to it: 'native title, though recognised by the common law, is not an institution of the common law . . .'.[38] It is not surprising that members of the Court should have expressed a range of opinions on the precise nature of native title. On this point, the judgement does give rise to uncertainty in the law with regard to the consequences of the recognition of native title. Under pressure from the mining and pastoral industries, the government has sought to reduce this uncertainty by its native title legislation.

Over and above this uncertain relation to the outside, the translation of indigenous property rights into common law native title exposes an inherent limit to this legal recognition of difference. By admitting the concept of a title grounded in indigenous laws and customs, the law provides a basis for the defence of indigenous property rights within its own courts and procedures.

Such indigenous rights are thus protected by, but not fully incorporated into, the body of Australian law. They are recognised, but at the expense of a more thoroughgoing recognition of the systems of law which, it is now admitted, governed Aboriginal and Islander societies before colonisation. There remains an irreducible difference between European and indigenous law. One of the Murray Island plaintiffs, Father David Passi, points to this difference in describing Australian law as 'an artificial blanket'. In other words, the common law is not the natural protection of land rights which is provided within Murray Island society by *Mabo*'s law. As Father Passi commented: 'the common law is not common to me because it has not reached me. It does not include me'.[39]

Equally, there remains an asymmetry in the relationship between Australian common law and indigenous law, in so far as this relationship is recognised within Australian law. The skeletal status of the doctrine of tenure means that the Crown's power to extinguish native title is preserved. While the common law thus recognises indigenous law as a source of title, it maintains its own pre-eminence with respect to the extinguishment of title. In this respect, the hierarchical relation of culture and power established by colonisation remains essentially unchanged. Equality before the law for indigenous people comes at a price. As Professor Detmold comments: 'Whilst [the High Court] recognised aboriginal difference in the matter of a different conception of title, they imposed the European valuation of it in the matter of its conditions of extinguishment'.[40]

From the point of view of justice, this irreducible difference plays a paradoxical role: it is at once both a precondition and a limit of the justice in the High Court's decision. In Derridean terms, the difference between indigenous title and common law native title is at once both a condition of the possibility of justice and a condition of its impossibility. Justice is realised in the *Mabo* decision to the extent that judgements of fact and law, which in the past have prevented forms of indigenous title to land from being recognised and protected, are no longer permitted to hold sway. Justice is not realised to the extent that Australian law still falls short of recognising indigenous law as another legal system, or series of such systems, that is as a body of law in its own right. Justice therefore reveals itself to be isomorphic to *différance*: at once present and absent in this historic judgement. The recognition of indigenous law is both accomplished and deferred. It is perhaps because of this essentially differential nature that the *Mabo*-event has the potential to deconstruct legal and political certainties.

Difference and the body politic

As we saw above in relation to the issue of equality before the
law, the High Court decision in *Mabo* possesses a remarkable
capacity to fuel contradictory responses. This is no less true with
regard to its perceived implications for the Australian polity as a
whole. On the one hand, it has been welcomed as an important
contribution to the process of reconciliation, where this is assumed
to be a means by which existing divisions within society may be
overcome. On the other hand, it has been alternately denounced
or hailed as contributing to the deepening of divisions between
indigenous and non-indigenous Australians. Right wing critics
such as Hugh Morgan and Geoffrey Blainey assert that *Mabo*
poses a real threat to the unity of Australia, while members of
the Aboriginal Provisional Government such as Michael Mansell
see it as adding legitimacy to the claim for Aboriginal sovereignty.[41] There is some justification for both of these responses,
which implies that both are ultimately unjustified because unduly
one-sided. In effect, *Mabo* is an agent of both unity and disunity
within Australian politics. In relation to the health of the body
politic, it possesses a dual potency akin that which Derrida
discerns in Plato's *pharmakon*: at once poison and remedy.[42]

Consider firstly the assimilationist response: there is no doubt
that *Mabo* will provide effective legal protection of land rights
for some Aboriginal and Islander communities. Equally, there is
no doubt that it represents a significant symbolic victory for
indigenous people and their claim to land. The judgement recognises prior occupation of the land along with the integrity and
sophistication of their culture. As such, the Council for Aboriginal
Reconciliation welcomed the High Court's decision as one which
'rights a distortion in the history of Australia'.[43] The federal
government has seized upon this decision as a unique opportunity
to reconstruct the fundamental relationship between the nation
and its indigenous people 'on just foundations',[44] and has pursued
this goal in its native title legislation. The legislative recognition
of native title, along with the proposed land acquisition fund and
other measures intended to benefit those communities unlikely to
gain anything from native title claims, will contribute to the
economic independence of a greater number of Aboriginal and
Islander communities.

On this basis, it can be argued that *Mabo* does represent a
step towards the reconstitution of Australia's moral and political
community, and that it points towards a society that includes
rather than excludes Aboriginal and Islander people. Such an
extension of moral community is implicit in much of the govern-

ment's rhetoric of fairness and reconciliation. However, as we saw above, there are limits to the degree to which *Mabo* represents a recognition of cultural difference rather than simply its assimilation. These limits appear starkly in the manner in which the High Court decision leaves intact the paramount power of the Crown to extinguish native title, thereby modifying but still preserving the supremacy of British common law over native law. This hierarchy remains in the native title legislation, which establishes a right of negotiation but not veto over mining and other uses of Aboriginal land. These limits also appear to the extent that native title is treated merely as another form of property right, since doing so fails to come to terms with the specific character of Aboriginal people's attachment to the land. Thus, Noel Pearson criticised the government's initial response to the High Court decision on the grounds that it treated the issue as simply one of land management, at the expense of recognising 'the fact that Aboriginal culture is inseparable from the land to which Aboriginal title attaches. The loss or impairment of that title is not simply a loss of real estate, it is a loss of culture'.[45] The legislative response to *Mabo* is likely to further enmesh native title with existing forms of property right and land management practices, thereby contributing to the further withering away of cultural difference.

Turning to the separatist response: here too, there are limits to the degree to which *Mabo* can be said to contribute to the dismemberment of the Australian body politic. On the one hand, it is true that the High Court decision recognises a form of property right whose nature and incidents must as a matter of fact be ascertained by reference to the laws and customs of indigenous people. It remains an open question just which aspects of Aboriginal culture might be recognised as incidents of land ownership under native law, but these may be extensive. For example, given the relationship between land and forms of painting, music and dance within Aboriginal culture, it has been suggested that forms of visual art, music and dance might be protected in this manner.[46] On the other hand, conservative critics such as Morgan and Blainey overstate the degree to which common law native title introduces a foreign body of law and threatens the integrity of the nation. In itself, foreign ownership of land poses no threat to territorial integrity. Extensive tracts of the country have long been foreign owned. In such cases, as indeed under the native title legislation, all normal State and Territory laws relating to aspects of land management such as quarantine, diseases and noxious weeds still apply. The recognition of common law native title does not *ipso facto* remove land from subjection to the framework of Australian law.

From a strict legal point of view, it is entirely false to suggest that *Mabo* provides any support for the claim to Aboriginal sovereignty over the Australian continent. Although sovereignty was not a central issue in the case, the Court reaffirmed the principle that sovereignty was established by an act of state within the field of international law, and that as such it cannot be challenged in any Australian court whose authority derives from that act.[47] Nevertheless, it can be argued that the judgement provides some implicit and moral support for the claim to some form of Aboriginal sovereignty, because of the manner in which it argues against the doctrine that the country was, for legal purposes, uninhabited at the time of settlement. Brennan J's judgement relies in part upon the critical examination of the theory of *terra nullius* by the International Court of Justice in its *Advisory Opinion on Western Sahara* (1975),[48] in which it was asserted that *terra nullius* should be understood in the strict sense of land empty of inhabitants. Given this rejection of the extended concept of *terra nullius* in international law, Brennan J argues that, contrary to the principle espoused by the Privy Council in *Re Southern Rhodesia*, 'the doctrines of the common law which depend upon the notion that native peoples may be "so low in the scale of social organisation" that it is "idle to impute to such people some shadow of rights known to our law" can hardly be retained'.[49] His argument thus establishes a link between the international law doctrine and the corresponding common law fiction of uninhabited land, and then rejects the latter partly on the basis of the International Court's rejection of the former. In doing so, Justice Brennan's argument implicitly raises the question of the legitimacy of the initial British assertion of sovereignty. As Professor Nettheim comments, with reference to the views of Mansell and others, 'if Australia was not *terra nullius* in terms of land ownership, how could it have been *terra nullius* in terms of sovereignty?'[50]

While the legitimacy of the British claim to sovereignty over the Australian continent may well be open to question, there are serious practical and political obstacles to the goal of establishing Aboriginal sovereignty in law, and even more so to its establishment in fact. These include the problem of gaining access to an appropriate forum in which such claims might be heard, and the problems associated with setting up and maintaining an Aboriginal sovereign nation in the unlikely event that they were upheld. Over and above such difficulties, there are philosophical reasons to question this approach. While there were undoubtedly indigenous societies with their own law and institutions of social governance prior to colonisation, it is by no means clear, as Noel Pearson has argued, that the concept of sovereignty as developed in European legal and political theory is an appropriate expression of this state of affairs.[51] Rather, the case for sovereignty appears to be an artificial attempt to reconstruct the relationships among Aboriginal communities in terms that reflect the structure of European societies. Moreover, at a time when the metropolitan European nations are actively engaged in renegotiating the limits of national sovereignty, it would seem pointless for indigenous people to be laying claim to complete autonomy in matters of economic policy, foreign affairs and defence.

Pearson and other Aboriginal leaders involved in the *Mabo* debate have argued that a positive recognition of cultural difference may benefit indigenous and non-indigenous Australians alike. Such recognition may take legal and institutional forms which fall well short of sovereign independence. From this perspective, both the right wing critics of *Mabo* and the proponents of Aboriginal sovereignty remain committed to a unitarian conception of the body politic which has already been overtaken by events. The experience of limited forms of self-determination by indigenous peoples throughout the former colonial world suggests that sovereign nationhood is capable of accommodating a much greater degree of cultural and political diversity than might have been supposed or allowed in the past. The choice is not simply between assimilation and separate sovereign identity, but rather between such exclusionary ways of thinking and acting and the task of finding new forms of internal political differentiation. From this perspective, both the assimilationist and the separatist responses remain bound to a logic of identity and to its counterpart, namely a simple dichotomous conception of difference. *Mabo* is neither a remedy for the divisions which already exist nor a recipe for producing further internal conflicts. Rather, it is a legal and political *pharmakon*, both panacea and poison at once. However, it is not the indeterminacy of this state of affairs that is of primary importance for political thought, but the need to find new forms of specific determination. It is not undecidability which matters but specific forms of differentiation. What is important is not simply the refusal of closure or containment, but the challenge to re-think our conceptions of society and of nationhood. The challenge of *Mabo* is to find ways of going beyond the choice between assimilation and separate political identity, towards the social and political co-existence of different ways of life. The task is to build a legal and political framework around unassimilated cultural difference.

PART II

The national-constitutional body

4 Law before Auschwitz: Aryan and Jew in the Nazi Rechtsstaat

David Fraser

> In the National Socialist state the law can only be a means for the maintenance, securing, and encouragement of the racial *volkisch* community. The individual can be judged by the law only from the point of view of his value for the volkisch community.
>
> Hans Frank, 1934, Academy of German Law

The history of Christian anti-Semitism is written largely in the body. We find not only a body of legal regulations in relation to dress, occupational restrictions, residential limitations, etc., all of which resurface in Nazi legality, but a body of myths which bear most importantly on the Jew's body.[1] The physical attributes of 'the Jew' become inscribed in myth, legend and eventually science and law as the paradigmatic traits of the Other. Over time anti-Semitism becomes the inscription of the body of the Jew in the body of the law.

The nose, feet, beard and especially the penis of 'the Jew' become body parts of a body of knowledge, marking and making his difference, his Otherness. The Jewess, unclean even within parts of her tradition, becomes the seductive temptress, whose exotic, erotic Otherness contaminates and calls up the fleshly, bodily urges of the non-Jew. More deeply embedded, historically at least, however, are even more subtly pernicious legal inscriptions of the Jew and the body.

According to the blood libel and associated legends, Christian children were sacrificed in secret Jewish ceremonies. Of course, these kidnappings, sacrifices and ceremonies were ordained by a secret Jewish body corporate, later the mythical Elders of Zion, but the importance of the myth for the body of 'the Jew' and the body of the Law does not lie there. It is in the reading/interpretation of the sacrificial ceremony that we find the vital and key issues. The myth inevitably involves the linking of Jewish and Christian bodies—the kidnapped youngster is sacrificed in a manner which at once mirrors and mocks the crucifixion and sacrifice of Christ. The martyrdom of the Christ figure finds itself rewritten again and again on the bodies of the innocent children. But the purpose of the sacrifice, in the most pernicious form of the blood libel legend goes even further into the body of Christ and Christians. The purpose of the sacrifice for the 'Jew' is to obtain Christian blood for the making of the matzoth. Not only, then, is the sacrifice of the Christian body linked to the cannibalistic consumption of that body, but the ritual sacrifice itself is a mockery of the high sacrament of the Holy Communion. The body not just of a Christian, but of Christ, is destroyed and consumed by the evil Jew.[2]

Two points of interest arise here for any study of the law of the body. The first and more obvious, is the position of 'the Jew' in relation to the body of Christians and to the body of Christ. 'The Jew' becomes identified as a cannibalistic enemy bent on destroying and consuming the Church, and in a logical pre-modern extension, the people who are 'the body of Christ'. The second point, now more easily recognisable following Sartre's analysis,[3] is that 'the Jew' is Christianised, i.e. the primary definitional aspects of what constitutes 'the Jew' exist in relation to the Christian body and to a body of Christian laws. His most secret rituals at one and the same time destroy and honour Christ. In the blood libel legend there is a strange and persistent juxtaposition between 'the Jew' as the murderer, both figuratively and literally, of Christ, and the Jew as secret admirer of Christ. Whatever the contradictions and potential resolution of the juxtaposition, 'the Jew' becomes intimately linked with the body of Christ and therefore with the body of Christ's followers. 'The Jew' becomes a Christo-centric creation but at the same time, a foreign body in the body politic of each and every Christian nation. A series of religious and secular edicts and laws regulating 'the Jew' occur, to be replaced temporarily and partially by the civil emancipation of the Enlightenment.

With traces of the volkisch anti-Semitism deeply embedded in European and especially Germanic culture and traditions, the rise of modernity does not replace the myth but simply displaces its metaphoric applications. With industrialisation, growing urbanisation, the rise of the nation-state and the triumph of a rationalised scientific world view, in short with modernity and the Enlighten-ment, the Jew's body is simply re-inscribed, over-determined, in the body of medical and biological theory, in racial hygiene and eugenics[4] and in codified legal prescriptions, as a threat to the Christian-volkisch body. This time the body under Jewish attack becomes the nation—the body politic.

The re-orientation of the discursive political attachment to anti-Semitism, to a re-positioning of 'the Jew', takes place primar-ily at the levels of the discourse of modernity. At the first stage, we witness the rise of medico-biological discourse which describes 'races' in terms of hierarchically ordered attributes and which sees the inferior almost purely in terms of the new internalised self-referential language of modernity. The body politic comes under threat from 'parasites', 'vermin', 'bacillus'.[5] The Aryan body pol-itic must be immunised against these foreign and dangerous bodies. The chief means for self-preservation come to be found in the newly emergent medico-legal discursive matrix.

At the same time as we find the re-orientation of the discourse from religion to racial hygiene which again defines 'the Jew' in terms of its relationship to the body of the non-Jew, we can witness the creation of a new political discourse which gives rise to the seemingly positive emergence of the non-Jewish body pol-itic, the Volk. The growth of political anti-Semitism[6] in Germany, coinciding with the arrival of the new racial science sees the creation of the most important concept in terms of Aryan-Jewish relations, the Volksgemeinschaft. The Volksgemeinschaft is pre-sented[7] as a positive embodiment of the Aryan race. The term 'anti-Semite', itself the creation of Jew-haters, with its clearly 'negative' aura is replaced by the more positive term volkisch. Of course the seemingly more 'positive' volkisch barely conceals its own inevitable negative connotation. 'The Jew' is not part of the Volk. But the Volk must necessarily define itself as excluding Jews. The Volk is non-Jewish. The Jew is not part of the Volk. No matter how one looks at it, the body of the Volk is threatened by Jewish contamination—the virus which threatens the Volksgemeinschaft insinuates itself even into the self-definition of the body politic. 'The Jew' is the unwritten and necessary Other of the Volk.

Aryan and Jew in the Nazi Rechtsstaat

'Mein Volk is alles, ich bin nichts', said Hitler. But Jews are not nothing. Jews are a threat to the Volk. Aryan/Germanic blood and soil are under a constant and imminent danger of contamination from this foreign body. Such a threat, against the present and future Volksgemeinschaft, can be dealt with by bringing together other bodies, bodies of Aryan knowledge and power, medicine and law. The Nazi Rechtsstaat is the protection of the racial state,[8] Volk, Staat und Rechts. The merger of medical and legal science in Nazi Germany becomes a logical and natural focus for prophy-lactic measures against the enemies of the body politic. Institutes for 'racial hygiene' were established and manned by the top German scientists. Leading constitutional lawyers wrote text books underlining the importance of a scientific/legal approach to the protection of the Volk.

The most important of the 'public health' measures undertaken by the Nazi regime was the passage of both the Law for the Protection of German Blood and Honour and the Reich Citizen-ship Law—the so-called Nuremberg Laws of 15 September 1935. These legal provisions codified the bio-legal nature of the rela-tionship between the Aryan and the Jew. The Blood Law stated inter alia:

> Entirely convinced that the purity of German blood is essential to the further existence of the German people, and inspired by the uncompromising determination to safeguard the future of the German nation, the Reichstag has unanimously adopted the following law, which is promulgated herewith:
>
> I.   Marriages between Jews and citizens of German or kindred blood are forbidden . . .
> II.   Sexual relations outside marriage between Jews and nationals of German blood or kindred blood are forbidden.

The Reich Citizenship Law provided further clarification:

> I.1.   A subject of the state is a person who belongs to the protective union of the German Reich and who therefore has particular obligations towards the Reich.
> II.1. A citizen of the Reich is that subject only who is of German or kindred blood and who, through his conduct, shows that he is both desirous and fit to serve the German people and Reich faithfully.

The First Supplementary Decree to the Blood Law of 14 November defines, in case there was any doubt, Jews as non-citizen (Art. IV). A Jew is further defined as someone who is descended from at least three grandparents who are racially full Jews (Art. V), or as someone who has two Jewish grandparents if he is a practising Jew, or if he is married to a Jew, or is the offspring of a Jewish marriage or an extramarital relationship with a Jew (Art. V.2) or, finally, if he is of mixed Jewish blood (Art. II.2 i.e. with one or two Jewish grandparents).

The importance of these provisions is clear—Jews are not citizens, nor are they German. German blood must be protected. German blood is to be protected from contamination primarily, at first, at last, through the prohibition of sexual contact between Aryans and Jews. The Blood Law was strictly enforced, although it would seem that the primary focus of law enforcement was on Jewish male-Aryan female relationships.[9] The body politic had to be protected from further contamination by the offspring of the Jewish male sperm/virus. Blood, sex, the Jew's penis—all must be inscribed in·the body of the law as the law of the body.

But this inscription of the Jew's body in the corpus of German law goes beyond the purely contraceptive and therapeutic protection of the Volksgemeinschaft through the proscriptions of various legal provisions. The inscriptions of 'the Jew's' body in juxtaposition to German blood replicates in the biological discourse of the Nazis the same contradiction/dependence of relationship we find in traditional volkisch anti-Semitism. Nowhere do we discover a legal definition of the German or the Aryan. The definitional thrust of the Blood Law is all in one direction—the delimiting of the Jew—the not-German. Like the term Volksgemeinschaft itself, the legal body of texts giving life to the Aryan body politic does so through a process of definitional exclusion—the Jew is not-German, but the German is even more, the not-Jew. Throughout the history of Nazi Germany, the search for racial purity was undertaken almost entirely in terms of defining the Aryan not positively (although there was a failed biological/eugenic attempt to delimit and propagate Aryan traits) but by demonstrating the absence of Jewish blood/contamination. Genealogical searches to declare an SS member fit for marriage focused, for example, on his ability to prove the absence of Jewish blood from his family tree.

Despite the occasional attempt at a systematic 'positive' definition of Aryan traits however, the entire Nazi racial/legal policy continued to focus on the negative, i.e., the exclusion of 'the Jew'. It does seem, however, that those so-called negative aspects always carried with them a mirror image. The Aryan was always the non-Jew, even as 'the Jew' was a non-Aryan. The thousand-year Reich, the policy of Lebenstraum, the Shoah—all Nazi racial policies were pursued with the goal of achieving a Europe which would be Judenrein—free from, purified of, Jews. Yet again, the Reich exists purely in relational terms, 'the Jew', even in, or especially by, his absence, will be the ultimate defining characteristic of the Nazi Rechsstaat.

But for all its careful legislative drafting and scientific, eugenic research, the Nazi state apparatus could still not quite define the

other. Because of its self-definition and therefore the very existence
of German blood in the body politic, the Volksgemeinschaft, the
problem of 'Mischlinge', the offspring of 'mixed' marriages,
became one of vital importance to the bureaucrats of murder and
extermination[10] and one which informed the entire operation of
the medico-legal apparatus of the Shoah. Again, the best Aryan
minds dedicated their medical and legal expertise to a delineation
of 'the Jew' and the Aryan.

Notwithstanding the difficulties and bureaucratic infighting
caused by the definitional and psycho-existential crisis of the
'Mischlinge' (half-Jew, half-German), the vital importance of 'the
Jew' and the Jew's body to the Volksgemeinschaft continued as
the Nazi regime began its seemingly inexorable path to the
medico-legal extermination of the Jewish people. Beginning with
the sterilisation program for those of unsound body or mind who
might infect the German people with parasitic life,[11] followed by
the euthanasia program which targeted 'life unworthy of life',[12]
again to protect the Volk from contamination, and culminating
with the transfer of staff from the euthanasia program to be
charged with the running of the Operation Reinhard extermination
camps,[13] Nazi bio-legal practice constantly inscribed 'the Jew' and
the Jew's body in an attempt to define him (and her)[14] as non-
German, the effect of which was always and inevitably to
reinscribe the German as the non-Jew.

It must always be borne in mind, and underlined at this point,
that the Holocaust was not, as many would have it, a lawless
barbarism. It was, on the contrary, a lawful barbarism. In other
words, the Holocaust occurred not as a mindless series of actions
without rules or limiting bounds but rather within a framework
of legal, scientific, rule-making. The problem which faces us when
we confront the horror and terror of 1933–1945 is the fact of the
historical, philosophical and legal continuity of this period both
with its predecessors and with its successors. The law of the body
which is the Shoah is forever inscribed in the body of the law.

The primary legal-ideological function of such juristic events
as the Eichmann trial in Israel or the trial of Klaus Barbie in
France is to convince us instead of the discontinuity, the radical
break of 1933–1945, and once that epistemological step has been
accomplished, to assure us of a return to the safety of modernity,
of the primacy of the rule of law. But the epistemological certainty
of such legal spectaculars is undermined not just by internal
critiques of the 'legality' and 'justice' of such events, but by a
more fundamental unveiling and derobing of the rule of law. As
Joshua Halberstam succinctly puts it:

> The Nazis were not a lawless bunch. To the contrary. Theirs was
> an inflated sense of duty. They revered the law too much.[15]

Even a cursory examination of the Nazi Rechtsstaat underlines
the cogency of Halberstam's comments. The so-called Nazi courts
simply applied standard legal techniques, rules and worldviews to
achieve what Frank called the 'encouragement of the racial
volkisch community'. While their goals may have been aberrant
(although the existence of racial and eugenicist worldviews in the
legal system of other nations might well belie this point),[16] their
techniques and substantive formulations of legal rules were perfectly consistent with much more widely accepted views of the
nature and function of law. One brief example from the plethora
of 'Nazi' cases will suffice to properly situate the body of law
and the law of the body within a broader juristic context and
continuous tradition.

Among the first anti-Semitic legislative measures of the Nazi
state was the Law for the Restoration of the Professional Civil
Service of April 7 1933. While this statute dealt only with racial
qualifications for government service, it came to be seen as
grounding a much broader notion of the racist ideal of the Nazi
Rechsstaat, to be given subsequent formal status in the Nuremberg
laws. In a series of decisions, German courts began to find that
divorces or annulments could now be granted on the grounds that
one's spouse was 'Jewish'. The logic of the judicial argument in
such cases is quite simple. The Law for the Restoration of the
Professional Civil Service evidenced, as a principle of public policy,
that one's 'Jewishness' was not only a fundamental personal
characteristic, but that it was a characteristic that carried with it
quite clear civil impediments. That the Reichstag as the body
corporate of the body politic had deemed it necessary to single
out 'Jewishness' as a negative personal characteristic could then
mean that the principle should be carried into other realms. A
'German' married to a 'Jew' would now realise that this characteristic of his/her spouse was such as to go to the very validity of
the marriage bond. Divorce or annulment would necessarily
become, for a loyal member of the Volksgemeinschaft, a necessary
step to ensure that all contaminating forces were to be excluded.
However, Article 1333 of the Civil Code permitted dissolution of
marriage only:

> . . . by a spouse who at the time of its contraction was unaware
> of personal qualities in the other spouse, qualities that would have
> prevented a person from entering into the marriage had he had
> knowledge of the true circumstances and a proper understanding of
> the nature of marriage.

Thus, in those cases (virtually all) where the spouse's 'Jewishness' was known to his/her partner at the time of marriage, Article 1333 would appear to pose an insurmountable barrier. The courts were not to be stopped, however. The argument which developed was a simple one. It was only in light of current and evolving scientific and legal standards and knowledge that one could know the true meaning of the 'personal quality' of 'Jewishness'. Therefore, the passage of the Law for the Restoration of the Professional Civil Service marked an important stage in the growth of both legal and general public knowledge about 'Jewishness' and the court could and should give effect to this new degree of awareness by finding as a matter of law that had the true nature of the spouse's 'Jewishness' been known at the time, the complaining partner would never have entered into the marriage. In other words, knowledge that the spouse was 'Jewish' at the time of marriage did not, as a matter of law, include knowledge of what the true impact of that 'Jewishness' really was.

Some, like Ingo Müller, have called such decisions 'perversions of justice'.[17] It seems clear, however, that while the underlying epistemological assumptions behind these decisions are indeed so offensive as to be beyond our full comprehension, the techniques and reasoning which the courts employed here are perfectly consistent with legal thinking in the civil law tradition. To find in legislative enactments general principles of public policy, to argue that literal interpretations of the Civil Code are to be replaced with a method of telelogical reasoning in the light of general scientific or specific legislative public policy propositions, these are not 'perversions', but actually techniques of judicial lawmaking which, in other contexts, are considered to be highly desirable and progressive.[18]

Moreover, the example of judicial rewriting of the epistemological and hence legal character of 'Jewishness' in marital annulment cases is but one of many. The legal history of Germany from 1933–1945 is full of laws, regulations and bureaucratic edicts which write the status of 'the Jew' in the body of law. In each case, written with/under/behind 'the Jew' is the Aryan who finds himself inscribed again and again as the not-Jew. As the Final Solution loomed ever closer, the writing of 'Jew' and Aryan in the body of the law became the actual, graphic, writing of the body of 'the Jew' in the body of the law. The yellow badge or Star of David became the actual mark of the Jew in law, replaced only by a more efficient form of legal bureaucratic inscription, the final solution to writing 'the Jew', the branding of the body with the tattoo as a (pre)inscription of death.[19]

To signal by way of vestementary regulations—the wearing of

a yellow star or piece of cloth—was simply to re-assert the historical legal relations between Jew and Christian,[20] to rewrite the body of the law of the body. The Jew was written on the body in some concentration camps—tattooed, number recorded, those not scheduled, not written down for immediate extermination. Everywhere the body is marked, marked for identification, for legal classification, for life, for eventual death. But the SS man, too, is marked, tattooed with SS sign and blood group, inscribed as Aryan, of Aryan blood, identified as pure, so as not to risk contamination in case of a required battlefield blood transfusion—another legal inscription for the preservation of German blood. Jews marked for life before death, SS marked for life. The Jew, survivor marked for life by death, everyday, a written reminder that s/he is a Jew, not German.[21] The body, a written remembrance of the gift of life, and/or death. A gift of the legal, medical bureaucratic process of the Rechtsstaat.

Law before Auschwitz

Let us not forget, then, if forgetting is possible[22] about the law. Let us remember that the Nuremberg Laws:

> . . . were the expression, concentrated in legal-textual form, of the verdict, 'Death to the Jews' which already earlier had been pronounced by German society.[23]

Let us also remember, by way of example only, Einsatzgruppe A which worked its way through the north-eastern areas of the former Soviet Union in the course of Operation Barbarossa, murdering hundreds of thousands of people. Of the seventeen group leaders of Einsatzgruppe A, eleven were lawyers. Nine of the eleven had doctorates in law. The mythology of the Nuremberg Trials and subsequent legal spectacles—the trial of Eichmann in Jerusalem, Barbie in France or Polyukovich in Australia, is grounded in the ideal of the period of Nazi rule, 1933–1945, as a lawless time of the barbarians. The Nuremberg Trials and their offspring are meant to legitimise the modern, civilised, rule of law by defining the Nazi period as not—not modern, not civilised, not the rule of law. Here we come to the crux of the issue of law 'before Auschwitz' and of the body 'after Auschwitz'.

'After Auschwitz'. Following Adorno, coming after him, the devastating critique of the Aüfklarung, thought, critical theory, philosophy, law, has entered, so it would appear, a new phase. The paradigm and period shift to what can be called, for the sake of brevity, postmodernity, has begun to be perceptible and to be perceived. We follow Adorno, we repeat, expand, discuss, bury, attempt to resurrect[24] the Enlightenment. We come to a body of theory, of knowledge, and of law, to debate the terms of the transformation. After Adorno and critical theory, Critical Legal Studies.[25]

'After Auschwitz'. In the present current of events, we write, speak and situate ourselves 'after Auschwitz' except perhaps, within Critical Legal Studies, where the debate has yet to find and locate 'Auschwitz'.[26] Nonetheless, as a larger body of scholars, 'we' follow, in a temporal sense 'Auschwitz'. This is a simple operation of periodisation, a timely situation of events and knowledges—first there was 'Auschwitz', then there was/is now.

Post-modern, post-'Auschwitz'. But beneath, or behind, or before 'Auschwitz', is another issue, the call of/to the Law.[27] 'Auschwitz', not as a time or place (or series of places really—Auschwitz, Birkenau, I.G. Auschwitz—labour/ capital/ extermination—law), 'Auschwitz' not as a time or place, temporal and spatial markers, but as signature, signatory—a signal event. Legislating. What law? Whose law? Whose body?

Post modern, post-'Auschwitz'. 'Auschwitz' = modern. Again, however, the temporal implies, perhaps or should imply, something beyond or before a simple periodisation. Is 'Auschwitz' operating here in a finite sense, marking the boundary, the end of modernity, the beginning of the 'post'? If the answer given is in the affirmative, affirming the end, then both modernity and 'Auschwitz' (will) have ceased to operate. If the answer is negative, negating the ending, then both modernity and 'Auschwitz', for they are, it would be appear, synonymous, continue, are present, present themselves, operate not as historical objects, artifacts and markers, but as presences. In other words, 'after Auschwitz', 'Auschwitz' is still here. We follow 'Auschwitz', not in temporal sense of coming after, but rather we follow 'Auschwitz' as a marker, a guide, a path, in legal terms, a precedent. The legal principle of 'Auschwitz'—'Auschwitz' as binding authority in the body of the law and the law of the body. 'Auschwitz' becomes, for us, now, a place where law was/is made.

'Auschwitz'—the legal principle '. . . a paradigmatic name for the tragic 'incompletion of modernity'.

'Auschwitz'—the corpus juris:

> . . . a whole people was physically destroyed. The attempt was
> made to destroy it. It is the crime opening postmodernity, a crime
> of løse-souveraineté [violated sovereignty]—not regicide this time,
> but populicide (as distinct from ethnocide).[28]

'Auschwitz'—a crime and a law. The crime, the law. The death of the subject and, so it would seem, the death of the Other. The place and time where, in the haze of the Zyklon B in the 'shower' rooms and in the smoke of the crematoria, the Law seemed to die. 'Auschwitz'—a place, a time, a metaphor, a crime, a legislation, after which we stand, seeking, in vain, perhaps, an ethical and legal point of view which does not sink into the mire and shit of 'after Auschwitz'. This was the goal of the Nuremberg War Crimes trials, to reinscribe a body of law 'after Auschwitz'. To write in the body of the corpus juris, the prohibition of crimes against humanity, to place 'Auschwitz' outside the Law and to re-integrate the bodies of the Jews and 'the Jews' (the Gypsies, Slavs, homosexuals, communists, Poles, asocials) into the law of nations. To save the Law through the spectacular of the trial, at Nuremberg, where the non-German 'Jew' was written in the Law, and later with Eichmann and Barbie, to place the Law 'after Auschwitz', which was lawless, after Nuremberg, which was lawful. But the Law was not absent from 'Auschwitz'. It was not a lawless time or place. 'Auschwitz' was lawful, it was full of law—lawful prescriptions of 'Aryan' and 'Jew', lawful sterilisations and euthanasia to protect the blood, lawful orders, from lawyers and doctors, for the extermination of those enemies of the state, those parasites who would infect the Volksgemeinschaft. The 'selection' on the ramp offers us the moment and place of medico-legal judgement par excellence. To seek, as we seem to do, an ethical/legal stand-point 'after Auschwitz', to stand 'after Auschwitz' (or to ignore it as do my colleagues in Critical Legal Studies), as lawyers who proclaim Law, we must first and last, stand 'before Auschwitz'. Again, this phrase may potentially lead to confusion. It has, perhaps for some, a double legal signification. It too implies and commands a periodisation, a temporal demarcation—before 'Auschwitz' there was . . . Before Zyklon B and medical experiments and Dr Mengele, and selection, and crematoria, what happened? This brief descriptive and slightly historiographical task has already been outlined. Where are the beginnings of 'Auschwitz'? 'Before Auschwitz', there was law, there was 'Jew', there was non-Jew. There were bodies before 'Auschwitz'. There were bodies of law, bodies of knowledge—science, law, medicine, institutes, universities. There were bodies—'Jews'. 'After Auschwitz', there were ashes. The second legal and ethical requirement seemingly imposed 'before Auschwitz' compels and commands a different type of judicial and historical process. It demands other judgements. We must stand 'before Auschwitz' so that we may be judged by 'Auschwitz'. This is the task undertaken, in a philosophical attempt to deal with philosophical complicity, by Lyotard and Lacoue-Labarthe.[29] But philosophy can be no more than an accomplice, before or after the fact, before or 'after Auschwitz'. The Law must be the principal offender and the offender in principle. 'Auschwitz' is, was, and will remain, a site for/of Law.

For Law, however, to be judged by 'Auschwitz', a fundamental and insurmountable difficulty presents itself—the différend.[30] The victim demands justice, the tribunal, even a tribunal as powerful as 'Auschwitz' can offer only law, if not Law:

> . . . the 'perfect crime' does not consist in killing the victim or the witnesses (that adds new crimes to the first one and aggravates the difficulty of effacing everything), but rather in obtaining the silence of the witnesses, the deafness of the judges, and the inconsistency (insanity) of the testimony.[31]

What can be more insane than testimony about 'Auschwitz'? What can be greater than the silence of forgetting the forgotten? Who could be deafer than judges of Law 'after Auschwitz'? But that is, I think, to pre-judge the case. We stand 'before Auschwitz' before 'Auschwitz'. The past, in a sense, presents itself for judgement. What can be more normal than this?

The case, then, comes 'before Auschwitz' and the case comes before 'Auschwitz'. 'Auschwitz' stands 'before Auschwitz' awaiting judgement and justice because 'Auschwitz' was legal. And the Law can judge its own.

Law before 'Auschwitz': bodies of evidence, evidence of bodies

Matters of proof. Such problems present themselves in every trial. Documents, testimony, presumptions, inferences. Proof does not equal truth, this is itself a truth known to every law student. But we are not looking for truth, we are looking for justice, or at the very least for law. As Lyotard reminds us, if we need reminding, the evidence was destroyed:

> The SS did everything possible to remove all traces of the extermination. Its orders were to make sure nothing was recorded . . . It had to be a perfect crime, one would plead not guilty, certain of the lacks of proof.[32]

The revisionists certainly note the claim. Where are the bodies? Zyklon B was a disinfectant, not a mass extermination weapon. Six million did not die. Where are the bodies? Where is the proof? Without proof, no trial. No trial, no justice. The laws of evidence will not permit the judgement of the Law.

Of course, there is some evidence, some evidence even of and after the complete destruction of Treblinka, Sobibor and Belzec.

The desire for efficiency required the keeping of some records,[33] so there is the beginning of proof. Bureaucracy always leaves a trace, a trace of law, a body of evidence, and in the case of the tattoo, marker of bureaucratic efficiency, evidence written on the body.

But the main body of evidence, the evidence of the bodies, the *corpus delicti*, is well and truly absent, gone in a cloud of smoke. But this ignores the rule of evidence, the burden of proofs, the litigation of the différend. 'The perfect crime' requires 'silence', 'deafness' and 'insanity' of witnesses, judges and testimony. In this case, the case of before 'Auschwitz' 'before Auschwitz', the witness is not silent, the judge cannot be deaf and the witness is not insane. The trial here is of the Law before the Law, before the Law of 'Auschwitz' which can see and hear itself. And on this level, the madness of the Law is proof positive of its sanity.

The most damning and irrefutable evidence which can be placed before 'Auschwitz' is 'before Auschwitz'. It is found in Jean Améry's realisation that the Nuremberg Laws were the legalisation of the extermination of the Jews remembered every day as he looked at his arm, a persistent legal text. The body of evidence presented here is evidence of the bodies—bodies of/in Law. Out of the gas and fire comes the body of evidence, evidence of bodies, proof positive of 'Auschwitz' before 'Auschwitz', a re-inscription of the Law as the place where the bodies of 'Auschwitz' are buried, before their death. The law stands condemned before the Law. *Corpus juris, corpus delicti.*

The evidence of the law 'before Auschwitz' requires and commands a re-ordering of 'before Auschwitz' and 'after Auschwitz'. Here we find the possible legal realisation of Martin Amis'[34] fictional dream of the Aryan as midwife of 'the Jew', of the crematoria as the birthplace of 'Jews' out of the flames. The law 'before Auschwitz' establishes this relationship as well as its mirror image, 'the Jew' as life-source of the Aryan. The Oedipal conflict, the castration anxiety of the Volk is here simply writ large in the bio-legal killing of 'the Jew', Father of the Volksgemeinschaft. 'Auschwitz' is written in the body of law 'before Auschwitz' as the Other is written always before.

The evidence of the law of Aryan/Jew, in essence the law of identification and differentiation carried to its logical, mechanised, biologised modern extreme is available for all to see. The causal chain exists, inscribed in legal text and practice, from the Blood Law to the crematoria. Documentary evidence, written in the body of the Law, the Jew's penis, on his forearm, under the arm of the Aryan, is there for all to see and read. Building a case 'for Auschwitz' before 'Auschwitz'. Inference, legal techniques, bodies of law, there is no différend, there is only Law. The tribunal and the crematoria are both *loci legis*.

The acts and actors which stand before 'Auschwitz' and which are inscribed 'before Auschwitz' are acts of law and acts of lawyers. The case to answer proceeds on the view that 'Auschwitz' was legal, that that status of legality can be traced in a body of law which circles back upon itself to reveal the bodies hidden in the smoke and ashes. In the politics (and law) of forgetting 'after Auschwitz' this case presents the first fact to be remembered. We return to Halberstam: 'The Nazis were not a lawless bunch. To the contrary. Theirs was an inflated sense of duty. They revered the law too much.'[35]

The Nazi social state was also a Rechtsstaat. The Holocaust, the Shoah, 'Auschwitz', these are all, beyond the horrific factual reality, metaphors, descriptors of what, as I have stated above, we can call modernity. And 'Auschwitz', is nothing if not modern and, therefore, lawful.

> Like everything else in our modern society, the Holocaust was an accomplishment in every respect superior, if measured by the standard that this society has preached and institutionalized.[36]

'Auschwitz' then, 'before Auschwitz', there was Law. A legally constituted state and a people which defined itself, legally, almost purely in terms of its Other, 'the Jew'. A Volksgemeinschaft in which membership was determined by the absence of contaminated blood. Blood and soil. A legal image from which Jews were excluded. They could not be of German blood (The Blood Law) nor could they be of the soil: 'Only German citizens of German blood or of that of a similar race . . . are eligible to be peasants.'[37]

Blood and soil—the body of the Volk—kept legally free from contamination, yet defined in terms which could not help but include 'the Jew'. Throughout the Nazi state was *Recht* and through the law—the Volk. Nowhere, but in the Nazi myth,[38] was there a positive, even if 'only' imaginary, constitution of the Volk—the Aryan. The constitution of the Aryan can be found only in one site—before 'Auschwitz', in the body of the Law, in the Law of the body and ultimately, in the body of 'the Jew'. What is truly constituted, what authentically and in the only real sense 'constitutes' the Nazi Rechsstaat and Volk, blood and soil, is 'the Jew'. Aryan blood must be freed from contamination, the land purged of the vermin, but 'the Jew' is the worm at the heart of the Aryan dream.

> Any rational assimilation or mystical communion between spirits that is not based on a community of blood is suspect.[39]

This is the truth of law 'before Auschwitz'. The Volks-gemeinschaft is that community based on blood and written in the body of the Law. The Law writes and delimits the 'subject' and 'citizen' not just in terms of merit and obligation, but finally, ultimately and primarily in the foundation of the blood and the body. 'The Jew' cannot be citizen because the citizen must be the 'non-Jew'. German blood and honour must be protected from the vermin 'Jew' but the parasite is insidious for German blood is the blood of the 'non-Jew', it is non-Jewish blood, purified, Judenrein. The SS tattoo testifies to the purity of the blood. But it testifies, first and foremost, to the primacy of 'the Jew', to the Juden of the Judenrein. It bears witness 'before Auschwitz' to the identifi-cation of the non-Aryan, 'the Jew' 'during' and 'after Auschwitz'.

The body of law 'before Auschwitz' is the law of the bodies 'before Auschwitz' before 'Auschwitz'. Neither 'before Auschwitz' nor before 'Auschwitz', not even after 'Auschwitz' on the body of the Law and the law of the bodies can we separate the Aryan and 'the Jew'. Derrida is right to doubt, to question, the possibility of separating:

> . . . all the shared portions and all the partitions that organize such a configuration, of the vertiginous proximities, the radical reversals of pro into con on the basis of sometimes common premises.[40]

'The Jew' and the Aryan, the destroyed and the destroyer are linked, inextricably bound, in the body of the law 'before Aus-chwitz'. In the mystical foundation of the authority of the force of Law which precedes law, is 'the Jew' and 'the Aryan', the Other whose call cannot be heard in justice 'before' or 'after' Auschwitz, but who must be heard, called before the tribunal of 'Auschwitz' which judges not the Other, not the ineffable, the différend between law and Law, between Law and Justice, but which judges itself, Law 'before Auschwitz'.

It is not, therefore, accidental that Derrida focuses on 'the phantom body of the police'[41] when turning his discussion of the Force of Law towards the question of spirit (Geist).[42] The 'phan-tom body of the police' marks the law and the body of 'the Jew', the policed, surveilled, subjected, disciplined body par excellence. The 'Jew', arrested, sterilised, deported, ghettoised, marked, enslaved, exterminated and now denied. The apparent aporia between law and Law, between the mystical and totalitarian founded on violence is written in the hinge of the 'Jew's' body. In the absent foreskin, the consideration given in the foundational legal document, the contractual constitution of 'the Jew's' pact with God, the Chosen People, who were subjected to a whole other type of 'selection', in the absent body gone in the smoke and ash, 'after Auschwitz' within the trace of Law and body are the body and the law 'after Auschwitz'. This 'entirely different blood or rather something entirely different from blood'[43] is the filiation, the brotherhood, buried in the contractually required disappearance of the hood of the penis, between Aryan and 'Jew', brothers-in-law, blood brothers. The constitutional violence of the Chosen People is mirrored in the constitutional violence against the Chosen People. Another choice, a medical-legal 'selection' is made. But the Aryan will remain, despite his best legal efforts, always a third party, always Other to the originary contractual arrangement written on the body of the Jew, the contract constituting the people of the Book as the people of the Law. The constitutive legality of the crematoria can only write upon a body inscribed in foundational Law.

But in the end, Derrida attempts to ellide the familial bond, to escape from the contractual nexus, to avoid being caught 'before Auschwitz':

> In other words, one cannot think the uniqueness of an event like the final solution, as extreme point of mythic and representational violence within its own system.
>   . . . it kept the archive of its destruction, produced simulacra of justificatory arguments, with a terrifying legal, bureaucratic, statist objectivity and paradoxically produced a system in which its logic, the logic of objectivity made possible the invalidation and therefore the effacement of testimony and of responsibilities; the neutralization of the singularity of the final solution.[44]

As an attack on the inexorable self-referentiality of the Historikerstreit and the ugly justificatory positioning of revisionism in rational debate and discourse, indeed, in law, Derrida is correct. The Final Solution writes its own denial in the rationality of the Aüfklarung. But it does not, in this denial, efface testimony or render the witness' account insane. The Law 'before Auschwitz' is more than simulation. It is its own witness. 'Before Auschwitz', there was 'before Auschwitz' i.e. a complex body of law on the law of the body of the Aryan and 'the Jew'. This is the body of evidence which presents itself 'after Auschwitz'. The Law 'before Auschwitz' cannot, it is true, offer justice, for justice is no doubt withheld, even, or especially 'after Auschwitz'. But the law does offer a body of evidence to be judged before 'Auschwitz'. 'Auschwitz', in other words, judges itself. But it stands its decision in abeyance, *curia advisari vult*. The court wishes to be advised. It must not, cannot be inadvertent. It must, but cannot, judge, for to judge rationally 'before Auschwitz', it must find itself guilty—the sentence—suicide/legicide. The death of the 'Jew'. But more importantly, the death of 'the Law'. To kill 'the Jew', to remove from the body of the law the originary constitutive arrangement of the Law, the Law must die. It cannot judge. *Curia advisari vult*. 'The Jew' is the Law of the law. The creature of law—the son-in-law; brother-in-law.

This is the impossibility and the possibility of law 'before Auschwitz'. A body of law which desires its own death but cannot act except by indirection. In smoke and ash. Judeocide, legicide. Law 'before Auschwitz'.

5 Of pleasure and property: sexuality and sovereignty in Aboriginal Australia*
Elizabeth A. Povinelli

In 1788 on the shores of Botany Bay, Australia, Watkins Tench, Captain of the British Marine Corps, had 'scarcely landed five minutes' when his party was met 'by a dozen Indians, naked as at the moment of their birth'.[1] Eager to aid in bringing 'about an intercourse between [the] old and new masters' of the continent and 'to take possession of [the] new territory',[2] Tench entices the Aboriginal group forward by 'baring' the bottom of a five year old convict boy and 'showing the whiteness of [his] skin'.[3] This enticing display of a small boy's bottom was not the only way in which the British used the body to take possession of the Land Down Under. During this same meeting, in order to make his own sex clear and to construct a distinction between old and new masters, Tench describes how he reached into his—or perhaps a convict's—breeches and pulled out his penis only to be met with 'the most immoderate fits of laughter' by the Aboriginal men. Or so I interpret the manner by which Tench made the sex of his party 'understood'—the text itself remaining ambiguous on this point by skating between reference to a direct, shameless display of anatomies and a performance of European reticence and modesty.

In Tench's *A Narrative of the Expedition to Botany Bay with an Account of New South Wales* and in other colonial officials' memoirs[5] this juxtaposition of bodily action and reaction will occur again and again; Europeans attempt to use bodies to effect a 'rational intercourse' across cultures only to be thwarted by Aboriginals' apparently immoderate and unproportional sexual

80

and emotional responses. Relying on discursive frameworks and narrative constructions of savage *sexual irregularis*, the civil government appropriated the Land Down Under on the basis of a social *terra nullius*, while the military used a narrative of emotional irrationality and sexual irregularity to make the continent an actual *terra nullius*.[6] While Tench first offers the hope of peaceful and productive relations between Europeans and Aboriginals, the reader soon learns that indigenous Australians' sexual and emotional irregularity 'signify' *terra Australis* is *terra nullius*—an empty land lawfully available for the expression of British land desire. Thus in a colonial memoir offered as 'amusement and information' to its readers, a military leader of the British penal colony in Australia imbricates racial, sexual, and national discourses that simultaneously construct British sovereignty and the Aboriginal and European bodies and passions on which that sovereignty will rest.

Almost two hundred and ten years later, the grounding of European dominion over Australia in a textual portrait of indigenous social and sexual irregularity would suffer a representational crisis. The textual accounts of race, sexuality, and nationalism[7] that in the 18th century produced a legal context for British sovereignty claims—accounts oriented toward other European nations not indigenous Australians—not only no longer produced sovereignty, but were becoming detrimental to the Australian state's standing in the international community. Not surprisingly, then, on 3 June 1992 the Australian High Court overturned the doctrine that Australian was settled as *terra nullius* (a land belonging to no-one). Writing with regard to *Eddie Mabo v the State of Queensland* the High Court found that the Meriam Torres Strait Islanders retained native title to the Murray Islands off north Queensland and, extending their findings, found that native title had never been completely extinguished on the Australian continent. Further, the majority of the Court found that the *terra nullius* claim had rested on a 'discriminatory denigration of indigenous inhabitants, their social organization and customs'[8] and that for Commonwealth, State or Territory governments to extinguish native title now, they must meet the non-discriminatory standards laid out in the Commonwealth *Racial Discrimination Act 1975* which, in effect, bars the taking of Aboriginal land without just compensation. The broad scope of this decision potentially subjected all unalienated Crown lands in Australia to a traditional Aboriginal land claim.

While the High Court did not contrast Aboriginal and European sexualities in as dramatic a fashion as did Tench, a discourse on race and sexuality remains in the seams of their discussion of sovereignty and native title. On the surface, the representation of Aboriginal sexual subjectivity has changed dramatically. Indeed, the contemporary court, politicians, and the media highlight this transformation; they emphasise the *difference* between past misrecognition of the meaning of 'traditional' Aboriginal sexual and social life and contemporary recognition of its value. Whereas in the colonial period Aboriginals were portrayed as culturally and sexually incoherent, in the postcolonial state the traditional Aboriginal acts as a symbolic repository of a heterosexual and gender conservatism that can be opposed to the public's perception of most contemporary Aboriginal communities as sites of decayed and dissolute cultural mixing. It is this traditional Aboriginal that the High Court recognises as retaining native title over unalienated land. The site of sexual and cultural incoherence has thus shifted from a location in traditional outlooks and practices to a symptom of their loss, but the site from which these sexual and cultural practices are evaluated has not. While the traditional Aboriginal man, steward of family, clan, and land, has replaced the naked satyricon as the nation's reference point for sovereignty claims, we should not overlook a deeper similarity between them: each has allowed the nation-state to consolidate and legitimate its power through reference to an imaginary Aboriginal social body.

A critical framework of the ongoing *Mabo* debate, and something that motivates my own interest in it, is its dual productivity in the legislative arena and public realm (as both a politico-jural and a cultural phenomena) and its specific discursive structure as apocalyptic—as a struggle against all odds, as a final reconciliation or disaster, as the end of cultural chauvinism and economic racism, and as a radical shift from misrecognition and misrepresentation of indigenous social practices to state recognition of and acquiescence to them. Indeed, most legal discussions of the *Mabo* decision and the subsequent *Native Title Act 1993* have assumed that, whether or not the specific legislation resulting from the High Court decision was a victory or defeat for Aboriginals and Aboriginal activists, the 'recognition' by the state of Aboriginal sovereign rights was a 'radical departure' from the past. Equally as interesting is the *Mabo* debate's orientation and discursive framing. We find in it political and economic leaders grounding their politico-jural stances in a diverse set of, often competing, anthropological, political-economic and social discourses: from cultural relativism, to social progressivity, to the universality of human rights and social justice. We also find a variety of material suasions accompanying these discursive frames, especially the economic trench warfare of national and international political communities and multinational businesses. What we see, then, is the resourcefulness and multifaceted nature of non-Aboriginal responses to *Mabo* and the symbolic, material, and discursive manner in which they are articulated.

I wish here to interrupt this narrative of recognition and reconciliation by showing, first, what *similarities* between the past and present the courts, government and media obscure when they contrast recent thinking on the relationship between Australian state sovereignty and Aboriginal socio-sexual practice to historical portraits of the same and, second, how the implementation of this 'new recognition' of Aboriginal land rights is restructuring contemporary Aboriginal socio-sexual practices as the courts claim to acknowledge them. In short, I show how the current government and courts are using a portrait of Aboriginal socio-sexual practices, as previous colonial governments did, for their own purposes, and why. On the way we see what imaginary 'Aboriginal traditions' serve as the measure for 'legitimate' land title claims, why these and not other 'traditions,' and why 'traditions' at all and not another conception of cultural continuity and change or of cross-cultural dialogue. My purpose here is, therefore, not primarily ethnographic even though, because of the constructive bent of legal texts and public discussions, I provide a counter-reading of them from my point of view on Aboriginal practice. These counter-readings—some narrative, some ethnographic—are speculative interruptions of 'grip,' of current accounts of Aboriginal sexuality and social practice. They should not be taken as *the* Aboriginal counter-discourse. Instead this chapter seeks to present a method of reading popular and legal texts to show how Aboriginal sexuality is constructed in the European social imaginary and how it functions as a critical pivot point in the Australian state's engagement with shifting discourses on nationalism and cultural value. I am interested, therefore, both in the mobile and multifacted uses of sexuality in nation-building and in its purposive failure to find referent in Aboriginal *praxis*. How and why does the state frame its actions with regard to indigenous rights as *resulting from* the cultural forms it *encounters* (Aboriginal sexual irregularity, Aboriginal sexual regularity) and the social and moral standards in which it lives (liberal humanism, cultural relativism, multiculturalism) even as it is *producing* the cultural forms and moral standards allowing it to re-entrench its power and authority over these minority communities? We will see that in democratic contexts such as Australia, appropriation of minority community rights occurs not through a challenge to the notion of 'social justice,' but through the creation of and then assent to standards of social justice. Finally, building on a developing literature examining the links between nationalisms and sexualities[9] and a growing critique of state sanctioned indigenous rights as unambiguously positive in value,[10] this chapter shows how this 'new era of reconciliation', in critical ways, is the *legatee* of a colonial discourse hell-bent on appropriating Aboriginal land 'by any means'.[11]

Land desires: 1966–94

In the two hundred and ten odd years since Australia was founded as a penal colony, it seems that social theory and international law has turned full circle in its understanding and valuation of indigenous social *praxis*. Traditional Aboriginals are no longer portrayed as sexually unregulated and irrational. Instead, modernist social theorists celebrate Australian Aboriginals' totemic marriage system as one of the most complex and interesting cross-cultural examples of the dominating nature of socio-sexual institutions in 'small scale' societies. Critical studies in Marxism (*Origin of the Family*), Freudian psychoanalytics (*Totem and Taboo*), Durkhiemian functionalism and Levi-Straussian structuralism (*Primitive Classification, Totemism*) have all turned to the dominating, domineering, constraining logic of Aboriginal totemism, kinship, and marriage (or descent and alliance systems) to solve much broader puzzles in human psychology, political-economy, and society.

Not only has social theory supposedly come around to recognising the inherent order in Aboriginal sexual and gender practices, so supposedly have international and national High Courts and parliaments. In Australia, no surer sign of this is there, we are told, then the series of legislative acts and juridical decisions that have occurred since the mid 1960s, culminating in the very recent decision *Eddie Mabo v the State of Queensland* in which the court rejected the doctrine that Australia was *terra nullius* at the point of European colonisation. Asking the critical question of 'whether the rights and interests in land derived from the old regime survive the acquisition of sovereignty or do they achieve recognition only upon an express act of recognition by the new sovereign', the court answered that the government's 'exercise of a power to extinguish native title must reveal a clear and plain intention to do so'.[12] It had not done so in the past and its ability to do so now was restricted by the *Racial Discrimination Act 1975*. In a policy discussion paper circulated almost exactly one year after the *Mabo* decision, the Keating government summarised the Court's finding for Aboriginal people and non-Aboriginal Australians:

> The challenge is how to recognise and manage a title to land deriving not from laws passed by Parliaments, but from the continuation by the common law of rights over land which pre-date European settlement. More broadly, the Mabo decision underlines the dispossession of Aboriginal and Torres Strait Islander people from their land. Its logic is seen as requiring further consideration by governments of measures to respond to that historical injustice, including for people who now cannot benefit from the decision because their connection with the land has been severed.[13]

Most Aboriginal leaders and activists have applauded the High Court's recognition that Australia was already peopled and possessed when the first boatload of Europeans stepped onto its shores. But this High Court decision did not come without heated response from the Aboriginal and non-Aboriginal communities. Popular media personalities, international business corporations, and the chief ministers of Australian State and Territory governments predicted that the Mabo decision would result in everything from the last breath of Australian racism, to the last gasp of the Australian economy, to the last stage of Aboriginal dispossession.

In the face of advice from some in his own party, the Australian Labor (although hardly leftist) Prime Minister, Mr Paul Keating, set for himself the daunting task of navigating stridently divided political, economic, and social communities and coming up with a legislative package that would, in some way, acknowledge the Court's decision. On 19 October 1993, seemingly 'against all odds',[14] Mr Keating persuaded his cabinet to approve a compromise package that recognised native title and provided 'social justice' for Aboriginals, while, at the same time, safeguarded, as an editorial in the Australian put it, the 'integrity of our land management system as one of the foundations of our economy'[15] [added emphasis]. On 22 December 1993, the Australian Parliament passed the Native Title Bill.

What then were the juridical grounds on which the High Court overturned terra nullius as a legitimate method for the British acquisition of sovereignty over Australia and its people? The reasoning in the Mabo decision, as in earlier acts of Parliament (Racial Discrimination Act 1975; Aboriginal Land Rights (Northern Territory) Act 1976), was that 'the theory that the indigenous inhabitants of a "settled" colony had no proprietary interest in the land . . . depended upon a discriminatory denigration of indigenous inhabitants, their social organization and customs'.[16] We are told that the High Court *now* recognises that 'traditional' Aboriginal people have a highly structured social system for regulating sexuality, marriage, and property that is the very opposite of irrational. It is rather the dominating institution in their lives. Moreover, all sexual excess—that is, all deviation from the model of marriage, sex, and reproduction that the courts recognise, homosexuality, single motherhood and, to a lesser degree, miscegenation being the most stigmatised examples of contemporary sexual 'disorders'—is seen as symptomatic of cultural upset and loss; symptoms, we will see, that the state can diagnose as internal social disease and thus the grounds for land dispossession.

Of course we should be suspicious of the motivations for this, if not sudden, nevertheless decisive turnaround. Few, even in the Keating government, would deny that this state flip-flop is motivated by social concerns other than mere justice, namely, the pragmatic constitutional issues raised by, and the national and international political-economic consequences of, the High Court's decision. Perhaps caring less about international human rights issues and more about local economies, conservative (Liberal and National Party) state leaders have foreground forcefully what they see as the catastrophic economic implications of *Mabo*. The *Australian* (3 December 1993) reported that the New South Wales Premier, Mr Fahey went out of his way to reassure Japanese investors about the *Mabo* decision, saying in Tokyo that no land titles in his State were under threat, while *The Sydney Morning Herald* (3 December 1993) reported that 'the Chief Minister of the Northern Territory, Mr Marshall Perron, warned that the Federal bill "set the scene for the greatest battle between Aboriginal and non-Aboriginal interests Australia has ever seen"'. Such a response by the Northern Territory's Chief Minister is not surprising given that many in the northern government and business communities lament racist attitudes towards indigenous people primarily because they scare away Asian investment.

While conservative state governments have foreground economic reasons for overturning *Mabo*, Keating has vacillated between social justice and constitutional pragmatism as the motivation for his proposed 'landmark . . . reconciliation'[17] between Aboriginals and non-Aboriginal Australians. In Keating's remarks on radio and television and before Parliament, social justice and human rights appear to be key discursive frames to his Native Title Act.[18] But while 'social justice' may be a better 'guiding principle' for the left than other minor- and meta-narratives,[18] it also provides political groups from the left, centre, and right with a discursive framework that masks other motivations for and

implications of social legislation. By framing his stance in terms
of social justice, for instance, Keating need not acknowledge any
inevitable right of Aborigines to determine land interests in
Australia, but can rather re-entrench nation-state rights in this
regard by resting his argument that *Mabo* must be squarely faced
on what he claims to be the inevitability of a legislative response.
Thus it is not 'social justice' or Aboriginal rights to self-determination *per se* that centres the public articulation of Keating's
vision—neither would be sufficient or persuasive—but rather a
strong constitutional belief that the High Court has the legal right
to decide issues of sovereignty and that this right has created an
economic climate of uncertainty that can only be rectified through
a concrete legislative response. It is the court's legitimate right to
rule and the economic legacy of that ruling that Keating claims
has forced the Australian government's hand in 'finally' solving
the indigenous legacy of the colonial period or, in a more flattering
formulation, has 'provided' contemporary Australians with the
'unique opportunity' of working for social justice.

However motivated or described, this new state strategy of
'recognising rights' and acceding to social justice is as restrictive
and transformative and as bent on representing Aboriginal sexual
and social systems in a way that would make them compatible
with governing needs as was the colonial strategy of producing
'civil order' from savage social disorder. Whereas in the colonial
period, the state gained international support by showing it could
produce order from cross-cultural and ethnic disorder and justified
its sovereignty claims by positing that no (and not dickering over
what degree of) social order preceded European settlement, now
the state gains international legitimacy by showing it can reconcile
itself to a multiplicity of cross-cultural social orders and can
discriminate among degrees of cultural authenticity. Tellingly,
during the initial political sallies over the Keating government's
policy paper—framed by some in explicitly racist and Eurocentric
terms—supporters of Sydney's quest against Beijing's for the 2000
Summer Olympics compared the two cities in terms of their
respective nation-state's record on multiculturalism and human
rights. And in non-Australian papers such as *The New York
Times*, issues of international political-economic orientation and
human rights policies are linked to national Aboriginal rights
issues.[20]

Much of the persuasive force of new land rights legislation
comes from its rhetorical framing as a monumental moment in
which Aboriginal people's traditions are 'finally' recognised. This
is opposed to the little that was once allowed and all that was
once misrecognised. With the same gesture, the courts and many

in government can reject European colonial 'traditional attitudes' as incorrect and unjust and can laud those Aboriginal traditional knowledges and practices that survived the colonial period. What 'traditions' then is the state recognising as the legitimate grounds for an Aboriginal land claim? How is reference to 'traditions,' on the one hand, creating a narrow chute that restricts Aboriginal access to land and, on the other hand, acting as a discursive virus that expresses state needs through Aboriginal social forms—a 'structuring structure', in Bourdieu's sense, that transforms Aboriginal socio-sexual practices into non-Aboriginal Australian desires. In other words, how is a discussion of 'traditions' restricting Aboriginal claims, legitimating the actions of European governance, and transforming Aboriginal practices in a nation-state increasingly economically, militarily, and politically oriented not to the West (Europe and the United States) but to Asia and the Pacific (Japan, Indonesia, Fiji, and Papua New Guinea), the latter watching closely the Australian state's legal and rhetorical twists and turns on multiculturalism and human rights?

No matter what they are, 'traditions' work simultaneously in a politico-jural domain in which legislation is enacted to ensure that only certain forms of Aboriginal practice are legally productive and in a cultural domain in which certain forms of Aboriginal sexual and familial expressions act in the public realm, if not in the jural, as a marker of cultural decay. Perhaps, the most useful and summary way of comparing the effects of these politico-jural and cultural domains is to discuss the quantitative restrictions of Aboriginal human-land and human-human relations imposed by land rights legislation and the qualitative alterations of them created by the cultural hegemony of western sexuality. Both these social arenas restructure culturally organised desire as they impute a recognition of the critical component of its difference.

Prior to the 1992 *Mabo* decision and the current Native Title Act rushed through parliament, legislation pertaining to Aboriginal land claims was primarily determined by the States. For instance, the South Australia reformist government was the first to pass, in 1966, land rights legislation (*Aboriginal Land Trusts Act 1966*) after the unsuccessful struggle of the Yirrkala plaintiffs against Nabalco Pty Ltd (*Milirrpum v Nabalco Pty Ltd* 1971[21]) and after the well publicised Gurindji strike from the Wave Hill cattle station. More recently the South Australian government passed the *Pitjantatjara Land Rights Act 1981* and the *Maralinga Tjarutja Land Rights Act 1984*. However, both these Acts were essentially private deals worked out in negotiation with the Aboriginal owners, containing no mechanism that allowed other groups to gain additional land.[22] In New South Wales the *Aborigi-*

nal Land Rights Act 1983 probably provides the most liberal grounds on which a land claim can be based. Unlike the *Aboriginal Land Rights (Northern Territory) Act 1976*, the Aboriginal Land Rights Act does not require proof of traditional ownership or residence on a reserve, relying rather on questions of historical attachment and need. However, this liberal law operates in a State with little claimable (unalienated Crown) land.[23] In contrast to these liberal bows to indigenous rights, in Queensland, Aboriginal human and land rights were only partially protected after a series of Commonwealth acts overturned State legislation that breached Aboriginals' 'internationally recognized basic human rights such as freedom of speech and freedom of movement'.[24]

The chute through which Aboriginal groups can gain access to land seems to have narrowed rather than expanded based on the preliminary legislative fallout of the *Mabo* decision. In perhaps the most drastic example of this narrowing, the Native Title Act overrides the Commonwealth *Racial Discrimination Act 1975* which was passed to reflect the United Nations *Convention on the Elimination of All Forms of Racial Discrimination* (CERD) and to which the High Court referred as restricting the ability of the Commonwealth, State and Territory governments to take Aboriginal land. By overriding the Racial Discrimination Act, the Commonwealth government is now able to extinguish native title without paying 'just compensation'. Less startling but equally as threatening to an indigenous group's ability to determine how human-land and human-human relations will be legally conceived is the proposed establishment of tribunals to hear Aboriginal claims. These tribunals, whose constitution is still not settled, would among other things determine whether the 'general nature of the connection between the indigenous people and the land remains' and thus whether a land claim is viable.[25]

While the Racial Discrimination Act applies Australian-wide, only in the Northern Territory has there been a Commonwealth Act pertaining to Aboriginal land rights, the *Aboriginal Land Rights (Northern Territory) Act 1976*. Examining how 'the connection between the indigenous people and land' was operationalised in it may allow us to imagine how Aboriginal claims might be assessed in the climate of a Native Title Act. In the Aboriginal Land Rights (Northern Territory) Act Aboriginal groups have to pass through a series of social and cultural tests before being granted traditional title to their country.[26] Specifically, an Aboriginal group must prove that it is the 'traditional Aboriginal owners' of the land under claim. In the Act, 'traditional Aboriginal owners' are:

a local descent group of Aborigines who—

(a) have common spiritual affiliation to a site on the land, being
    an affiliation that place the group under a primary spiritual
    responsibility for that site and for the land, and
(b) are entitled by Aboriginal tradition to forage as of right over
    the land.

In more common parlance, the local descent group is a heterosexually defined genealogical family group reckoned through
the mother or father's line (or, in some recent decisions, both)
which has as its apical ancestor a Dreaming (or totem, say a long
yam Dreaming) whose spiritual centre is on the land under claim
(say a rock or banyan tree). The Dreaming is defined as the
Aboriginal belief that the extant world was formed by the actions
and travels of Dreamtime men and women (say, the Blue Crab
Man and the Stringbag Woman) who, at certain places in the
countryside, left a mark (e.g., stone, banyan tree, waterhole) and
remain there today. In a marriage of social theory and western
law, it is a conceptual method for reckoning a group's relationship
to land and each other. In the best of all legal worlds, land
commissioners, anthropologists, and local indigenous groups construct a genealogical map, draw a circle around the descent group,
locate that group's Dreaming (totem) on a map and the case is
settled. That group owns that land. Nowhere else; no-one else.

Ian Keen has described the relationship between the definition
of 'traditional Aboriginal owners' and 'the 'orthodox model' of
'Aboriginal land tenure'.[27] In particular, Keen draws out the
connections between the Act's use of the phrases 'local descent
group', 'common spiritual affiliation', 'primary spiritual responsibility', and 'to forage as of right over the land' and
structural-functionalist discussions of the differences between
Aboriginal land-holders and land-users.[28] Land-holders were posited to be an exogamous patrilineal descent group (or 'clan'). In
contrast, land-users (bands or 'hordes') were thought to be a
looser confederation of families and friends ('the residential unit
was thought to have been almost identical in membership to the
patrilineal totemic clan, give or take a few women'[29]) actually
living on and using the clan territory. Land-holders were a heterosexually and genealogically defined group with spiritual ties to
a stretch of the countryside, while land-users were defined by their
affective relations to one another and their economic interests in
the land.

Thus, as others have long noted, indigenous land rights legislation quantitatively restricts the type of group and the number
of people who can make proprietary claims to an unalienated piece

of land.[30] The Australian Parliament's and the courts' recognition of 'the local totemic descent group' (patrilineal or matrilineal) as only the legitimate basis for land-ownership under the Land Rights (Northern Territory) Act, allows the state to restrict Aboriginal understandings of human-human and human-land relations in a way that best fits emerging 19th and 20th century western notions and institutions for the descent of rights and goods.[30] By only recognising the 'local totemic descent group' the state is provided with historically predictable and delineable, relatively immobile sets of heterosexually defined families through which and only through which property is passed. When these narrowly defined groups die or change their beliefs 'significantly' land reverts to the state. Thus when the state says it recognises the local totemic descent group, it is in fact recognising its own needs, compatibilities, and wants within it—it recognises the distribution of property rights through human reproduction anchored in the cultural topography of the Dreaming.

Dialogical sexualities

Human sexual reproduction and the heterosexual form of the family within a totemic framework (often portrayed as 'mystifying' or ideological, but never granted a real nature) are, therefore, the underpinnings of European legal recognition of Aboriginal traditions. But while the law specifies a type of sexuality and a form of cultural belief as defining Aboriginal legal rights to land, it does not account for the action of culture on the production or delimitation of sexuality; in this case, it does not account for the fact that humans are not the only subjects involved in reproduction and eroticism and that rights do not only accrue through the heterosexual family. This is not to imply that, after all, Montagu was right: traditional Aboriginals did not understand that sex makes babies.[32] But rather, it is to point out that there are severe problems in delimiting the realm of sexuality cross-culturally and that this delimitation has a productive effect on Aboriginal and European understandings of land rights and land relations. While a full articulation is beyond the scope of this chapter, examples of these problems can be seen in north Aboriginal human-human and human-land relations.

Aboriginal understandings of human-human sexuality and erotics are usually described as fitting within a kinship and alliance system. For all practical purposes, all persons are socially fixed to one another by kinship and Dreaming (totemic) references. Both references are, in part, a set of prohibitions and commands. For

instance, sexual relations in a cross-cousin system are figured as
such: all your mother's brothers' (and those structurally similar—
so your mother's mother's brother's sons or anyone who your
mother calls sister's [so, her mother's sisters' daughters] sons)
children are your cousins, while your mother's sisters' children are
your siblings (with the same crossing principle working on your
father's side). These 'cousins' are 'wives and husbands'; or the
terms themselves mean 'marriageable person'. This 'marriageable'
group is further narrowed by restrictions on the degree-of-relation
(you should not sleep with your actual mother's actual brothers'
children for instance) and by Dreaming (in some Aboriginal
communities you should or should not 'marry' certain Dreamings).
Importantly, within an Aboriginal system, the mode- and degree-
of-relation is the critical diacritic of sexual desire and erotic
relations, not the sex of the body, remembering that rare is the
place in Australia, Aboriginal or otherwise, where sexuality
defined in terms of kinship and alliance is not in dialogue with
sexuality defined in terms of sex object-choice; a dialogue that
invalidates the pure place of 'within an Aboriginal system' and
produces in everyday Aboriginal life interesting supplemental discourses on the meaning of eros.

Human-human desire, eroticism, and sexuality do not simply
work to produce 'marriages,' even granting an expansion of one's
marriageable choices from cross-sex to cross- and same-sex part-
ners. Desire and eroticism are also tools Aboriginals use to build
mobile and diffuse affective relations between groups vis-a-vis
individuals. For instance, after periods of intense emotional stress,
people often demand that the community come together for 'play'.
At these times, corroborees are sung and danced and people urged
to tease each other sexually and otherwise. Women dance erotically toward each other or men, perhaps mocking the dance style
of a male suitor or a female 'rival'. Adult same-sex cousins will
urge each other's sons and daughters to dance together erotically,
teasing them and each other mercilessly, often in explicitly sexual
terms—both teasings a form of emotional and bodily pleasure,
recognition, and alliance. Old people will pursue young people
and everyone will be urged to 'be serious' as they throw dog, cow,
or horse manure at each other, and are uproariously mocked and
laughed at. These mandatory pleasures are just formalised examples of the constant erotic teasings and bodily interactions that
occur on northern Aboriginal communities and that create the
dense same-sex and cross-sex, generational and cross-generational
emotional networks that can be relied upon to secure economic
and social assets. This pleasure, this sexual excess—which is seen
in everyday conversation and joust and is composed of sexual

discourses from putatively Aboriginal and non-Aboriginal sources—is not simply the topsy-turvy world of Bakhtinian carnival because it does not simply invert the normal order. Instead, it performs the available 'tracks', not all of which are utilisable for adult reproduction, that cement alliances, make contacts, connect persons and through them places. Human-human relations are, in large part, discussed as a question of how to get people and places to desire one another, sexually or affectively, and thus form a flexible, but dense, community of resources—an abundance of affectivity rather than the thin line of descent that courts and parliaments now recognise. These dense networks of affectivity/sexuality/eroticism are part of the reason that certain people are found in certain places and subsequently form the human-land attachments described below.

While Aboriginal understandings of human-human sexuality and erotics provide some problems for current legislative attempts to delimit the realm of property, Aboriginal understandings of human-land relations provide somewhat different problems. Human-land relations (reproduction, desire, bodily pleasures), or the Dreaming, are implicated in, but escape current legislative definitions of sexuality in three main ways. First, northern Aboriginal groups do have what are usually called descent Dreamings (totems). And, the reproduction of human life (having children) is the occasion for descent Dreamings to maintain their here-and-now being in the world with their there-and-then origination at a site. An example helps. The long yam is, through my father, brought to life in me. Through my mother's family Dreaming, I am the red kangaroo. I, the temporary human manifestation of the Dreaming yam and kangaroo, may travel anywhere, but my origination site, where I-the-Dreaming yam and kangaroo emerged from, travelled to, and submerged in the Dreamtime, is marked with one or a series of geological features, such as one or a series of waterholes; i.e., descent Dreamings are a place and a being.

But while the courts essentialise Aboriginal human-land relations to this form of reproductive heterosexuality—conversant with its own notions of the genealogy of emotional obligations and legal property—Aboriginals have many forms of human-land, or Dreaming, relations none of which are essential in the sense of reducible to the other. For instance, northern Aboriginal groups also recognise a Dreaming relationship between persons and places based on conception.[33] In many Aboriginal communities conception Dreamings are said to 'catch' people hunting, camping, and travelling through the countryside. As people go along, a conception Dreaming hears them or smells their sweat, then manifests itself as a food. Sometimes men are said to catch the food and give it to their wives; at other times women are said to come upon the Dreaming, hidden in the food, themselves. Either way a woman unintentionally eats or otherwise comes into contact with the Dreaming. It then creates a child, marking the foetus in the process with a birth anomaly. Through this sign, parents or other knowledgeable persons establish a link between the child, the Dreaming species, and the place where the Dreaming appeared. The child then has potential rights and obligations, affection and duties towards that place. The relationship between persons and the places where they were conceived, like the relationship between persons and their descent Dreamings, is described as the place/landscape/Dreaming wanting ('being hungry for') the persons—a subjective Dreaming seeking out its human object.

Thus more important than the quantitative restriction (from many totems to the one totem) that the courts impose is the qualitative perversion of the meaning of the Dreaming in relation to Aboriginal notions of bodies, desires, and land. It is a narrowing of the sense in which land-human affectivity and desire is understood, as a contextually based, emergent and ongoing relationship between people and places: something that cannot be known *a priori* or fixed by genealogical referent. Northern Aboriginal people discuss human-land relations, like they discuss human-human relations, as a problem of how to get people and places to desire one another and thus form flexible but dense bonds of attraction—an abundance of affectivities for a multiplicity of places, rather than a dependency on one single site or region.

Locating traditions

Irrespective of these cultural conceptions of human-land relations, in the context of a post-*Mabo* tribunal system, future land commissioners or tribunal members would, arguably, turn to the wording of the High Court and parliamentary debate to determine the scope and meaning of 'traditions' (how 'traditions' were conceived as a cultural litmus for land rights). As land commissioners in the Northern Territory have turned to parliament and court discussions to understand the meaning of 'traditional Aboriginal owners' and 'local descent group', tribunal members would be looking for some way of deciding what constitutes 'traditions': what would be the essential component of cultural continuity or the critical diacritic of cultural loss? They would find an ambiguity that, Solan has argued, is an inherent part of the judicial process.[34] Court opinion on the meaning of 'traditions' wavers between an 'autonomous and continuous cultural system' and an 'invention' in the sense of fabrication.[34] At first glance the High Court seems to provide some mobility for cultural expression. For instance, Brennan argues that:

> Native title has its origin in and is given its content by the traditional laws acknowledged by and the traditional customs observed by the indigenous inhabitants of a territory. The nature and incidents of native title must be ascertained as a matter of fact by reference to those laws and customs.[36]
>
> Where a clan or group has continued to acknowledge the laws and (so far as practicable) to observe the customs based on the traditions of that clan or group, whereby their traditional connection with the land has been substantially maintained, the traditional community title of that clan or group can be said to remain in existence.[37]
>
> However, when the tide of history has washed away any real acknowledgement of traditional law and any real observance of traditional customs, the foundation of native title has disappeared. A native title which has ceased with the abandoning of laws and customs based on tradition cannot be revived for contemporary recognition.[38]

Contrast this emphasis on an essentially unsevered maintenance of tradition in the imaginary context of cultural and social floods[39] to Deane and Gaudron's attempt to reconcile historical change to traditional content and to resist seeing traditions as frozen in a precolonial period:

> Ordinarily, common law native title is a communal native title and the rights under it are communal rights enjoyed by a tribe or other group. It is so with Aboriginal title in the Australian States and internal Territories. Since the title preserves entitlement to use or enjoyment under the traditional law or custom of the relevant territory or locality, the contents of the rights and the identity of those entitled to enjoy them must be ascertained by reference to that traditional law or custom. The traditional law or custom is not, however, frozen as at the moment of establishment of a Colony. Provided any changes do not diminish or extinguish the relationship between a particular tribe or other group and particular land, subsequent developments or variations do not extinguish the title in relation to that land.[40]

What are we, let alone future tribunals, to make of these images of frozen and flooded traditions? More important for my purposes, how might this 'reconciliation' of cultural history to contemporary political-economics be a re-entrenchment of the state's rights to evaluate and value Aboriginal 'lifestyles'?

The Court re-entrenches state authority as it proposes to force it to acknowledge indigenous traditions by necessitating the sorting and valuing of contemporaneous Aboriginal social and cultural practices and, through such, by re-establishing the dynamics, if not the explicit discourse of a theory of cultural stagism and social progressivity. For instance, Brennan's and Deane and Gaudron's discussion of 'traditions' differentiate between those contemporary social practices which have legitimate ties to 'traditional law or custom' and those which do not. At the surface, some leeway is provided for cultural change. For instance, Brennan's discussion of cultural change seems quite broad; for traditions to maintain their legal veracity Aboriginal groups must simply continue 'to acknowledge the laws' and 'to observe the customs' *so far as practicable*. Likewise, Deane and Gaudron bow to the dynamism of culture, apparently acknowledging current trends in cultural theory in which traditions are seen to be fluid rather than frozen and where ethnography and law are always 'caught between cultures'.[42] In their view an Aboriginal society can change and still retain traditional rights to their land *provided any changes do not diminish or extinguish the relationship between a particular tribe or other group and particular land*.

By establishing a testable, factual basis for a claim that looks at degrees of change rather than at frozen cultural states, government rights are re-entrenched as they are represented as liberal accommodations. Arguing that there are degrees past which the grounds for 'special rights' pass into the grounds for 'equal rights'—'our traditions are different but equal thus laws relating to us differ' to 'our traditions are the same thus laws relating to us must be the same'—courts and parliament gain the backing of the 'reasonable person' who does not want to turn a cold eye to the atrocities of colonial history but also wants some contemporary basis for the differential treatment of Aboriginal people. By framing Aboriginal land rights as 'special rights' that can be extinguished either by previous acts of sovereignty or by the ongoing process of cultural change, the state gains the benefit of recognising the rights of authentic Aboriginal cultural subjects (acting on principle for 'social justice' in classic cultural relativistic terms: culture should be seen to be legitimate *in its own right*) as it maintains the right to evaluate that subjectivity—to distribute the rights the authentic cultural subject retains. For the state also *only* recognises Aboriginal cultural subjectivity as legitimate if it is *in its own right* (viz., as 'special' and 'other') and if *it is seen to be* by official institutions (in this case the state or Commonwealth tribunals). This 'multicultural'[43] turn in Australian law can thus be seen to mask a malignant institutionalisation of European discrimination of Aboriginal social organisation in the imperative sense of 'distinguish as distinct' if not 'denigrate as degenerate'. For, even if the Court recognises that Aboriginal traditions are not unchanging or static, it still grounds Aboriginal authority ('native' rights) in an ideally static cultural synchronism, while attributing government authority to a dynamic cultural and economic diachronism. Why denigrate the indigenous cultural subject if it is always and already undermined by the question of cultural corruption and cultural tainting? Like sexual misconduct, cultural corruption need not be proven or even pressed for the possibility of taint to undermine the unity of an authentic voice—to have to be a culturally authentic subject is always possibly not to be one, thus always to be subject to state evaluation and certification.

A decisive double-speak, is, therefore, the state's supposed movement past a 'discriminatory denigration of indigenous inhabitants, their social organization and customs'[44] even as it relies on the ever-possibility of socio-economic and cultural change to discriminate among land claims, on the national and international business communities to provide a discourse of social progressivity that can act as a counter-weight to 'militant' Aboriginal reactions to parliamentary compromises, and on the wider dominant society to provide the standard for assessing what counts as 'special' in the realm of culture. Thus, for example, the business community was sure to frame its responses to *Mabo* using a model of socio-economic progressivity, and it did. Mr Rob Davies of the investing banking house Lehman Brothers told the AAP in London that the *Mabo* decision threatened Australia's ability to maintain a '*modern* economy': 'If this decision stands, Australia could *go back* to being a Stone Age culture of 200,000 people living on witchetty grubs'.[45] And, we can be sure that, as they did in virtually every land claim case in the Northern Territory, local governments and businesses will, in the post-*Mabo* world, challenge every Aboriginal claim on the basis of its social referent's social, cultural and historical authenticity. Critically, then, three spheres of state power—the political, jural, and the economic—can be disarticulated but still function as a whole against minority communities.[46] Indeed, so unhinged they can better conspire together under similar cultural assumptions while seeming to be agreeing from multiple objective points in the social community, thereby isolating oppositional voices as 'fringe'.

While political and jural activities catch most people's attention as that which bears on Aboriginal practices, it is the working of culture that conspires both to value Aboriginal practices from the outside and to change the meaning of these practices from the inside. 'Fringe' increasingly becomes an interior position: what is within the group that cannot be shown outside and what itself is or seems to have been changed by dominant cultural views. For example, if an Aboriginal community attempts to create dense affective networks of relations predicated on a kinship system that weighs more heavily degree-of-relation than sex, but also knows from the public realm that sexual identity is a form of subjectivity that overrides kinship ('I am a homo-poof' versus 'that is my same-sex marriage partner'), into which system will it place the name of same-sex desire and eroticism? And how will this name differ within the community, the courtroom, the media? Whereas, in Western society 'at large' homosexuality is a counter-discourse to the hegemony of heterosexism and hetero-presumptions, in an Aboriginal context this oppositional framework undermines and transforms local systems of desire, sexuality, and economy and thus land use/ownership. And how much more stigmatised is same-sex eroticism and desire than single-motherhood and miscegenation which the non-Aboriginal public sees as evidence of the breakdown of 'traditional Aboriginal values'? Over and over, on television shows, in public welfare pamplets and in scholarly essays, the single Aboriginal mother of multiple children is described as a 'social condition' produced by unemployment, the loosening of belief in the Dreaming, and the devastating effects of drug addictions. It is not proclaimed, as it is in some Aboriginal communities, a new form of polygamy. Likewise, the lightening of skin is metaphorically linked to the draining of culture: miscegenation is an inevitable loss of cultural authenticity, not a new form of cultural inclusion. For the single mother herself or the two same-sexed cousins or the child of Aboriginal, Anglo-Celtic or Asian parents, the cultural condition of 'single-motherhood', 'homosexuality' and 'half-caste' becomes that which distinguishes between authentic and 'buggered-up' Aboriginal subjects; thus, that which can be told, known, accepted, embraced. These are the cultural discussions of sexuality and the family that provide the critical means by which land rights as a discursive framework is inculcated in and transforms local communities and insinuates itself into popular evaluations of Aboriginal cultural subjects. The western discursive opposition between heterosexuals and homosexuals as types of people, between single mothers and married mothers as more or less valid expressions of Aboriginal traditions, and between levels of miscegenation as retaining more or less culturally viable elements undermines the operance of kinship and the Dreaming in the domain of attraction and desire and, thus, in the creation of networks of same-sex and cross-sex resource sharing even as the dominant non-Aboriginal society is 'working for social justice' by recognising the value of Aboriginal traditions.

'Homosexuality', 'miscegenation', and 'single motherhood', not only function within Aboriginal communities as hegemonic rearticulations of the social imaginary, but also, from a western legal perspective at least, function as a sign of cultural decay, the loss of 'specialness' in the realm of culture, and thus the loss of any basis to claim land rights in Australia.

What guilt allows: a conclusion

In many ways, this chapter is simply an elaborate discussion of how a discourse of guilt allows the contemporary state to keep while giving away and the role that sexuality plays in this game of fort-da. Rather than position itself as opposing Aboriginal land rights, easily redeployed by Aboriginal activists as oppressing Aboriginal people and thus easily entangled in a human rights controversy, the Australian government positions itself as, on the one hand, expressing sorrow for the effects on Aboriginal people of past European misunderstandings (although those Aboriginal groups who suffered most gain least) and, on the other hand, supporting multiculturalism in the form of Aboriginal traditions. But in the midst of elaborate displays of remorse and appeals for reconciliation, the state has managed to maintain its control over both the type of Aboriginal sexuality that will be legally productive and the manner by which sovereignty (ultimate authority over people and places) and sexuality will be articulated. Whether portraying Aboriginal 'traditions' and Dreaming-inscribed sexual and gender relations as inherently disordered or ordered, the non-Aboriginal government and public have not altered their understanding of their own principles of governance: the notion that ordered familial relations serve as the basis of an ordered civil society. Loosely articulated, mobile but dense, same- and cross-sex, human-human and human-land desires and affectivities have no place in an ordered society or the law that seeks to uphold it; even though, in the post modern context of current national and international business communities, mobile worker populations and facile commodity desire figure strongly.[47]

As, hopefully, even a brief discussion makes it clear state manufactured Aboriginal sexuality has no real social referent. In short, state representation and implementation of legally recognised 'traditions' serve to restructure the Aboriginal social system and articulate it to state needs even as it purports to be recognising Aboriginal traditional institutions and legalising a multicultural approach to land tenure. The sexuality that government officials overtly and covertly invoke is but a marker and site of non-Aboriginal uses of culture as a means to power. The sexuality and social organisation that contemporary Australian public figures deplore or defend—but do so in either case in the name of Aboriginality—are their own. And while I have suggested that western constructions of sexuality bear on Aboriginal understandings of human-human and human-land relations, Aboriginals' rearticulated, dialogical conceptions and practices of eros and affectivity will never be Western but will always slip outside it because it will always be speaking with and against something which is itself always moving.[48] Thus, hopefully, this chapter suggests the need to 'synthesize an understanding of local movements and class culture, on the one hand, and large-scale state dynamics, on the other'.[49]

The discussion of *Mabo* also helps make sense of how culture, power, and history are implicated in the maintenance of state authority over minority, here indigenous, communities. *Mabo* certainly shows how contemporary interpretations of history are one set of actions turned on or towards another, a present event ordering and making sense of a past event; that is, *Mabo* is a 'discourse on time [that] is in time'.[50] The portrait of European and Aboriginal relations and traditions is a production geared towards current thinking on sovereignty. How surprising is it then that the current High Court and government represent colonial descriptions of Aboriginal traditions as misunderstandings? Why not admit that colonial writers and officials were not misunderstanding *per se* but producing a form of sexuality that was conversant with then current understandings of sovereignty (the legal implications of social progressivity and vacuity, sexual order and disorder); on the contrary, they were demonstrating a keen understanding of what were the necessary components of Aboriginal socio-sexual organisation to ground British sovereignty over *terra Australis* as *terra nullius*? To recognise that representing Australia as *terra nullius* at the point of settlement did not depend 'upon a discriminatory denigration of indigenous inhabitants, their social organisation and customs',[51] but rather on a necessary production of indigenous inhabitants, their socio-sexual irregularity and irrationality, the contemporary court and government would need to skim too closely to the similarities between colonial and postcolonial periods.

Finally, while much of my discussion has focused on hegemony in the sense of a rearticulation of the social imaginary[52] and while from an indigenous perspective political-economic discourses are anything but transparent,[53] I do not mean to imply that political and economic issues are absent. Quite the contrary, international and national corporations and political bodies were all critical influences on the form Keating's and other politicians' rhetoric took. However, the particular form of their rhetoric lies within dominant cultural assumptions about the legitimate basis of a civil society, the role of the state as ultimate guarantor and arbiter of rights (whether special or equal), and the orderly form socio-sexual organisation (even for those 'other cultures'[54]) can take. Because of the taken for granted nature of these assumptions, three sites of dominant power—the political-economic, the cultural, and the jural—can be unhinged without any serious threat to the current social order; indeed, it can work more effectively and appear more democratic and just as it makes critiques seem more outlandish and militant.

PART III

Rethinking bodies as property

6 Patent pending: laws of invention, animal life forms and bodies as ideas

Cathryn Vasseleu*

PATENT: Open to view, exposed to sight; hence exposed to the mental view, clear, plain, manifest, obvious; = OPEN[1]

1988 was a significant year for the mouse. In April of that year the United States Patent and Trademark Office (US PTO) granted Harvard University a patent on a genetically engineered version of the small mammalian species; a version which was highly susceptible to cancer formation and thus desirable as an object of cancer (or oncology) research. The 'OncoMouse' was the first multicellular organism to be protected by patent. Broadly speaking, patent law is the legislation which recognises the activity of invention. As a pursuit whose reward combines wealth, ubiquity and value to humanity, invention has been classically expressed as 'the quest to build a better mousetrap'. From this perspective, the granting of the OncoMouse patent announced a change in patent law which appeared to be one of epochal proportions. It had the effect, as one commentator describes the action of the US PTO, of instituting a shift in the focus of invention from building a better mousetrap to building a better mouse.[2]

Until recently, patent law has applied unproblematically to life forms because patent law does not distinguish between living and non-living things.[3] There are many instances in the history of the US PTO of patents being issued for living things. For example, patents were routinely granted for fermentation processes, and a patent was given for a vaccine in the form of an altered virus. Louis Pasteur was issued a patent for a yeast.[4] It was not until

105

the patent examiner denied a patent for a genetically engineered bacterium which degraded crude oil that the patentability of inventions of living matter became an item of dispute within patent law. The denial of the patent claim, which was based on the finding that a bacterium is a living, naturally occurring thing, was subsequently overruled by the US Supreme Court.[5] The Court's decision in 1980 was based on the argument that the critical distinction within patent law wasn't between living and non-living things, but between natural and man-made. Both of these categories included living and non-living things. The PTO Board's subsequent interpretation of the ruling was that the Congress intended patent law to apply to 'anything under the sun that is made by man'.[6] The qualifications to this 'anything' are that human beings could not be patented because no-one can own another human being, and that nuclear weapons could not be patented because the public disclosure required by patent law might be detrimental to national security.

The affirmation that life forms could be 'man-made' opened the way for patentable biotechnology as we know it today, from gene splicing and recombinant DNA to transgenic animals.[7] Although the invention of life subsequent to the Supreme Court ruling has been stranger than fiction, I am not qualified to directly address the myriad debates and complex issues surrounding the interpretation and applicability of patent law to biotechnology.[8] There has been both vigorous support for and opposition to the patenting of animal life, but discussion of the various positions has been left aside for the purposes of this chapter. My interest is directed towards an interpretation of the functioning of various philosophical terms in patent law.

Patent law is distinguished from copyright law by a tenuous line which is drawn between the *expression* and the *idea* of a thing. Although the distinction is contestable,[9] copyright affords its owner a monopoly over the *expression* of a piece of work, while a patent grants, for a limited time only, a monopoly over the exploitation of an *idea* embodied in a process, machine, manufacture or composition of matter. In the case of copyright, the material itself (which is deemed to be words, images, or any work which has been fixed as a tangible medium) is protected, but an independent creation using the same idea will not be an infringement. A patent holder on the other hand, does not have any exclusive rights over the matter in which an idea is expressed. Nor does a patent authorise an inventor to make, use or sell an invention. Any exploitation of the idea is subject to the restrictions of other regulatory bodies. However, for the duration of a patent, any unauthorised *use* of the patented idea is an infringement, even

in the event of its independent discovery. Paradoxical as it may
seem, an example of the difference between these two forms of
intellectual property is that Mickey Mouse is a material expression
of a mouse, but OncoMouse is an idea.

It is worth considering how the distinction between expression
and idea can be established in the invention of life forms. This
distinction applies to the body of the inventor before it applies to
the invention. Patent law relies on the Cartesian mind/body distinction, which posits the body as an idea of a disembodied mind.
In Cartesian dualism the body exists as an idea, and as such, can
be an object of knowledge. As I intend to discuss, this concept of
the body is fundamental to patent law, which authorises the use
of the idea, not its embodiment.

An example of the use of the idealisation of the body in law
is the attribution of paternity rights in the case of artificial
insemination by donor (AID). Paternity is established by the
principle of substituting a legal relationship for a biological or
natural one. The man whose semen is donated is presumed not
to be the father, while a husband or de facto partner is recognised
as the legal father. Fatherhood becomes a legally rather than a
naturally determined relationship. It is arguable that in law, this
has always been the case.[10]

The idealisation of the father's body in the example of AID
occurs as an effect of substitution. Paternity is established by a
symbolic link with semen, which signifies man's agency in fecundity rather than a particular body. Once it has been proferred as
a gift, the material specificity of semen can be rendered irrelevant
by an institutionally authorised concept of patrilineality. Legislation for AID has been a relatively uncontroversial affair despite
anomalies which have resulted.[11] Such ease of substitution in AID
does not occur in the instance of surrogacy, which has not only
met with widespread outcry and concern, but also, since the
infamous *Baby M* case, defied legislation.[12]

Concern about surrogacy arrangements has focused on the
issue of control. The expression of this concern has ranged from
predicting the opportunities for unethical exploitation, to stressing
the unenforceability of contractual arrangements between parties.
The current trend in legislation is to confirm that surrogacy
contracts will be unenforceable, but that no criminal sanctions
will be imposed where they are made. The contradictory nature
of the arguments against the legalisation of surrogacy arrangements (that it will lead to exploitation and that it defies
exploitation) reflects the ambiguity of a woman's relationship to
her body in law.

This relationship can be addressed in ideational terms. In the instance of AID, where semen is given away as a gift, its symbolic duplication of the paternal body in the embodiment of a child is upheld in law. However, a maternal relationship to offspring of a surrogacy arrangement, which includes a woman's body as well as gametes, defies such representation. It appears that the substance of semen can be idealised, but the substance of a woman's body cannot. While semen is regarded as a concept in AID (man's agency in fecundity), the maternal body-link in surrogacy is a unique material relation. There is an ineffable bond between a woman's body and the product of her womb. While offspring can be adopted if they are given away as a gift, any familial relation to offspring based on the substitution of 'rearing' or even 'gamete-producing' parent for uterine mother cannot be upheld in law.

AID and surrogacy are instances of the effectiveness of the law's mediation of the material body and the body as an idea. In AID, the law can act as an inventive transitional agent, acknowledging the idea of paternity in its expression as offspring. In surrogacy, the law fails to act as a transitional medium, thus preserving a material relation between a woman's body and its creations. Both consequences are the effects of the inventiveness of the law. The inventiveness of the law in AID relates to its capacity to grant a legal status based on an idea. The invention is limited to *the usage of the idea as an inventive link*, not the idea. Legal texts stress that ideas belong to everyone, and as such cannot be the prerogative of anyone in particular. In contrast to invention, the maternal relation is called a natural bond. A natural bond is implicit and indefinable and has no substitute.

A patent is regarded as the intermediary between the private disposition and public circulation of an idea. Insofar as it grants its holder the right to exploit the unexploitable for a limited time, a patent is the middle ground between the use of an idea as a commodity and the use of an idea as a gift. The institutions of patenting and licensing, which relate to 'applied science', are essential to the commerce of ideas. Patented uses of ideas are proprietary concerns and do not circulate without a fee. The common justification of patent law is that it both rewards and stimulates invention, and in doing so, it advances and institutes new knowledge. Exclusive rights to use are given in return for public disclosure of the means by which the invention can be reproduced. After the statutory time limit of the patent, the invention (that is, the inventive link, or operational possibility) becomes common knowledge, or the property of all. In comparison, it is generally argued that the ideas and resources which circulate within a community of scientific scholars are treated as gifts. Such free exchange of ideas and resources is essential to 'pure' or 'basic' (and less well remunerated but more prestigious) research. The ideal function and effect of this gift giving is the creation of a community of a 'common mind'.[13] Although the two groups supposedly stimulate and contribute to each other, that is increasingly not the case. As scientists feel that their 'gifts' are being exploited without due credit, and proprietary groups turn to trade secret provisions for their investments, the more prophylactic effect of patent law is that 'People are no longer sharing their strains of bacteria and their results as freely as they did in the past.'[14]

The demand for *acknowledgment* of ideas circulating as gifts in the scientific community indicates that this concept of gift is operating in terms of exchange. A reconsideration of gift as a form of exchange is made by Jacques Derrida, with reference to the work of Marcel Mauss[15] (a human and therefore unpatentable Mauss). According to Derrida, Mauss's analysis of the gift is caught in the contradictory insistence that there is no gift without the bind of obligation, and yet, unless the gift is free of contractual obligation and the imperative of return, it is not a gift. Rather than supporting economic exchange, the gift cannot be figured in economic terms and is thus an impossibility:

> By the impossible, what ought one have understood? . . . If we speak of it we will have to name something. Not to present the thing, here the impossible, but to try with its name, or with some name, to give an understanding of or to think this impossible thing, this impossible itself . . .[16]

Instead of mediating between the circulation of ideas as gifts and ideas as commodities, the impossibility of gift suggests an alternative mediating function of patent law. That function would be the assignation of a name to the impossible. I will develop this point in the following discussion.

The moment of invention

In deciding the issue of whether biotechnology should be included within the definition of 'invention,' courts have argued that failure of existing legislation to specifically nominate biological inventions is not sufficient reason to deny them patent. Instead, courts stress that patent law is framed to include future ingenuity, which it could not possibly anticipate. One of the three basic requirements of patentability is *novelty*. If an invention can be anticipated it is unlikely to be a novelty. The United States Supreme Court held in 1980 that '[a] rule that unanticipated inventions are without

protection would conflict with the core concept of patent law that
anticipation undermines patentability'. The intentional use of general terms in the patent statutes is 'precisely because inventions
are often unforeseeable'.[17] In Australia, the High Court has also
recognised that any attempt to define 'manufacture' would be to
ignore the fact that the purpose of patent law 'was to allow the
use of the prerogative to encourage national development in a
field which already, in 1623, was seen to be excitingly unpredictable'.[18] In other words patent law has the impossible task of
anticipating its application. It must anticipate what it cannot
anticipate, or legislate for the unforeseeable.

The temporal enigma which is brought together in invention
is the novelty of a first time and the arrival of the future, or
time-to-come:

> Never does an invention appear, never does an invention take
> place, without an inaugural event. Nor is there any invention
> without an advent, if we take this latter word to mean the
> inauguration for the future of a *possibility* or of a *power* that will
> remain at the disposal of everyone.[19]

An invention has to be recognisable and evaluable and reproduc-
ible by another party. Its status as invention depends on the
certification of its public, open, clear identification, of its being
patently obvious. The law confers the status of obviousness.
Without legislation, there can be no invention.[20] The relationship
between event, adventure and convention in the production of new
operational possibilities has been characterised by Derrida as
follows:

> Advent there must be, because the event of an invention, its act of
> inaugural production, once recognized, legitimized, countersigned
> by a social consensus according to system of conventions, must be
> valid *for the future (a—venir)*. It will only receive its status of
> invention, furthermore, to the extent that this socialization of the
> invented thing will be protected by a system of *conventions* that
> will ensure for it at the same time its recording in a common
> history, its belonging to a culture: to a heritage, a lineage, a
> pedagogical tradition, a discipline, a chain of generations.
> Invention begins by being susceptible to repetition, exploitation,
> reinscription.[21]

The three aspects of this relationship can be found in the three
basic requirements for the granting of a patent. First the event of
an invention, or its act of inaugural production is determined in
the requirement of *novelty*. Second, the advent of an invention,
or the validation of its potential value is determined in the
requirement of *non-obviousness*. Finally, the convention of inven-

tion, or its cultural establishment, is determined in the requirement of *usefulness*.

The requirement of novelty in patent law validates the uniqueness of an event. The uniqueness of the event, which applies to human ingenuity, is conditioned by its difference from nature. Unlike nature, which defies all limits, invention must have a unique moment of origin. The production of an animal or protein or genetic fragment is not a unique event if it can be found that way in nature. It is merely copying nature. Discovery re-presents a prior existential claim. It is the uncovering rather than beginning of something. Invention is a reflexive structure which speaks of itself, not as a presence, but as an instant which is both already past, and yet to be realised in future productions. Hence, the novelty of invention is caught in the paradox of being a once-only and yet repeatable operative possibility.

The requirement of non-obviousness in patent law recognises the adventure of invention. To qualify as non-obvious an invention must bear no resemblance to anything already known. It must be unconventional. At the same time, it is proposing that it can be known, as a power potentially available to all. It is necessary to submit a written account of an invention which would allow someone 'skilled in the art' to be able to reproduce it. Interestingly, in the case of biotechnology, written accounts give insufficient guidance for the reproduction of the invention. Despite their facility in the language of genetics, biotechnicians have been unable to formulate a separate metalanguage or 'blue-print' which suffices as a description for the material reconstitution of invented life forms. The expression of genetic material is unaccountably more variable than the functional correlation between genes and traits which is often asserted. The requirement has presented so many problems that it, more than any moral, theological or ecological arguments, may act as a limit to the patenting of animal life forms.[22]

The provision that has been established for biotechnology has been to deposit an example of the invention in material form. This is based on the assumption that there is communication of ideas within genetic material. Once lodged with the patent office the sample is accessible to anyone to use without profit. As a piece of DNA or the gametes of a multicellular organism, the invented matter 'advances itself' as the means of expression of the patent idea. However, the effect of the deposit requirement has been an undermining of the desirability of seeking a patent. Compliance with the deposit requirement is tantamount to relinquishing to competitors the means of production along with the invention. During the life of the patent, the deposit requirement encourages the practice of copying and counterfeiting.[23] There is no need for expenditure on production of the invention, which can be quickly and cheaply exploited once the patent has lapsed. It can be exploited indiscriminately in countries where there is no patent. The value of the distinction between the means of expression and usage of the idea is lost. The invention creates/discovers/produces/copies/counterfeits itself without crediting the inventor.

The requirement of usefulness in patent law establishes order in place of a difference in the order and the impropriety of the not-yet normal use of an idea. Invention refers both to a power of discovery, and to a power of producing what is.[24] As such, it oscillates between truth and fabrication, disturbing the facticity of those unequivocal ideas we know as conventions and norms. Invention has no status without its reinscription within a system of technoscientific, economic, and humanist conventions, which will establish its obviousness to all. It is not sufficient for an invention to be novel, it must have a proposed application, a causal relation, an end in mind. Some scientists working on the human genome project have failed to patent the gene fragments which they have discovered because they have been unable to propose a use for their discoveries. Their discoveries, or 'snippets of sequence with no known biological function', remain just that without the power of inventive connection.[25] The requirement of usefulness gives invention a means of association with institutional stability, and limits the effects of its impropriety. The unconventional becomes progressive. There is a normative mechanism which operates between developments in genetic engineering and the explosion in numbers of applications for biotechnology patents. Where invention begins by being susceptible to repetition, exploitation and reinscription, conventions assure that patent law itself generates this kind of invention. Life, as we know it today, is genetically recombinant, translatable, reiterable, sequential. Rather than overrun the bounds of convention, 'life' comes to resemble patent law—that is, susceptible to repetition, exploitation and reinscription. The mouse comes to resemble the mousetrap.

Title to invention

As mentioned earlier, patent law does not distinguish between living and non-living; only between natural and man-made. Patent law was originally framed within a structure of rationality which viewed nature as the basis of the order of material things. Products of human manufacture were differentiated from those products, both organic and inorganic, which were authorised by nature.

An idea of life which is dissociated from nature was proposed by the late 18th century pathological anatomist, Marie-François-Xavier Bichat. As Michel Foucault has described the shift, in considering the notion of 'pathological life', Bichat overturned the structure of rationality which viewed nature as the basis of the order of things. Bichat's idea placed life at a deeper ontological level than nature. Life was not a quantifiable or qualitative issue which could be distinguished from the inorganic. It was the basis of the opposition through which the living and the non-living organism could be perceived (the presence or absence of life). Arguments between vitalists and mechanists as well as notions of pathological life were all reducible to the fundamental priority of life.[26] On the same basis, it is possible to conceive of 'patent life forms' as organisms whose life is not naturally bestowed. Furthermore, the diversity of matter included in that notion will range from the proteins of molecular biologists to the animals bred by transgenic manipulation.

Bichat's proposition reiterated that life is a gift, which is given by an unknowable other. No person can claim life as their invention. This aspect of patenting life forms is passed over in the exchange view of gift which I have referred to earlier. Life does not enter into invention, except as the statutory time limit prescribed for the claim to a patent. Life itself cannot even be entertained in patent law. Instead, claims for biotechnology patents are based on the manipulation of matter (biomass), in a way which would be impossible in nature. It can be argued that the impossibility in nature referred to here is the impossibility of manufacturing an origin. Things are *created*, not invented, in nature. Their origin might be inexplicable but its authenticity is never in dispute. These products are called 'gifts of nature', but they are gifts understood in economic terms, that is, of *recognisable* (natural) origin. The paradox is that an origin *is* manufactured for this unmanufactured matter. The impossibility of gift is forgotten in the very naming of matter as a product of nature.

Invention is a self-referential initiative, whose origin is technically determined and thus always in dispute. As has been discussed, an invention is not simply discovered, nor is it simply produced. As such, the status of its existence is never finally settled. An invention is a fabrication which must authorise itself in terms of something other than itself. It is this something other which makes invention a uniquely human activity. The patency of invention is upheld by the normative view (convention) that any human is capable of invention:

Man himself, and the human world, is defined by the human
subject's aptitude for invention, in the double sense of narrative
fiction or historical fabulation and of technical or technoepistemic
innovation . . . No one has ever *authorized* himself—it is indeed a
question of status and convention—to say of God that he invents
. . . and no one has ever authorized himself to say of animals that
they invent. On the other hand men can invent gods, animals, and
especially divine animals.[27]

Insofar as the originality of an invention is an attribute given to
a human (being or group) by other humans, the thing made patent
is the *inventor*. A patent authorises its holders to say of themselves, on the basis of discoveries which others can repeat, that
they invent. In other words, patent law establishes the patency of
the inventor rather than the invention. I will discuss this assertion
by referring to issues which have arisen in the patenting of animal
life forms.

One of the most complex issues which has arisen from the
patenting of animal life forms has been the extension of patent
rights to the offspring of patent animals and future products which
might arise from them. Reproduction is a capacity inherent in
living things, which makes the question of patent claims in this
area difficult to resolve. Unlike non-living inventions, patent life
forms can often sexually reproduce themselves. The issue has
extensive economic ramifications in areas such as agricultural
production and availability of breeding stock, particularly in the
case of smaller farming operations.[28] However, I will limit my
discussion to the OncoMouse patent. The patent was licensed to
DuPont,[29] which distributed the mouse in two ways. Researchers
were charged a fee per mouse. They were permitted to reproduce
only a limited number without paying a licensing fee. Commercial
groups were charged a fee per mouse, as well as a licensing fee
and royalties on all offspring reproduced. Furthermore, a 'reach
through' clause entitled DuPont to claim an economic interest in
any drug or therapy which resulted from the mouse's use, on the
basis that the mouse would have contributed to the value, because
it speeded up research.[30]

Licences to reproduce other strains of laboratory mice have
been partially modified since the now-notorious DuPont policy,[31]
but the general principles allowing DuPont's claims are worth
considering. The patent for the OncoMouse did not cover the
reproduction of matter. It covered the reproduction of an operative
possibility. Each mouse was considered as merely the embodiment
or evidence of the patent claim. The mouse's capacity to reproduce
is a property of a living thing and thus not at issue in a patent
claim. The fact that not all genetically altered mice express or

reproduce the desired characteristics has raised the question of whether they must be paid for. The reproduction of the capacity of a human to produce a mouse is the issue in a patent claim. I am referring here to biology as a reproductive technology, which invents a mechanism in place of an origin. The mechanism of reproductive technology, as analysed by Walter Benjamin,[32] can be characterised by its displacement of the 'originality' of the unique, and the erasure of the difference between original and repro-duction. The intention of a genetic biologism is ultimately the eradication of the unaccountable differences inherent in the repro-ductive capacity of living things, and the production of an infinite reiterability of the biological sameness of living things. The human genome project, and all that it can offer humanity, is the example *par excellence* of this principle.

The rights over offspring of the OncoMouse patent are based on the acknowledgment of the originality of the inventor in every different embodiment and each new generation of the mouse. The patent establishes a causal relationship or inventive link between a subject, or inventor, and the predicate of invention, or embodiment of the inventor's idea. There is no possibility of knowing where the difference between the mouse's invention and the mouse's existence starts and ends. The inexplicability of material reproduction is both *essential* and *incidental* to the patent process of the inventor. Furthermore, DuPont was determined to capitalise not only on the offspring of the mouse, but even on the *time*, or future 'saved' by the inventor in the adventure of the mouse. Neither of these things is entertainable as property (time and matter are simply given), yet this impossibility is exploitable *additionally* to (in support of) a contribution attributable to an inventor. The only property right which is recognised in invention is the use of the inventor's title to invention.

The invention of humanity

Another issue which is raised by claims to animal invention is the patenting of human life. The US PTO announcement in 1987 that it would accept applications for patents on animals specifies 'non-human' life forms,[33] and the *Australian Patents Act 1990* explicitly excludes the patenting of 'human beings and the biolog-ical processes for their generation'.[34] In Europe, even the continued patenting of non-human animals is under challenge. The general explanation for making an exception of human life is that the ownership of another human being is prohibited by different law (in America, this is the Fifth Amendment, which is the law used

to abolish human slavery).[35] Another interpretation of the exception is that it is intended to quell objections that animal patents
demean life and invite the patenting of humans.[36] Nevertheless,
this exception has highlighted the impossibility of drawing a line,
not only within biology, but also within law, between human and
animal life. There have been many instances of patenting human
genetic material. The development of transgenic animals and
proteins by recombinant DNA involves a variety of combinations
of genetic material from different species and micro-organisms.
Commonly, human genes are used. For example, the production
of proteins which have medical applications (such as insulin)
involves the inclusion of the human gene for that protein within
the genetic makeup of a micro-organism or a domesticated animal.
In order to be patented, any organism which includes human
genetic material must be identified as 'non-human'. Another, more
curious instance is the acceptance of a surgeon's application to
patent a cell line from a patient's spleen. The application prompted
an ownership dispute between patient and surgeon, inspiring a
memorable case comment title: 'Moore v Regents of the University
of California: *Was He Merely Vending His Spleen?*'[37]

Commentary on the problems of drawing the line between
human and non-human life includes questions of ownership and
'species integrity'.[38] It also includes discussion of the spectre raised
by the possibilities of 'near-human' life. These range from 'less-
human' vehicles for medical research to surrogate limbless bodies
functioning as artificial wombs.[39] These arguments consider the
consequences of the inability to distinguish between the human
and the animal in law. Such arguments emphasise the ineffectual
nature of the qualification concerning human life in patent law,
and presume an ideal human form is being violated. The fear of
the hybridisation is often expressed in terms of the animal being
given human intelligence, and the human being reduced to a more
animal body, over which it has no control. Exception to this
argument is made in the case of animal rights lobbyists, who are
more concerned with the violation of animals. I prefer to relate
this point to the argument that justifies the qualification in patent
law, that is, the prior existence of a different law that prohibits
the ownership of another human being.

This alternative point is that the exclusion of human life from
patent law highlights that the uniqueness of human life is dependent on the establishment of its difference from invention. If human
life transcended 'all things under the sun which are made by man'
then there would be no need for the qualification of 'non-human'.
The exclusion reveals an inventor whose body is perilously close
to becoming an invention. In other words, the integrity of the law

which precludes the ownership of human life is itself threatened without the qualification in patent law. Without the difference between human and 'non-human' matter, the human body would be *nothing other* than matter, and thus merely a vehicle for invention. One of the more novel if not bizarre responses to this indeterminate existence of the human body in law has been a call to anticipate the need for a theory of constitutional personhood for transgenic humanoid species. This is an 'invention' which humanises and *liberates* the mouse. It would guarantee the rights of hybrid humans yet to be created, and these rights would effectively prohibit their patentability.[40]

Cartesian dualism guarantees that the human body as matter acquires an extreme naturalism. The idea of the body originates in the mind of subject. The matter of the body originates in nature, and as such cannot be the subject of invention. There is, however, another way of interpreting Descartes' proposition, which opens up the possibilities of the body as an idea. Maurice Merleau-Ponty, for example, has referred to Cartesian dualism as 'perhaps the most profound idea of the union of the soul and the body'.[41] This accolade is an unexpected one from a philosopher whose work represents a radical attempt to renegotiate subjectivity through the phenomenon of embodiment. According to Merleau-Ponty, in referring to the body as an idea, Descartes proposes a human body which is open to conjecture. A human body is irreducible to natural matter, because thought predetermines its existence. A body has a human form only in a different form (a thought) of itself. At this point Merleau-Ponty makes a distinction between Descartes' and his own interpretation of this difference. In Descartes' case, the idea of a human body is achieved in a 'mental' view or thought of itself. Merleau-Ponty proposes that the idea of one's body is achieved in the view or perception of others.

Merleau-Ponty's interpretation of Cartesian dualism draws attention to the mediation of others in the naming of one's body as one's own, thus bringing the indeterminacy of the body closer to invention. One's body represents an operative possibility, or a means of linkage, which is unique yet inseparable from its historical and material circumstances. The lived-body is a reflexive structure, but it is not simply an idea which is co-incident with one's self. Its reflexivity, or the means by which it can be claimed as one's own, is an idea which is mediated by cultural perceptions. My body is not a projection of mine. My body is only mine insofar as it is given to me, both in the sense of givenness and being given by others:

> The central phenomenon, at the root of both my subjectivity and

my transcendence towards others, consists in my being given to myself. *I am given*, that is, I find my self already situated and involved in a physical and a social world . . .[42]

By insisting on the origin of the body as a question within the terms of perception, rather than a thing uncovered by it, Merleau-Ponty proposes a body which is produced by the perception that dawns through it.[43] Invention is as much a skill of placing or contextualising itself as it is a skill of linkage. The law institutes a body of common possibilities for those who have skill in that art. As with invention, any normative concept of a body must be susceptible to repetition, exploitation and reinscription, by the cultural establishment of its patency.

Despite his intention to overcome a distinction between the body as subject and the body as object, Merleau-Ponty's reflexive subjectivity has been criticised by various feminist theorists for its perpetuation of that very distinction.[44] Although maintenance of the distinction is critical in patent law, its indeterminacy becomes apparent in the case of pregnancy. The problem which the 'non-human' qualification reveals as it solves in patent law is the use of the inventor's own body as a medium of the ideas of others. This disclaimer against the use of one's body as a medium or host is complicated by the example of pregnant subjectivity. In the case of a patent for the production of a protein by biological means, the altered animal or micro-organism which produces the protein is referred to as a host. For the purposes of a patent claim, usefulness is expressed in terms of the commercial benefit which will follow from the invented, or *mediated* material (host/product) interaction. In the case of pregnancy, there is an irreducible difference between a woman's body and her body as a material host. As a pregnant woman, the connection between her own self and her pregnant body is materially determined. As a human subject, a woman's body is her own, but this cannot account for the difference between her body and a child. Her/pregnant body is neither her own or another's. Nor can anyone exploit it. On the other hand, the use of the idea of genetic matching can be the basis for establishing the patency of a claim in paternal interventions against abortion. As Germaine Greer writes: 'The most staggering development in the opening of the womb to public gaze . . . was not echosound or endoscopy, but the discovery of a way positively to identify the genetic father of any embryo.'[45] Such in(ter)ventions are at the expense of a woman's inviolate humanity, effectively reducing her body to a host, or object open to the use of others.

The Cartesian proposition—that the human body is an idea—

sustains the law of invention and AID, yet its objectivity is consistently defeated by the materiality of subjectivity in, for example, pregnant embodiment. The ambiguous determination of a pregnant woman's body/matter as both hers and an other's defies the transcendental idealised subjectivity of legal invention. But nor would it be appropriate to insist on the autonomy of feminine embodiment in terms of material states. Maternity is hardly the ultimate definition of female humanity. The problem, as Luce Irigaray describes it, is the necessity for positive rights to an *idealised* human identity of one's own, which is irreducible either to the value of matter or to any medium of exchange.[46]

In recognising the extent to which the Cartesian idea of embodiment has defined both the possibilities and limits of the the law's inventiveness, there is potential for that invention to be reconsidered and reinvented. Merleau-Ponty's interpretation of Cartesian dualism is just one step which can be been added in that direction, as is any evaluation of the underlying philosophical assumptions concerning the use of an idea of a body in law. However, another essential feature to pursue is that patency is equally conditional on its impossibility, or the indefinability of its claim to existence. Indefinability is not a condemnation to infinite dispersibility, nor is it an irrational dead-end. Rather than being a limit to law, patent law demonstrates the immensity of its generative powers.

Invention has been the abiding metaphor of the innovative and destructive power of modernism. By way of contrast, my point in considering the body as invention is to argue for a reconsideration of the indefinability that prefigures its self-defined autonomy. Indefinability is the condition of both a clarified openness and an opening of possibility. On the other hand, the establishment of patency is always contingent on the effacement of the indefinable possibilities of a medium in the name of a particular, attributable one.[47] Where the uniqueness of a body is considered as an invention, the law's assumption of its patency is itself a constantly contestable issue, and one which must acknowledge any claim's exploitability, limitations and operative specificity. Patency begins by being non-obvious, unrepresentative and disorderly, and yet with institutional support, ends by becoming a conventional idea. It must be added that the procedure of investigating a patent claim is often lengthy and cumbersome, requiring extensive expert research of the conventions and practices in the field of each claim. Furthermore, in the interests of a new 'humanity,' the body of the law would become the mouse.

7 The gift, sexed body property and the law

Rosalyn Diprose*

Certain developments in medical technology over recent years have tended to increase the alienability of human body products and parts. The ability to transfer cells, zygotes, body fluids and organs from one body to another, via some kind of storage facility, is one of the wonders of modern medicine. But as we wonder, the viability of the alienation of these substances has become less a medical than a legal and moral problem. Something as trivial as a homeless cell can raise questions about matters as significant as ownership, identity, legal responsibility and morality. Who, for example, owns the cell line produced from the cells of someone's pancreas: the owner of the pancreas or the manufacturer of the line? Who owns the zygote held in storage after its genetic parents become estranged? What moral status does the zygote itself have? Who has ultimate claim over the foetus in a surrogacy arrangement: the genetic parents, the intending parents or the surrogate? Does a sperm donor have any claim to, or responsibility for, the product of his ejaculation? Should the product of that event have the same rights to know their genetic origin as an adopted child? Should a person be permitted to sell their blood or kidney to the highest bidder? And so on.

A pattern is beginning to emerge in legislative responses to such questions. The responses share with the questions the assumption that the corporeal substances at issue are someone's property. In keeping with the tradition of thought based on social contract theory and liberal individualism, it is taken for granted that the human body is owned by the particular self to which it

120

THE GIFT, SEXED BODY PROPERTY AND THE LAW

is attached, as is that part of 'nature' transformed by the body's labour.[1] Accompanying the concept of property in one's person is the assumption of natural freedom and autonomy: the equal right of individuals to be free from subjection by others and the right to do with one's body what one wills providing that action does not bring harm to others, either directly or via harm to oneself.[2] On the one hand, the idea of freedom as autonomous, rational self-government renders the human body inalienable under laws which prohibit slavery. On the other hand, the idea that a person's body and the products of its labour is their property supports an image of social relations as the shared government and exchange of this property. The role of the law is to protect this property and to ensure that the disposal of it, and the access of others to it, is equitable. Social relations are said to be equitable, and individual freedom and autonomy preserved, if the exchange of body-property is based on fair contract or informed consent.

It is on the basis of this model of individual autonomy and equitable social relations that the invisible cell is understood in terms of personal property. And, given that the law exists to protect individual autonomy, while ensuring the equitable exchange of personal property, it is not possible to legislate, in any blanket fashion, against the biomedical alienation of body products and parts, particularly when this is said to create or save lives. So the law is called upon, not to determine whether alienation of body property is viable, but to determine to what extent and under what conditions body property can be justly alienated. Two alternatives have emerged in answering this call: either the transfer of body property is allowed under the terms of a contract, in which case money can exchange hands, or it is only allowed in terms of a gift.

The following analysis of these alternatives will reveal some problems in legislation governing the alienation of body-property, particularly when the body involved is sexed. I will argue that endorsing the transfer of corporeal substances in terms of contract is unjust in its determination of sexed identity. And, while the model of the gift appears to remove some of the difficulties surrounding the alienation of body property, it does not guarantee justice. Insofar as giving is understood in terms of relations between self-present, autonomous property owners it underscores an inequitable 'exchange' of corporeality in the creation and maintenance of life. Only by opening the gift beyond these terms is justice possible. Yet, to do so challenges the very foundation of the law.

At stake in the battle between contract and gift as paradigms for the biomedical alienation of body tissue is the need to avoid commodification of the person (which would negate their 'natural' freedom) while preserving the individual's autonomy as sovereignty over their body (which implies the right to use their body as they will). This balance seems to be achieved by giving the transfer legal status in terms of a contract, providing the contract is understood to be governing the provision of a service.

Such a contract is said to be between the owner of the body providing the service and either the manager of the facility for storing the body product or its intended recipient. Given that the recipient of the service can, under the terms of the contract, determine the working conditions necessary to ensure a quality product, the person providing the service does temporarily relinquish the sovereignty they are said to have over their body. However, autonomy is apparently preserved insofar as the service provider has consented to the terms of the contract. And commodification of the person is seemingly avoided: the corporeality being transferred is viewed as the product of work done (transforming 'nature' through the body's labour) rather than part of the substance of the worker. Hence, as in any service or work contract, the worker can receive payment for their service and apparently does not incur any personal loss in the transaction. What this service contract effectively constitutes is the uniform, intentional, linear transmission, through objective time and space, of a corporeal unit originating in one atomised, static individual and arriving in another. What remains to be assessed is what is written out of the contract in the name of equity and justice.

On the basis of this model of contract, it is possible to sell your blood in some democratic states (the United States for instance) and your organs in others. Surrogacy can also be given legal status in these terms. While there has been a lucrative and apparently unproblematic trade in some body products for centuries, such as hair for the production of wigs, and while the sale of blood and organs does pose certain legal and practical difficulties,[3] the exchange of sexed body property under a service contract, for procreative purposes or for pleasure, has proven to be particularly controversial. The surrogacy contract generates far more bad press than the sale of hair because of its challenge to assumptions about sexed identity, biological origin and personal autonomy.

The notorious case of *Baby M* (New Jersey, 1987) serves to illustrate the difficulties. The case involved a contract between 'intending' parents, Elizabeth and William Stern, and a surrogate, Mary-Beth Whitehead. In exchange for a fee, Whitehead agreed to carry a foetus to term and relinquish the child to the Sterns after birth. However, Whitehead struck a blow against the foundation of contract by breaking her promise. Also up for challenge, at least potentially, in the legal battle for Baby M which followed, was the property status of the human body and the products of its labour, the individuation of persons and the corporeality said to pass between them and the assumed linearity of corporeal exchange.

Even if we grant that cells and tissues are owned by someone and can be alienated in terms of a service, who provided the service for whom in this case was, to say the least, ambiguous. A child was transferred from a body to the world, blood was transmitted to and enhanced a zygote, a gamete was transferred from William Stern to Whitehead, her gamete enveloped his, and so on. Determining a singular outcome and its proper owner in such a process of production is frustrated by the indeterminate constitution and multiplication of cells, the formation, transform-ation and crossing of borders, the fluidity of identity and difference. However, in the case of Baby M the presiding Judge, Harvey Sorkow, undeterred by the cloudiness of the issue, ruled in favour of the Sterns. He argued, among other things, that this was not a contract governing the exchange of a child for cash (thus avoiding commodification of one body). He deemed it to be a service contract between the genetic father and Whitehead, a contract she, as the provider of the service, was obliged to honour. In effect, this determination commodifies the surrogate's body, by reducing it to a storage facility, and secures the genetic father as the origin and destination of procreative property.

The surrogacy contract, upheld as it has been by this and similar judgements, has been widely condemned as unjust, particu-larly by defenders of women's rights. There have been two common arguments posed against it. Firstly, it is said that the surrogacy contract extends patriarchal control over women's reproductive bodies. This is based on two different observations, both of which assume that the recipient of the service is male. One is that the surrogate loses control of her body for the duration of the contract given that the recipient of the 'service' can deter-mine, under the terms of the contract, what she does with her body (that she exercise, not smoke or drink alcohol etc.).[4] This concern is otherwise put in terms of the (immoral) commodific-ation of the surrogate's body or the unjust treatment of it as a means to an end. The other observation is that upholding the contract amounts to the extension of paternity rights.[5]

The second kind of argument against the surrogacy contract is the one which proposes that a woman's decision to enter it as a surrogate is not autonomous. This is based on the claim that a decision is only autonomous if the person making it is fully informed of its consequences for her future wellbeing and, as experiences of pregnancy vary, an intending surrogate cannot know in advance what traumas her decision may bring (in giving up the child and in the 'usual risks' of pregnancy).[6] If the surrogate's decision to enter the contract is not autonomous in this sense then, so the argument goes, the contract is unjust. This objection implies that the intending surrogate is subject to some kind of coercion even if she actively seeks the arrangement. The types of 'coercion' cited include the undue influence of economic need and the social imperative to procreate upon the intending surrogate's decision, influences to which women are particularly susceptible in patriarchal society.

Without denying the import of these objections, one immediate problem with them is that they are, for the most part, just as applicable to other service contracts but are raised as if they are not.[7] Am I, for example, any more in control of my body than the surrogate given that I am not allowed to smoke or drink alcohol at work? Is economic need a form of 'coercion' peculiar to surrogacy or does it also inform decisions to enter other work contracts? If the social imperative to procreate compromises the autonomy of an intending surrogate, can this also be said of all women involved in procreation? Despite the wider applicability of these objections, their use against the surrogacy contract is rarely accompanied by arguments against other work or service contracts (such as those for selling blood) and never directed against procreation in general. In raising these problems I am not endorsing the service contract as a model for the alienation of body property. I am suggesting that these objections to the surrogacy contract fail to locate why such contracts are unjust. In fact by relying on the model of autonomy as control over one's body and by restricting the charges to some sexually specific contracts, these kinds of arguments risk reinforcing a tradition which excludes women from social exchange on the basis of the sex of our bodies.

I want to suggest that the injustice of the surrogacy contract lies not in an extension of patriarchal control over women's reproductive bodies nor in its failure to uphold women's autonomy understood in terms of informed consent. If the law fails women here it is for the same reason it fails in all service contracts: because it is based on a contradiction. While the law exists to preserve autonomy and freedom within social exchange, social exchange rests on the negation, by 'consent', of autonomy and freedom as they are understood within this paradigm. On this model of the individual and of relations between individuals, you can only be fully autonomous and free if you keep your body to yourself and your consent to lend your body to others can only be fully informed (and therefore autonomous) if you have already lived through that experience. However, if we begin with the assumption that we are always already, dwelling with others, rather than originally independent and self governing, then injustice can no longer be located in the law's failure to achieve the impossible. The injustice of surrogacy and other service contracts can be located in the law's determination of sexed, embodied identity and difference.

In 'The Child's Relations with Others',[8] Merleau-Ponty, for example, argues that the self does not carry, in isolation from others, a distinction between the inside and outside of itself, between external perceptions (the extroceptive body as it is seen and touched by others) and introspective perceptions (the body as it is lived, feels, sees and touches). The distinction between self and other is based on the experience of a difference between introspectivity and extroceptivity. This occurs through recognising that one's body is an object for, and therefore distinct from, the other. However, the distinction from the other cannot be absolute. Through objectification of one's body by another, a system of indistinction is established between the introspective body, the visual, extroceptive or objectified body and the body of the other. Insofar as the child identifies with its image of the Other's image of itself, it cannot easily distinguish between what it lives, what the other lives and what it perceives the other is doing.[9] This tripartite system is one of 'syncretism': the interbody transfer of movements and gestures.

So, the emergence of a body we can call our own occurs, not prior to, but through the 'alienation' of corporeality. And this constitution of the body-subject through the other occurs through mimesis and transitivism rather than by conscious intervention.[10] This indistinction between self and other is reduced by saying 'I', by taking up one point of view as the subject of language.[11] In language, the transfer of thoughtless gifts is diminished, that unconditional giving of the self to the other inherent in the confusion between the 'two'. Yet the structure of language is such that each person, while being an 'I' for themselves, is also a 'you' for others. As the self, as a lived body, remains caught between subject and object, syncretic sociability structures an adult's embodied existence even with a lived distance between self and other.

This account of embodied dwelling-with raises two points against the model of autonomy assumed in the service contract. First, the body is not a natural object given to, and governed by, its proprietor outside of social relations. The lived body, which is the self, is socially constituted: it is built from invasion by the gestures of others who, by referring to other others, are already social beings. The conducts which constitute the body-subject and, hence, its potential projects and modes of being will vary depending on with whom it associates and under what rules. So our 'freedom' (which is never absolute) is not limited, in the first instance, by others taking over control of our body but by 'the lessening of the *tolerance* allowed by the bodily and institutional data of our lives'.[12] Our tolerance to embodied projects, and hence what we are, is limited by the style of our embodied existence, a style subject to 'sedimentation' according to the institutional setting in which it is constituted. Insofar as we may be 'coerced' into sex specific projects, this is grounded in the social constitution of differences between sexed bodies.

Second, as the body subject is constituted through the 'alienation' of corporeality, then corporeal identity is never singular and always ambiguous. The lived body is only itself by virtue of being an object for others and yet by identifying with, and differentiating itself from, this image of itself, which it is not, the self lives through another. So, while the self is constituted through the building of a partition between the inside and outside of the body, it is also by virtue of this differentiation that my corporeality is given to, and takes place in, the world of the other's body as they live from and with me. As lived bodies are constituted and live as an interworld of potentiality opened onto others, our 'freedom' is compromised rather than guaranteed by keeping our bodies to ourselves and we have no means of 'knowing' or 'owning' a body other than through a familiar dwelling-with. Further, as identity is reconstituted through this dwelling-with, our living of any particular situation, and what we become as a result, is open to possibilities. Finally, as the 'alienation' of corporeality grounds rather than follows after the constitution of self, then the difference between consent and coercion is at best indeterminate. For the most part you cannot either consent to or be coerced into the process of corporeal 'exchange' which makes you what you are.

Just as the 'alienation' of corporeality does not begin with the medicalisation of the body, nor does the tendency to place a value on different body tissues. As Nietzsche suggests, the most fundamental social relation is that where 'one person first *measured himself* against another' in terms of the value of their flesh.[13] As I argue in more detail elsewhere, this process of corporeal evaluation is, like corporeal alienation, constitutive of embodied identity and difference.[14] If we take justice to be the realisation of equal value in the constitution of identity and difference then, again according to Nietzsche, this is only possible if it is already actual: if we already 'belong to *one* body',[15] that is, if we share a mode of evaluation by which the body-subject is constituted. The law embodies a community's shared mode of evaluation but, insofar as the law imposes absolute values equally upon all, it perpetuates injustice.[16] And this is because, in its constitution of embodied identity, the law legislates against difference. Or, to put this otherwise, injustice arises when, rather than allowing indeterminate possibilities in giving to the other through the labour of dwelling-with, the law makes the other familiar by denying the ambiguity of their difference. And it is this kind of injustice which governs the constitution of women's embodied modes of existence in relation to men in patriarchal social relations.

Merleau-Ponty notes two general ways in which the ambiguity of the relation to the other can be effaced: through 'social dichotomising' by which the other's difference is reduced to the negative of the self or by assuming the other is identical, thus ignoring differences which pertain to the cultural situation in which the other received their 'training'.[17] Both involve atomistic dualism and 'intellectual rigidity': the other's identity is assumed to be fixed, natural, given and knowable apart from, and unaffected by, my embodied dwelling with them. While Merleau-Ponty often implies that this reduction of the other's difference (through language, intellectual rigidity or representational knowledge) occurs after the event, his account of syncretic sociability suggests otherwise. That is, the objectification or partitioning of bodies, which divides as it constitutes identity, takes place through the same process of objectification which would close off open ambiguous possibilities for existence: through language, representational knowledge or any other mode of atomistic dualism.

The law participates in this partitioning of bodies in two ways. As I have indicated, in determining who transfers what to whom, the service contract atomises and commodifies corporeality. In doing so, it also determines the who, the what and the whom of social exchange. That corporeal identities are reconstituted and divided in this process is denied in the interests of propriety, interests which cannot entertain selfless gifts. Secondly, the law, in determining which forms of corporeal exchange can be governed by contract and which cannot, effectively determines which bodies so constituted accrue property and value and which do not. In both these ways the law constitutes identity and difference and distributes property according to norms about what is proper to bodies. And here I evoke a familiar theme: when dealing with sexual difference, the norm around which corporeal property is distributed is male. Either the law treats sexed bodies as if they are identical in their difference and, as the case of *Baby M* indicates, upholds a contract which, while apparently sexually neutral, deems the male body to be the origin and destination of procreative property. This effectively renders woman and her gifts selfless in relation to man. Or women's bodies are deemed other to what is the proper subject of social exchange and are excluded accordingly.

It is also here that the law determines consent and coercion. In partitioning bodies, the law also designates what is proper to each such that the accumulation of property by the body deemed to be its proper owner is said to occur by the consent of the other; the subtraction of property from that which is said to be its proper place is held to occur by coercion. So, for example, if the law assumes that procreative property belongs to men then its arrival at this destination appears to be with the consent of women. Under similar conditions the law has had difficulty recognising rape: 'no' cannot mean 'no' if it is assumed that what is extracted by men from the sexed bodies of women is destined for its proper place. What is at stake in these encounters between the sexes is not a woman's control over her body or her informed consent. If this were the issue, no self-respecting woman could have sexual relations or children. What is at stake is the legal determination of sexed identity and difference whereby men accrue property and therefore identity through a subtraction from the corporeality of women, a gift which cannot be recognised.

I have suggested that an alternative paradigm to contract for the medical alienation of body tissue is the gift. I turn now to consider whether this manages the determination of sexed identity and difference any better.

I have found fault with the way the claim of loss of control over one's body is applied to sex specific contracts rather than service contracts in general. Those who oppose surrogacy on these grounds often justify their narrowing of the field by the claim that the relation between a woman and the body tissue involved in pregnancy is more intimate than that involved in other kinds of contracts.[18] Carole Pateman singles out the prostitution contract for criticism on the same grounds: a woman is involved in the sex act 'in a different manner from the involvement of the self in other occupations'.[19] What is implied here is that certain body tissues, products and parts, particularly those which are sexed, are not as alienable as allowed in a service contract. The claim also highlights the risk in legally endorsing economic contracts to do with the human body: the potential for commodification of the person and, hence, the dehumanisation of social exchange. A possible way to avoid this is to suggest that insofar as a corporeal substance is thought to belong to someone's personhood and yet alienable in theory, it should only be alienable in practice as a gift.

This paradigm of the gift for the transfer of body property is favoured in Australia over contract for its legal, practical and ethical advantages. In giving away an organ, body product or part, the original 'owner' cannot be held legally responsible for the quality of the product nor for any consequences after it reaches its destination. (This is also true of the service contract, depending on where you are positioned within it.) So, for example, in terms of either an Artificial Conception Act (NSW, WA, ACT), a Status of Children Act (Vic, Qld, Tas, NT) or a Family Relationships Act (SA), donors of gametes used in various reproductive technologies have no legal rights or responsibilities in relation to any children resulting from such arrangements. A practical advantage of the gift as a model for governing the alienation of body tissue is that it reduces the temptation to give too much of one's body away, to the detriment of one's physical well. On the basis of such considerations it is illegal in Australia to sell your blood and organs, although you are encouraged to give them away. The moral advantage is that allowing the gift rather than sale of body products seems to minimise the commodification of the body and hence the potential dehumanisation of social exchange.

On the basis of these perceived advantages, the gift is the model used currently in Australia for legislation in relation to surrogacy. In terms of the Surrogacy Contract Act 1993 (Tas), for example, private, 'voluntary' surrogacy is permitted, providing, one assumes, it does not contravene the Status of Children Act 1974 (Tas). However, the legislation prohibits surrogacy contracts as well as any payment, advertising and provision of professional services in connection with a surrogacy arrangement. One advantage of this legislation, besides those already mentioned, is that it allows the surrogate to change her mind thus acknowledging that intimate link which may develop between a woman and her body during pregnancy.

While this legislation seems reasonable, given the objections to the surrogacy contract, it is, on closer scrutiny, merely the reverse side of contract and, hence, is no guarantee of justice. If we examine the National Bioethics Consultative Committee's (NBCC) 1990 report on surrogacy (one of two reports upon which the Tasmanian legislation is based) we find that the reasons for recommending prohibiting a surrogacy contract, while allowing private surrogacy, retain all the assumptions of atomised individualism upon which contract theory is based.[20] Besides the practical impossibility of preventing people from making private surrogacy arrangements, reasons given for not prohibiting surrogacy altogether include the principles of freedom and autonomy: the right of people to 'create a family by appropriate means except where the interests of others may be jeopardized' and an intending surrogate's right to 'use and control her body as she sees fit'. The reasons given for restricting formal surrogacy include the risk the surrogacy contract runs of treating children like commodities, of treating women as a means to an end (by, for example, implying a division between her reproductive capacity and her whole being) and of doing harm to the surrogate by 'the breaking of the mother/child bond which develops *in utero*'. On the role of the law, the report notes the state's 'right to intervene in this area to ensure that any such arrangements do not violate the personal autonomy of the parties involved or involve harm being done to others'.

The problem with the gift as it is conceived of here is that it remains caught within the logic of identity assumed in contract theory: the idea that everything is identical with itself and that difference is an external relation. As a consequence, in legislating in favour of the gift, the law fails to realise its purpose (to uphold the autonomy of individuals). The law fails in this respect for the same reason it fails under the condition of contract: you can no more realise control of your body if you give it away than if you lend it out as a service and your consent to do so is no better informed ahead of the event. However, if, as I have argued, identity and difference are constituted, bodies are partitioned, through this giving of corporeality, rather than prior to it, then the only conceivable advantage of legislating in favour of the gift is if nothing inequitable or final is determined about sexed identity and difference in the process.

If the law says no to contract in the case of surrogacy on the grounds that the self who signed the contract to give herself away is not the same as the self asked to fulfil the contract, then no harm is done. All that would be implied is that the lived body, held to remain identical with itself through the duration of the contract, has altered substantially through the labour of dwelling with. However, if the law says no to the surrogacy contract while remaining faithful to the concept of autonomous identity, then a problematic determination has been made. The contract is negated on the grounds that another contract has been formed with a child *in utero* or on the grounds that maternity is proper to a woman's body and hence inalienable. Giving is contained to the moment of relinquishing the child and we are back to where we began.

If giving a child to another involves breaking a contract, different to the service contract only in being more original, then the 'surrogate', while not legally culpable for breaking her word, would be morally culpable for keeping it. Or, if we say that maternity, or female sexuality, is proper to the woman's body then we may circumvent the tendency for procreative or sexed property, to accrue towards men, at least temporarily. But removing this difficulty opens the way for others. The giving by women of this property, while no longer conceivable in terms of automatic consent, starts to look like surrender under duress. That giving what is said to be proper to women must involve coercion accounts for the widespread resistance to 'noncommercial voluntary' surrogacy. The same assumption risks reducing all heterosexual sex to rape (or it at least requires that explicit consent be given for every sexual encounter).[21] And with the determination that maternity is proper to women, on what grounds can abortion be justified except through recourse to the problematic claim to sovereignty over one's body. Finally, in a context where some sexed body property attracts value (you can sell your sperm in Australia under a service contract) to rule that women can only give away what is deemed proper to her amounts to allowing that man's body can accrue value without responsibility while women's cannot. When the gift is understood to be the other side of contract the determination of sexed identity and difference is no less problematic: a woman is free only if she gives nothing of herself away and a norm of male body-property is both produced and maintained by holding that women's body property lacks currency within social exchange.

A connection can be made between the social privilege enjoyed by men and the legal distribution of body property if it is acknowledged that sexed identity and difference are produced through the gift rather than before it. This productive aspect of the gift is addressed by Marcel Mauss insofar as he takes issue with the contract model of social exchange and its atomised individualism.[22] For Mauss, the circulation of a gift, which can be an object, a ritual, a woman or a child, is in the order of a 'potlatch' (to nourish or consume). The gift bestows social rank and prestige on the one who receives it and a moral obligation towards the giver which cannot be repaid in ways other than by maintaining a social bond.[23] The power of such gifts to constitute a social bond lies in their spiritual status: they carry the significance of being part of the personhood of the giver.[24] And if the gift has the power to establish a social relation it is because it *remains* part of the personhood of the giver such that its circulation is one which seeks a return to the place of its birth.[25]

There are several ways in which the gift, as a model of social relations, challenges contract theory. A social relationship is effected, not through the exchange of corporeal commodities, but through the gift of part of oneself to another. To the extent that this gift has something to do with the body or the product of its labour, this body cannot be understood in terms of property distinct from the self. It is the self *per se*. Second, social identity is not given in isolation prior to exchange. As what is given is in essence part of the substance of the giver and, as the social identity and status of the recipient is enhanced by the gift then, contrary to the logic of identity in contract theory, what is constituted through the gift is the social identity of each in relation to the other. Finally, the giver does not pledge obedience with this gift in exchange for its protection. The debtor in this relation is not the giver but the recipient. The gift constitutes the social identity of the parties and an enduring social bond which obligates the recipient to the donor.

This model of social exchange acknowledges that, if men accrue social value and prestige it is via a gift of the substantial identity of women. It also finds contracts unethical insofar as it is assumed that the recipient of the gift can pay it out and thereby sign away their obligation to the donor without any further thought of return. On this model of social relations, surrogacy would not be unethical but a profound expression of the gift. However, the surrogacy contract would be unethical insofar as it allows the social obligation to the birth mother to be paid out.

There is however, a problem with Mauss's model of the gift. He assumes that, under ideal circumstances, the gift can arrive at its destination. In the case of sexual difference women may give to men their social identity and status but the favour is supposedly returned if the man maintains his obligation to the woman (or her family) through financial and other material support and if, with this, she receives an identity in relation to him. The marriage contract would be valid within Mauss's model of the gift, whatever internal inequities that may involve, as would the ruling in the case of *Baby M*. In the case of surrogacy, if the genetic father is deemed to be the origin of the gift, then the debt and hence the burden of obligation falls upon the surrogate. Even the Tasmanian legislation in favour of informal surrogacy would not prevent such an inequitable determination of sexual difference: the arrival of the gift, while not governed by a surrogacy contract, can be determined by the Family Law Act in terms of what is deemed to be in the best interests of the child. As Linda Singer points out, such custody rulings tend to favour the father to the extent that interest is measured in terms of social and economic privilege.[26] The circulation of the gift, as Mauss sees it, would allow the unity of identity and difference where woman's difference is contained within man's identity and her gift to him is not only selfless but invisible.

Jacques Derrida claims that, insofar as Mauss assumes that the gift is a commodity which can be separated from its donor and returned through a bond of obligation, he remains caught within the economy of contract and is speaking of 'everything but the gift'.[27] (Or, more exactly, Mauss reverses the terms of the contract, giving the donor more credit, but ultimately retains the contract logic of identity.) According to Derrida, if the condition of the possibility of the gift is its exchange between an already constituted self-present donor and an already constituted self-identical donee, then this is also the condition under which the gift is destroyed.[28] That is, if the gift is recognised as a thing separate from the donor and the recipient then a debt will be incurred by the recipient (the gift is no longer a gift as such) and the gift can be annulled by gratitude or some other form of return.

The gift is the gift of identity and has the impossible structure discussed earlier. As identity and difference is constituted through the giving of corporeality, self-present identity is deferred. So the realm of the gift is that of an ambiguous relation to the other, the open possibilities inherent in dwelling-with or, to return to the issue at hand, the realm of incalculable sexual difference. And the possibility of the gift rests on not determining anything about the other's difference ahead of or during one's encounter with them. Insofar as the law commodifies the gift and determines its point of departure and arrival it also determines sexed identity and difference in ways already discussed. And to the extent that self-present identity is said to have arrived or been determined in the opposition man/woman then an injustice has been done: the gift of an incalculable sexual difference is effaced and woman is constituted as the second sex.

Having said this, it would be a mistake to assume that justice can be restored through lawlessness, through forgetting the gift entirely, as if other possibilities for existence would emerge from the free play of the gift after suspension of the law's determinations. For, as I have already suggested, the ambiguity operating in embodied dwelling-with others is opened through the same law which governs the commodification and determination of sexed bodies. It is not that the gift should be forgotten. Rather, what should be remembered is that the giving which is consistently forgotten by the law is woman's and the gift which the law consistently remembers and recognises is man's.

The possibility of justice then rests with the law's ability to remember this giving of corporeality without naming or determining the lived embodiment which 'is' a woman. As Drucilla Cornell

suggests, following Lyotard, injustice is 'damage accompanied by
the loss of the means to prove the damage'.[29] A law which
normalises, a law which assumes self-presence and (woman's)
difference as a secondary relation and which, following this,
attempts to neutralise differences (in the name of equality), damages women. In a culture 'scarred by gender hierarchy', a theory
of justice which assumes or seeks sexual neutrality ignores the
harm done to women in the production of this scar and doubles
the injustice by insisting that harm be translated into the terms
of a system which does not recognise it.[30] For Cornell, justice
requires the interrogation of this system of injustice, a questioning
which opens up the operation of the gift, of that deferral towards
other possibilities which resists normalisation. Or, as Derrida puts
it, justice is not a matter of neutralising differences but, rather,
requires us 'constantly to maintain an interrogation of the origin,
ground and limits of our conceptual, theoretical or normative
apparatus surrounding justice'.[31]

So where does all this leave the law on surrogacy, rape,
prostitution, IVF or any other form of 'alienation' of sexed
corporeality, medically assisted or not? It leaves the law with the
task of recognising that women already give corporeality to the
world in the mode of dwelling-with which constitutes us as sexed
beings in relation to others. Some women 'give' children to
themselves, to others and to the world (simultaneously). The
difference between this and 'surrogacy' is in a name by virtue of
which the woman, rather than the law, determines an (interim)
destination of the gift. Some women 'give' sexual pleasure to
themselves, to men and to other women. The difference between
this and prostitution is that the woman, rather than the law,
attaches a value to the gift. There is nothing immoral about
'surrogacy' or prostitution that would not also be immoral about
procreation or sexual relations in general. And in legislating
against this giving, the law serves only to uphold its own authority
in the determination of womanhood. It does not serve women or
justice.

While some women already give in these ways, through sex
for pleasure or procreation, it is unjust to force any particular
woman to do so. The surrogacy contract is unjust for forcing the
gift, as is rape. And this is not because maternity or something
called female sexuality is proper to woman's body and therefore
inalienable. Giving involves a metamorphosis, a structuring of a
particular situation through incorporation and corporeal reconstitution, the possibility of which is dependent upon the tolerance
to it allowed by the lived body involved. A woman, or anyone
for that matter, can say no to giving because her body, which is

her indeterminate self, cannot tolerate the gift. (And as this assumes nothing about a proper body, there is no implication that an explicit yes must precede the gift. Yes is implied in the giving itself.)

What is being questioned in these suggestions is the authority we invest in the law to determine the origin and destination of gifts and, hence, sexed identity and difference. The medical alienation of corporeality makes the question more urgent only because of what it exposes about this authority. As if to drive home the point, the Victorian Parliament has just denied passage of legislation on surrogacy on the grounds that it permits its 'non-commercial, voluntary' form. It seems that while we can consider giving a zygote in a test tube the status of a person and have no problem attaching monetary value to a male gamete, we cannot tolerate acknowledging the gifts of women. Women disappear as the invisible becomes real in the interests of someone else's autonomy.

8 The taxpayer's body: genealogies of exertion

Judith Grbich*

> That she can finally become your mirror is today your chief article of faith . . . And if, at the end of your hour, she has again to carry the load of what you have created—a mere simulacrum of becoming—what do you care if her back is broken by the weight, as long as she still has the strength to give that present back, in the shape of a sounding echo that the voice of her flesh fills out . . . From this 'yes' of her flesh that is always given and preferred to suit your eternity, you draw your infinite reserves of veils and sails, of wings and flight . . . Of sublimation and dissimulation. For this flesh that is never spoken—either by you or by her—remains a ready source of credulity for your fantasies.[1]

The aim of this essay is to flesh out the double bind within which ontologies of being are located in western discourses of modernity, and to ask questions of the juridical qualities of this double bind. It is an essay on the retrieval of the theoretical formations of the everyday practices of understanding the self as a productive or economic subject in late modernity.

The practices of proper identities in western capitalism are located within formations of scientificity, these include the proofs of the productive self generated by the scientific reasoning of economic theory and the legal reasoning of juridical practices. In this essay I will flesh out two different formations of scientificity, two different 19th century accounts of the measurement and proof of the value of human exertion. Spivak has argued that if masculinism in western reason has named the conditions of truth

practices as 'woman' then we must maneouvre within these practices, that masculinism must be negotiated with. She says:

> Yet the name of woman as the non-truth of truth can have a
> significant message for us if we, refusing fully to honor the
> historically bound catechresis, give the name of woman to that
> disenfranchised woman who is historically different from ourselves,
> the subjects of feminist theory . . .[2]

I have borrowed these questions from Spivak's text and am
pursuing the possibility that one advantage of naming the already
saturated and coded body of the modern subject as 'the taxpayer's
body', rather than as 'man', (or rather than naming the surplus
of meanings within these codes as 'woman'), is the retrieval of
embodied forms of these codes of economic value. Naming the
coded body of the proof of the economic self as that of the
'taxpayer', may contribute to an understanding of how practices
of fiscal naming are about the ways in which bodies and their
actions have been marked and hierarchically ordered.

The promise of naming the subject of the technologies of
governance in late modernity as 'the taxpayer' is to generate a
dialogue within which the learned ontologies of productivity—the
sense of creativity which we have tied to commodification—can
be understood as having a human past. We can enter their claims
to scientificity and negotiate within them. Identities of productivity
within western capitalism seem to have lost their sense of themselves as imaginative subjects, and the possibilities of imagining
an ontology in which consciousness of self does always not arrive
with legal titles of ownership of the body seem to be lost.

In the extracts from Irigaray's *Marine Lover of Friedrich
Nietzsche* at the beginning of this essay Irigaray provides a reading
of Nietzsche in which 'woman' is courted by Nietsche for her
metaphorical capacities to renew mankind's sense of himself and
his order in the world, an order in which feminised bodies are
constituted as the proof of that order, provided of course that
they do not speak of the experience of that order or of different
meanings of female bodies. Nietzsche's narratives of Man's courtship of Nature and himself, and Irigaray's commentaries upon
these narratives provides a focus for my own questions about
women's refusals to continue to agree that their labour is less
valuable than men's, and their refusal to accept the official proofs
given by the legal order that their household labour is unproductive. Women are saying that they will no longer stand as proof
of the modern model of economic man, that their bodies will no
longer remain with meanings of 'economic man' uncontested
by women.

One aim of this retrieval of the embodied forms of the codes
of economic value, and this reading of the imaginative qualities
of the scientific accounts of human exertion is to be able to write
as the imaginative character of the tax law textbooks. Why should
the feminist scholar be excluded from this imaginative practice of
writing the modern proofs of the self? Why should the poetics of
volition[3] be reserved for the tax lawyer with masculinist credentials, or the economist writing about maleness in the guise of 'tax
policy'?

The focus in this paper upon the taxpayer's body is one way
of engaging with these themes of feminist writing about the
contemporary social practices of embodiment,[4] feminist themes of
pursuing the models of corporeality which have supported the
Enlightenment project of knowing human engagement with the
world through the practices of reason.[5] In the fiscal or taxation
discourse of everyday life of western economies female bodies are
often spoken of as unproductive, as unresponsive to market forces,
as having greater elasticity. They are both too elastic and not
elastic enough. While fiscal discourses about taxation liabilities of
people and corporations are produced by the legal and adminis-
trative apparatus of the state. They have become the discourse of
everyday life in their hegemonic qualities, their power to specify
the exact productive capacities of human actors and their imperative that the subject positions of productivity and nonproductivity
thereby deployed be confirmed as the self.

The modern economic subject, the subject of Foucault's
episteme of modernity,[6] is required to assess the economic value
of his labours and declare that the self so assessed is accurate,
that the economic value of his labour rightfully represents the
social measure of his contribution to the common good. These
are practices of selfhood in which the taxpayer's body is calibrated
by the state. The economic subject is asked to recognise himself
using a measure of human exertion calibrated upon the price of
other commodities, including the commodities of capital, the new
financial products of modern economies. The modern economy is
one in which self is diminished in the eyes of man, the value of
the human body shows a diminishing rate of return. In modern
economies we actually believe that there is a parity of measurement between human labour and the performance of financial
actors. How can we understand a social order in which people,
mostly male, trained in the management of the common good,
actually believe that tightening controls on the money supply and
the consequent devaluation of human labour can produce a better
form of human practice and social growth? How can the planned
measurement of human bodies as having no value or diminished

value be understood as a condition of economic progress? What kind of human is the economist who believes in the calibration of human exertion according to the needs of financial actors, those imaginary persons and imaginary objects of economic discourse, of the 'gold' standard, and of the legal order?

Legal regulation of taxpaying practices changed in western economies in the late 19th century. They became a technology for proving that the stories of neoclassical economists about human exertion, as an instance of more general laws of variation between economic actors and objects of desire, were true. Taxpayers were required to adopt 'exertion' as the practical, and metaphorical, account of their capacity to contribute to public revenue. Exertion became the required explanation for economic capacity, and the body of the human taxpayer, already calibrated to produce author-ised explanations of the regularities of intensity of labour and fluctuations in prices, provided the proof that there were natural laws of 'the economy'.

This new technology of collecting taxes and proving the truth of the neoclassical economist's story of the normative human body is our present discourse of income taxation. Income taxation laws are usually represented as simply the rules for the collection of revenues from individuals and corporations for the purpose of financing state activities. In Anglo-European societies they were invented in the late 18th century and used variously and unpopularly throughout the 19th century before becoming the major revenue collection base in countries such as Australia, in the 20th century. Income tax laws do more than create liabilities to contribute to public revenue. They are discourses of productive capacities in which there are subject positions for human and non-human economic actors.[7] They are capable of creating iden-tities and subjectivities for non-human actors, the imaginary characters of finance capital, provided of course that you believe the analogies and allusions of the economists that financial charac-ters are capable of 'effort' and conform to the same physical and sensory laws of variability as human bodies.

The income taxation legislation introduced in Victoria, Aus-tralia in 1895, an example from my local practices, contained no account of the measurement of the taxpayer's earning capacity.[8] The taxpayer was to be taxed on 'income' and the English common law supplied the interpretation that 'income' was what-ever 'comes in'. 'Income' was in effect the only measure of liability to pay tax provided in the Act. The Act provided two ways of calculating the tax payable in respect of 'income', the lower rate relating to 'income from personal exertion' and the double rate

relating to 'income the produce of property'. These different
modes and rates of assessment were described as follows:

> 'Income derived by any person from personal exertion' or 'Income
> from personal exertion' means all income consisting of earnings
> salaries wages allowances pensions superannuation or retiring
> allowances or stipends earned in or derived from Victoria and all
> income arising or accruing from any trade carried on in Victoria.
>
> 'Income derived by any person from the produce of property'
> or 'income the produce of property' means all income derived in
> or from Victoria and not derived by personal exertion.[9]

These two ways of calculating tax payable instituted a dichotomy,
an oppositional concept in which personal exertion, an energetics
of bodies, was the dominant interpretative mode for assessing the
taxation liabilities of human and corporate taxpayers. The definition of 'income the produce of property' provides only that it
is whatever is not income from personal exertion. The interpretive
uncertainty instituted by the measurement of taxation liability
using this exertion/non-exertion formula could be resolved by
recourse to human bodies, and the prices paid for the exertion of
human bodies could confirm the naturalness of using 'exertion'
or effort as the metaphorical account of the basis for revenue
liabilities of non-human taxpayers.

This interpretive mode or practice of an energetics of bodies
which the income tax discourses instituted was the same analytic
of muscular finitude invented by the neoclassical economists. That
gains from human labour became taxable was the political effect
of the growth of a middle class, that personal exertion or energetics should form the interpretive mode for the measurement of
gains from human labour and property ownership was the effect
of the successes of positivist explanations of human and scientific
progress in the 19th century. The next part of this chapter is
concerned with the retrieval of some of these positivist explanations of human progress and a mapping of their inscriptions of
standards upon bodies, standards of performance designed to
relegate some bodies to practices without value.

Writing on corporeality is a way of contesting the limitations
and boundaries of these inscriptions of standard measurement
upon human performance, a way of contesting the modern
episteme of finitude. A finitude or limit or calibration of the body,
by which the practices of human activity have become the
resources for proving the ahuman and atemporal character of
economic activity. Inquiries into the corporeality of practice locate
the meanings of bodies in a human framework, a space of human
perspectives and human times. My inquiries into the model of

corporeality embedded in the taxation narratives of energetics is also a way of contesting the limited forms of agency which these practices of energetics continue to replicate. These stories of energetics in taxation discourses limit the possibilities for understanding the self as productive for many women and feminised others.

In taxation law discourses the taxpayer is imagined as a kind of person always in a state of inaction, like a machine which has been wound up but is unable to start itself. A person who has a tendency to action but cannot act. This state of being is expressed as having an 'earning capacity'. The taxpayer as machine is imagined as having an internal order regulated by external events or stimuli, earning capacities need to be 'kick-started' by market forces or market players. Taxpayers are persons who are activated by 'structures of incentives', stimuli capable of releasing the spring of the body machine. These stimuli are imagined as pleasures of a monetary kind, such as wages, or perhaps cash transfers from the state such as a family allowance supplement. Liability to pay tax on income is regarded as a 'disincentive', a stimulus or displeasure of a monetary kind, and capable of blocking the action of the stimulus which activates the spring. These narratives about taxpayers are maintained in spite of alternative theories of being. There are other accounts of the self in everyday understandings of human nature, but this ontology of the reactive person has acquired a hegemonic quality in the relations of late modernity.

Persons with no 'income' can be described as having failed to respond to the prevailing structure of incentives, or as having decided that the disincentives of taxation were sufficiently great to block their response to market forces. Some persons with small amounts of 'income' or no 'income' are regarded as having such weak desires for action that these can be blocked by minute amounts of tax liabilities. They are characterised as it were as slothful automatons and required on moral grounds to prostrate themselves before better primed machines. The legal technologies of the calibrated body award identities of nonproductivity and moral deficiency to many women and men whose labour is otherwise immeasurable and valuable beyond price and upon whose gifts of life and trust the social order is maintained.

Imagining a calibrated body: the analytic of muscular and kinesthetic finitude

The modern economist acquired his techniques of calibrating the physical exertions of human bodies in the decades of the 50s and

60s of the 19th century. While 1871 has been given as the spontaneous and simultaneous conception of neoclassical economics in three separate sites in western Europe and three separate minds, the techniques of calibration were developed in the physical and biological sciences of earlier decades. In the 1850s the German physiologist Fechner had postulated a general law which quantified the sensations of bodies.[10] Bodily sensations were found to vary logarithmically with the strength or intensity of a physical stimulus, or at least the experience of a difference or change in sensation could be correlated with differences in magnitude of the stimulus.

In the words of a modern 20th century text:

> Every measuring system must be provable; i.e., it must prove its ability to measure reliably. The procedure for this is called calibration. It consists of determining the system's scale.[11]

In this same text 'measurement is the act, or the result, of a quantitative comparison between a predefined standard and an unknown magnitude. If the result is to be generally meaningful, two requirements must be met in the act of measurement: (a) the standard which is used for comparison must be accurately defined and commonly accepted, and (b) the procedure and apparatus employed for obtaining the comparison must be provable'.

The modern 19th century economist was able to prove that there was a physical and sensory regularity between the quantity or amount of physical exertion a human body would perform during a single day and the quantity or amount of money offered in payment, but only if some limit or finitude was set to exertions of a human body. A standard was needed for the 'normal' human body against which variations in effort of individuals could be allowed for by the assumptions of statistical thinking. The system's scale needed to be set. While statistical thinking provided the notion of the 'normal'[12] it was the 19th century political economist who clothed the daily labourer in this garment of 'normality' and thereby transformed himself into the modern 'economist'. The system's scale became those units of labour inherent in the 'normal' labouring body.

If a standard or normal amount of exertion in a labourer could be posed, and a monetary price fixed for the amount of daily sustenance that hypothetical labourer needed to survive, the performance of labour could serve as the measure of that seemingly 'natural' law of variation between effort and the price received. While the economist's proof that variations in prices paid for labour were caused by variations in human effort or exertion depended upon first calibrating or fixing a hypothetical and ideal limit to the physical capacities of the labourer, beliefs in these proofs were instituted by many different practices, including the intuitive and historical accounts of the productive contributions of human labour to economic progress.

The technique of the calibrated body invented by the modern economist provided the standard against which the efforts or activities of other commodities could be shown to follow the same natural laws of physical and sensory variation, including the financial actors of the 'gold' economy. The modern episteme of the 19th century was an analytic in which Man's labour became the measure of all things. Man's labour became the unit of measurement for all commodities, including the fantasies of financial property. Men dreamt of new financial relations and Man's body, his limits to exertion, could provide the unit for measuring the value of these new relations. But this was possible only so long as some men and some women could no longer speak of the different forms by which their selves were known to them, of their different practices of giving meaning to human labour and social progress.

These different forms for experiencing selfhood, forms for producing identities of value and productivity, were not erased by the hegemonic discourses of neoclassical economics, but were managed by various techniques of the modern state: in the mechanics institutes for the working man the naturalness of the new form for understanding the self was propounded; in the campaigns to introduce domestic sciences to the working woman, female labour in households was presented as naturally unresponsive to the new laws of the economy and as unproductive; and in the introduction of the new legal rules for measuring taxation liabilities to the state, the calibrated body, invented by the modern economist, became the form in which the human was measured as having a productive capacity for social life.

The technology of the calibrated body has a history in 19th century narratives of human progress, narratives in which sensations of exertion were a theme within which to negotiate ideas of corporeality and selfhood. In the next section of this chapter a genealogy of sensations of exertion is undertaken as a method of inquiry into these different practices of corporeality and progress. This method of inquiry is described by Foucault as the retrieval of an 'indispensable restraint',[13] a recording of the singularity of events, undertaken not to trace any gradual curve of the evolution of meaning to some present Truth, but to isolate the different scenes where the elements of Truth engaged in different roles. It is a genealogy which seeks to present the indispensable restraints of what is here called fiscal energetics, for the modern subject of economic life. It is a genealogy which seeks to understand how the economic subject of modernity has been divided from knowledge of pleasures, and divided from knowledge of the bodily form of objectivity in the world. How did the discursive formations of fiscal energetics achieve the standard of the 'normal' human body, the interpretive mode of a machine-like body with which we are impelled to recognise the value of our selves? The texts of Jennings[14] and Mach[15] on sensations of exertion provide two different scenes from mid-19th century narratives of human progress in which the corporeal elements of Truth are envisaged differently. The aim is to learn how to write a different bodily form of objectivity, a form in which the regularities of belonging are reclaimed as human attributes.

One question which always impells itself to consciousness when I try to complete this chapter is, how can I separate the stories of fiscal energetics which I find in contemporary revenue law texts from the stories of 'homo psychologicus' as told by Freud and Lacan. All share a conception of the human as a body structured as if it were a machine with electrical nervous pathways, pathways in which images and ideas of the body are conducted and renewed by condensation and displacement in a process which can not be spoken authoritatively by its owner. The circulation of these freely flowing energies lies in the unconscious. While my retrieval of some of these coded forms of these currents and equivalences seems to be a history of the economic subject, in another light they appear as the lost memories of Freud's economy of the sexed subject.

A poetics of electromagnesis

In the 1855 text of Richard Jennings, *Natural Elements of Political Economy*, corporeality is envisaged as a form of ownership, the matter of the body is under the control or possession of the mind. In the discursive formation of the mid-19th century human sciences, the natural sciences of physiology and comparative zoology were adopting the questions and conceptual structures of the physical sciences in order to pursue inquiries into the dominant social questions of the nature of human life and the origins of human societies. The sciences of mechanics and electromagnetics provided the broad conceptual frameworks within which to question the relationships between human bodies and their spiritual origins, and between human bodies and other human bodies.

In the mechanical epistemologies of physics, with their machine analogies of pressure, stresses and forces, the flesh of human bodies was envisaged as obeying natural laws of machine-like regularity and predictability. Questions about the capacities of human beings for changing the 'natural' course of development and progress could safely be asked, without unduly transgressing the conventions of divine order, if it were assumed that this divine order was immanent in the regularities of human bodies. Questions about the capacities of human beings to cause social change, and to be understood as rightfully subject to social change, could be safely asked within, what is here termed, a discourse of corporeal mechanics and a poetics of electromagnesis. Questions of the human and proximate causes of social change could safely be asked, provided the body of corporeal mechanics could be understood as an instance of a broader mechanical structure—the natural laws of social life, the natural laws of 'the economy' or, what was known as the 'Laws of Nature'.

Knowledges of the electrical circuits of the human nervous system and supporting musculature provided a metanarrative within which to challenge, and contain, natural orders of bodies and peoples. This metanarrative of the energetics of the flesh contained creative parts for the new social actors with fiscal, corporate and regulatory identities. Banking, Treasury and municipal corporations—the new managers—were naturalised by their necessary material existence in a scenario of bodily exertions. Owners of capital found for themselves a conceptual position of harmony with labour in the new science of bodily energetics, labourer's bodies could be measured and paced for that degree of effort which matched the 'natural' laws of the economy. Jennings's focus upon the nervous system of human bodies and their musculature was shared with his contemporaries in the natural, social and economic sciences. The human being was imagined as a being of living matter and soul whose practice in the world could be understood by an empirical study of the bodily movements of effort, the experience of the sensations of muscular exertion in working bodies.

This knowledge of the human sensations of effort and exertion provided the scenario of the new 'natural' relations between bodies, and these new knowledges provided an image of the self which came to be known as 'homo economicus'. In the poetics of electromagnetics it was imagined that human musculature could be owned by each and every mind and stimulated by each and every Will, provided the Will could adapt itself within the natural order of the species.

In Jennings's text on the 'natural elements' of political economy (the psychology and physiology of bodies) a new science of economics was created. It lacked only the symbolic proofs of the mathematical relations set out as explanations of human progress, symbolic proofs which were provided some sixteen years later by Jevons, often called the 'father' of neoclassical economics. The knowledges of sensations of exertion in Jennings's text produced an account of human agency in the lower orders which suggested that many of these lower order bodies were not acting as if owned/controlled by each mind. Their musculature was enervated by a reflex nerve network or arc in which the higher brain functions associated with the Will could be bypassed.[16] But the bodies of higher orders, the knowledges of their sensations of effort, were able to demonstrate a musculature which was enervated by the cerebrum, the mind in its material form. It was in relation to Ideas of economic Value that the exertions of these higher order bodies had become adapted and thereby created the 'natural', and normative, order of Value essential to the economic health of the body politic.

However, in Jennings's text there was some hope for the lower orders in achieving the new possibilities for agency, for achieving that sense of self as productive which the 'natural' order of Value made available. If the minds of the lower orders were educated about the new principles of economic order, what they had failed to achieve by the natural processes of mental adaptation across generations could nevertheless be achieved by learning the requisite Ideas about Value within a single generation or lifetime. Bodies which had learnt the new ideas about Value were imagined as capable of achieving a musculature stimulated by the Will as if the cerebrum had been naturally adapted to the principles of survival of the fittest bodies. In the Jennings metanarrative of the energetics of the flesh, lower order bodies were capable of demonstrating identities of self-possession, they were capable of exerting themselves beyond the needs of their 'common senses' for food, warmth and shelter.

Jennings's study is an example of the 19th century formation of energetics in which technologies of statistics or governmentality were able to reverse previous conceptions of causality of human history. Causation was now imagined to come within human control, rather than having a godly bearing. History and the progress of civilisation was imagined as a practice of the observation of instances of human productivity, it was imagined that the addition of these instances of productivity—in the form of numerical data on wages, prices of goods bought—could provide accurate and objective proof of the causes of economic Value. If men's individual ideas of utility or usefulness to the individual could be observed, and added, the natural and rational laws of development could be found. These rational laws of social development, what Jennings called the 'secondary laws of the mind', were based upon the assumptions that individual ideas of progress were of a sensory nature. Ideas were sense-data of the mind, they were the 'primary laws of the mind' and ascertainable by observation of muscular exertion.

In Jennings's narrative, his conception of corporeality as one of a living machine was one he shared with his contemporaries in the natural sciences. Within this conception of the organised body, volition is conceptualised as different from voluntary movement. The problem of the volition of machine-like bodies provided fertile ground for inscribing scientific accounts of the physiological capacities of bodies into the sense-data of political economy, a task made easy by the presence already of the problem of volition of machine-like people in the scientific texts of the physiologists. In the contemporaneous physiology text of Carpenter volitional behaviour was distinguished from voluntary: the term volitional expressed 'the character of an action proceeding from a distinct choice of the object, and from a determinate effort to attain it'. In Carpenter's words, it was an:

> essential condition to every Volitional action that a distinct idea should exist of the object to be attained, and that there should be also a belief in the possibility of attaining it by the means employed.[17]

In Carpenter's text the physiological qualities of the volitional body were organised around the concept of the Will, Ideas, musculature and nervous apparatus. Anomalies of movement were resurrected as occasions upon which the consciousness of the body was a problem to be explained. Set in motion within this narrative of the need to specify an object to be attained before the explanation of volitional anomalies could be given, was a need to explain the precursor of the Idea of the object. In Carpenter's text 'biologised' subjects were used to explain the 'dominant' power which the concentration of attention upon an Idea could give over the body, and 'not only over the mind'.[18] A person might be conscious and appear to be awake, but the musculature was not under the control of the Will. Movement of the muscles which impelled the body forward could be the effect of ideo-motor action. In ideo-motor action 'the mind is possessed by a succession of ideas':

> which may be either spontaneously evolved by its own operations, or may be directly suggested through the senses, or may be the products of the mental activity of the individual, exercised upon the promptings which it has received from without.[19]

In ideo-motor action the Will has no direct participation in producing muscular movements, these movements are 'the spontaneous manifestations of Ideational states excited to a certain degree of intensity, or in physiological language, the reflex actions of the Cerebrum'. Carpenter uses the account of the 'biologised' or mesmerised subject to explain the phenomenon of a conscious person whose musculature could be controlled by the directions of another. These contemporaneous scientific explanations of the physiological qualities of the human nervous system and musculature provided the expert knowledges on the internal mechanisms of the machine-like bodies called upon by Jennings to provide the sense-data of economic and human progress. They gave a scientific credibility to Jennings's stories about the diminished capacities of lower order bodies, and the mesmerising effect that commodities could exercise over the will of the conscious person.

Jennings's text provided a narrative of conscious and volitional bodies whose actions were separate and natural instances of ideo-motor action in which the Value socially ascribed to commodities so fixated the minds of some human actors that their behaviour could be studied as instances of the regular laws of Value. The Social Value of different commodities, or more correctly the bodies' memories of past sensations of pleasure associated with each commodity, acted as if to mesmerise the Will of the subject.

But how could learned habits of the subjective sensations of pleasure in individual bodies provide an account of the different pleasures felt between commodities? Why was the social Value of food less than the value felt in conjunction with the Idea of a luxury commodity? If bodies were living machines how could it be explained that the Idea of food was sufficient to keep some bodies exercising their musculature for five hours a day, whereas other living machines undertook exertion beyond the labour necessary to achieve the satisfaction of the consumption of food?

Jennings used the instances of money or prices paid for commodities as instances of each body's memory of the past sensations of pleasure of consumption. It was the commodity, that object which impressed itself upon the nervous pathways—and whose chain of stimuli caused the reaction of ideo-motor action—which was now imagined as the cause of human activity. The commodity was imagined to so stimulate the electrical pathways of the musculature and in such intensities that it provided the natural balancing mechanism of human effort or toil. Human exertion in the practices of production—now a natural component of progress and civilisation—was now always imagined as an internal physiological balancing of the energetics of toil (the electrical circuitry of receiving stimuli to muscular activity, the sensations of exertion and of fatigue consequent upon prolonged effort) against the emotional intensities of impressions of past commodities. This balancing was the actions of the electrical pathways of the nervous system and it was imagined to follow the principles of electromagnesis.

Bodies were naturally attracted to objects they desired, as if iron filings to a magnet. It is these bodies which Nietzsche was later to name as those of 'Man'. Intensities of sensation associated with the memory of past commodities could outweigh the sensations of pain and fatigue experienced in labouring bodies. As the measurement of muscular effort in bodies could be shown to have a natural daily limit, the mechanism of sensation of effort could be standardised, individual variations in effort during a day could be shown to follow a standard form of 'deviation' or variability from the mean or average or normal body. The assumptions of statistics provided the belief that these individual variations would, as it were, cancel out each other and thereby preserve the norm as standard. Variations in intensity of effort by the normal human body could then be left to demonstrate the regularity of variation with or between the commodity desired, that is the pleasure anticipated. Progress was created, and confined, as an effect of the human body's reaction to the single variable of the commodity. The normal labouring body with a natural daily limit to exertion was the calibrated body, henceforth available as both the origin of sense-data and the proof of the regularities which this data 'disclosed'. As the Values of commodities differed each was an index of an idea of Value held by the body politic. Progress and the course of history was now caused by belief in the Ideas of Values—the ideational state of anticipation of consumption, beliefs which could only be observed within a measure calibrated or standardised to allow for the very variations in sense-data that it was designed to measure. Bodily exertions were mapped as the standard or limit against which commodities might soar in the social imaginary. Wealth was imagined to depend upon the analogy of a body which could recognise sovereignty or ownership of itself only through a sensation of painful exertion, always paced or measured against the commodities of its own subsistence or nourishment.

In this fiscal energetics of bodies of Jennings and his numerous collaborators and disciples, a dismal finitude or limit to the human imagination was inscribed or engraved into the musculature.[20] Human exertion was commodified and in line with the beliefs in the naturalness of the laws of quantity of commodities, with each successive addition of a human commodity to the pool of humanity its Value was imagined to dissipate 'like a circle in the water, till by broad spreading it disperse to nought'.[21]

It was Jennings' evolutionary notion of mental adaptation within a single individual which provided the explanation of the differing capacities of human bodies for the sensations of pleasure and the anticipations of satisfactions from commodities. It required, however, a model of a base corporeality, a lower order body, a body whose satisfactions were satiable because it was imagined as naturally and physiologically unable to anticipate a pleasure or satisfaction beyond subsistence physical needs. The technology of the calibrated body needed a body which was imagined to labour only in relation to the physiological require-ments needed to sustain that amount of labour defined as the natural and normal daily limit. Without this model of base or brute corporeality, a type of body which could not appreciate the refined pleasures perceived by other types of bodies, the technol-ogy of fiscal and monetary energetics, which was made possible by the notion of mental adaptation, could not be inscribed into the flesh. Fiscal energetics needed a body with an instinct for mental adaptation, it needed a body which was restrained by its own electromagnetic circuits, its own nerve pathways and habitual ideo-motor impulses, from acquiring the innate mental adaptation of other bodies. Fiscal energetics needed a model of base corpo-reality in which the inscriptions of species' pleasures were erased and had to be relearned in each generation. The problem is that we are still required to live within the thrall of this brute, a brute which needs to be activated by a structure of incentives before exertion will commence, and a brute whose ideo-motor exertions can be blocked at the thought of a disincentive. A brute whose actions and inactions confirm the beliefs of modernity in an ahuman motor to human progress.

The placental economy

In contradistinction to Jennings's brute, in Mach's inquiries in the 1870s and 1880s into analyses of sensations of exertion, cor-poreality is envisaged as conventional, the body is understood as having its being as living matter, its mode of being in the world, by virtue of its beliefs in the different qualities of sensation conventionally termed the Will, the sensory organs and the mus-culature. In Mach's 1885 text *The Analysis of the Sensations* on the methodologies of physics and the new psychophysics, ques-tions of causation and the progress of peoples and histories are given a biological mode, causality becomes the biological need for causality.[22] Mach has, as it were, adopted his own epistemology, his own model of corporeality as an interpretive practice. He imagines causality as a biological need, a need to complete the deficiencies of sense data, because his contemporaries did believe that human action, the exertions of human musculature was 'really' caused by the external objects of commodities.

As the conventions of his period, in regard to human action in the world are the positivist and reductionist notions of the energetics of nerve pathways, then Mach adopts these conventions as the imaginary and real practices of action in the world. In Mach's writing, the possessive model of corporeality, in which the Will comes to an awareness of consciousness of its own body, its possession of a body, only through the belief in an outside origin of human action, is replaced by another model of corporeality. The character of this different corporeality, implicit in his positioning of the illusory character of the possessive model, is one of gestational being. The body is within a space which is no longer separate from what is to be known, and the modes of being are imagined as practices of enrichment, nourishment and supplementation.

The promise of interrogating Mach's phenomenology of knowing the self is that the kind of objectivity which his scientific proofs of identity have created are no longer tied to an essentialised and masculinised self. These proofs which the subject provides for the self to know itself as an object, to be other for others, can be located as contingent and conditional. Mach's gestational model of corporeality provides a metanarrative within which the western cultural mode, of signifying action and proof of identity as economic subject, can retain its imaginative character as a masculine sexual economy alongside another western cultural mode of signifying action, a feminine sexual economy. Mach's phenomenal epistemology/ontology is set out in the following pages in some detail. The aim is to make visible the places within it for the components of the contemporary practices of objectivity in the scientific proofs of economic identities. Here are the places for the subject of economic narratives, places for the slices of character compiled within statistical proofs of price theory, and places for writing the scientific proofs of a different self, a self respectful of the gifts of others.[23]

In Mach's phenomenal psychology of the subject, the imaginative practices of knowing the embodied conditions of volition and being in the world, the biological need for causation, are sexualised. I am of course reading the western codes of sexualisation into his phenomenal analysis of the sensory and semantic conditions within which the subject perceives itself as a self. I am

reading the dependence of the recognition of self, upon a possess-
ary model of the body with its ontology of electromagnesis, as a
masculinised and sexualised code for action, rather than as an
asexual economy. This kind of reading has the aim of making
visible another morpho-logic, the imaginative possibilities of a
feminine sexual economy. It is, of course, Irigaray's project of
inscribing the richness of humankind's life properties into
culture.[24]

My focus upon Mach's psychophysics has the purpose of
learning how to write a sexed psychophysics, that is, a psychophysics in which the sexualised codes for action are explicit. I
want to learn how to write a scientific proof in which the subject
is both one and the other within, a proof in which the female
body provides a model of tolerance of an other's life within itself.[25]
I want to be able to enter the double bind of this sexed psychophysics and rework the practices of objectivity. It is not to be a
repetition or renewal of origins in the name of 'woman', because
'woman' is the name we read to mark that body whose gifts of
abundance and spirit have been taken without acknowledgment
of authorship or parenthood. 'Man' claims the fruits of ownership
of the body in the name of a masculine sexual economy. This
reworking of the practices of objectivity aims to speak of and
with a language in which the gifts of life of female bodies are not
already written over and written out by the imaginative investments of western economies. It is to be an ontology named for
'the taxpayer'.

It is an ontology of being already existing in the narratives of
fiscal energetics. In the discursive formations of contemporary
taxation practices in western economies, the positions of gestational
being are occupied by the characters of fictional property. Capital
is often imagined to give birth to profits, but the fruits of capital's
exertions are animated by the same poetics of electromagnesis that
limit the meaning of capital's labour as instances of that grand
machine called 'the economy'. In the new narratives of a feminine
sexual economy, the female body and its placental economy provide
a model in which belonging is an attribute of neither one nor the
other.[26] It is a practice of mediation in which the maternal immune
system both recognises the other as other and is enabled to accept
it as an other. Here is a poetics of antigens and immune factors
which has not been colonised in the name of 'man'.

Gestational bodies

In Mach's analysis of the sensations of movement he interrogates
the phenomena of illusory movement in order to explain the

biological dependence of perception of the ego, the subject, upon beliefs of a conventional nature in an outside of the subject. In this methodology of studying the sensations of sight and space he theorises the space sensation as the sensation of height, breadth and depth. Space sensation in his analysis, the perception of an object as outside the body, is a threefold enervation of the senses, it is the 'three optical space coordinates', vis, the sensations of height, breadth, and depth. The perception of outside is explained by the sensations of optics, but they are sensations guided by the conventions of thought and language by which the subject organises the perception or sensation of the form of objects, the form of the outside. One sees an outside in which the self is situated because one has learnt the cultural modes within which the forms of outside can be organised as separate from the self.

Mach's analysis of the sensations of exertion are set within the 19th century interrogation by natural scientists of the claims to truth about the naturalness of the laws of human progress. Just as the English political economist cum physiologist, Jennings, posed analyses of volition as occasions for claiming the truth of natural laws of social development, so the physicist cum philosopher, Mach, poses the problems of illusory exertions as occasions for claiming another Truth about the nature of human progress. Mach disagreed with his German contemporaries in psychophysics that the sensory processes of the human body could give instances of natural sense-data, instances conforming to natural laws. He disagreed that the technologies of statistics about individual characteristics could provide proofs of the natural and divine order of progress. Mach was contesting a view of history, a scientific model, believed by its adherents to be capable of settling the basis of all history. In the scientific model of human progress of his contemporaries, it was a requisite that 'every man whose mind is unbiased by system' was expected to concede the following:

> that when we perform an action, we perform it in consequence of some motive or motives; that those motives are the results of some antecedents; and that, therefore, if we were acquainted with the whole of the antecedents, and with all the laws of their movements, we could with unerring certainty predict the whole of their immediate results.[27]

In this view of history it was explained, by the English historian Buckle in 1857 that, 'as all antecedents are either in the mind or out of it, we shall clearly see that all the variations in the results, in other words, all the changes of which history is full, all the vicissitudes of the human race, their progress or their decay, their happiness or their misery, must be the fruit of a double action: an action of external phenomena upon the mind, and another action of the mind upon the phenomena'.[28]

Mach contests history as the effect of antecedents by posing the problem of illusions of movement, such as the subject's erroneous belief of moving backwards after travelling in a moving train which has stopped. The illusions of forward direction are also posed as a problem for analysis of the sensations of exertion. Can the mind be understood as separated from the antecedents, is causation a question of accumulating instances of sense-data, when belief in the cause of bodily movements seems to be a matter of belief itself, rather than the sensations which are to count as instances of natural laws of progress?

In his experiment, from everyday experience of a stationary person gazing at a fast flowing river from a bridge, Mach notes that 'prolonged gazing' invariably results in the sensation that suddenly the bridge, with the observer and his whole environment, begins to move in the direction opposite to that of the water, while the water assumes the appearance of being at rest'.[29] If one is riding forward, another simple experiment, the sensation of forward motion arises he notes, 'only when I resist following the objects with my eyes'. How can the sensations of forward movement be understood as caused by the antecedent of the objects passing on the left, rotating like the hands of a watch, when the sensation only arises when the rider resists following the motion of these objects? It appears as if the sensation of bodily movement is under the control of the Will, but the illusory nature of the sensation of exertion must disturb the dichotomy of the mind and causal antecedents.

In Mach's analysis of the sensations of exertion all beliefs of motion become the illusions created by the qualities of sensations of space and movement. Both the sensations of exertion attendant upon actual movement and the sensations attendant upon 'illusory movement' are characterised as the illusions of sensations of space. Volition can be understood, as if 'like three animals', or three kinds of innervations or sensory modalities. What the Will experiences as voluntary movement is a quality of 'sensations of space and movement arising in the province of sight and touch during the change of place, or even as a shadow in remembrance of locomotion, or at the thought of a distant spot'.[30]

Mach's study of the sensations of movement associated with the ventricles or canals of the ear completes his threefold enervation account of the conventional understanding of the experience of the Will in volition. It is the sensations of bodily movement which are 'the Will to perform movements of the eye'. But how can this analysis of the sensations of space and movement be the experience of the Will, the sense of voluntariness under the control of the Mind, when the sensations of movement must arise before the sensations of space given by the optic modalities of the retina? Mach's explanation, of what is in effect a reversal of naturalistic understandings of time and space in notions of causation, is developed within an account of the conventions of perspective involved in Western perceptions of space.

He asks what are the sensory qualities of perceiving distance when the modalities of the senses involve only light, colour and movement? How is distance organised within sensation? In Mach's study it is the 'aesthetic impression', the impression 'of unity' which gives the appearance of a near figure as similar in form but distant from a far figure. This aesthetic impression, by which geometrically similar figures are perceived as optically similar is a question of the perspective or direction of the perceiver in relation to the objects of perception and the concepts and words with which the bodily movments of the perceiver are connected to the different objects. In Mach's perspectival model of space perception: 'our body, like every other, is part of the world of sense: the boundary-line between the physical and the psychical is solely practical and conventional.'[31]

Mach proposes that new paths of investigation would open for us if we assume that 'there is no rift between the psychical and the physical, no within and without, no sensation to which an outward, different thing corresponds'. He proposes that:

> there is but one kind of elements, out of which this supposititious within and without is formed—elements which are themselves within and without according to the light in which, for the time being, they are viewed.[32]

In Mach's perspectival model of knowledge of the world outside the subject, the time and space of antecedents thought to cause human action have been reversed. The lens through which human progress is to be understood is a sensory interpretive mode of corporeality in which the subject can know itself within a biological need to become, to be in the world. Mach explains this model of knowing the world using the psychophysical methods of measurement of sensations derived from the German psycho-physicist Fechner.[33] Just as the subject of the psychophysical experiment provides a sensory measure of his or her own sensa-tions through the use of the method of limits (in order to provide a standard or base against which intensity of stimulus can be mapped in the behavioural responses of the subject) so Mach's knowing subject provides for himself a sensory measure of the

space outside himself with which to perceive the character of the
self within that outside world.

In Mach's phenomenological and biological epistemology it is
because the experience of the self has been constituted by a
possessive corporeality (in which the Will is understood via an
external and causal antecedent to the body's existence) that the
subject's sensory measure of the world outside is a conventional
one. What appears to the subject as the sense-data of the outside
world is the conventions through which that subject provides
himself with a standard or base ground for knowing the practices
of progress and change within that world. But in Mach's perspectival or sensory perceptual model of knowing about personal being,
the possessive model of corporeality has become the real illusion
with which we negotiate the sense of self, an illusion replaced
within Mach's theory of knowing by what is here called a gestational model of corporeality. It is difficult to trace a precise
genealogy of Mach's perceptual principles to particular methods
for measuring sensitivities devised by Fechner. Mach does not give
precise directions in regard to his intellectual traditions, but he
does acknowledge Fechner and other psychophysics researchers
writing in Germany during the 1850s.[34]

At this point in my writing Mach's analysis of sensation and
perception begins to merge in my mind with Freud's writing on
the functioning of the psyche, with its primary processes in which
energy flows freely and ideas cathect or charge other ideas,
exchanging an energy which is always conserved. In Freud's
economical mode of writing/theorising Fechner's stability principle
or constancy principle becomes the pleasure/unpleasure principle
in which pleasure is a constant process of maintaining a balance
between quantities of excitations or affects.

Mach applies Fechner's measures of sensitivity in his own study
of the sensations of space and on the principle of adapting his
own mental processes to suit the task, pursues a sensory epistemology in which the knower takes on the same substance as that
to be known. Knowing becomes a practice of enrichment and
nourishment and the subject of knowledge, a gestational being.

Mach creates several principles by which to describe the knowledge practices of what Fechner would term outer psychophysics.
The sense-data which we understand as the physical facts of the
outside world—the facts of space and time—appear as an absolute
constant by virtue of our intuitive practices. Intuition and the
mental adaptation of concepts to new conditions is impelled, as
it were, to provide common elements by which variations or
differences between sense-data will be perceived as instances of a
general kind. Intuition's own principle of continuity provides, as

it were, a sensitivity threshold against which variations in sense-data can be allowed for. Intuitive knowledge, in Mach's words, 'impresses itself upon the memory and makes its appearance there in the form of recollections which spontaneously supplement every fact presented by the senses'.[36] The sensory processes of perception constitute the variations in sense-data as constants, or constant errors, because we forget that our sense-data is always in relation to our body: 'We attain the idea of absolute constancy only as we overlook or underrate conditions, or as we regard them as always given, or as we deliberately disregard them'.[36]

This forgetting of the body, this exclusion of the body as the condition of constancy because it is familiar might provide an 'undisturbed and economical conception of the world, but it is certainly not the only legitimate method'. In this framework it is the forgetting of the body's relational position within the conditions for reaching a consciousness of self, that the world outside takes on the appearance of antecedent to our understanding. In Mach's framework, human action has been theorised as the biological need of causality which confronts us 'like a power from without', but a power: 'which continually accompanies and assists us, as a thing of which we stand in need, in order to supplement the deficiencies of the fact'.[37] Human action is no longer theorised as the effect of an antecedent cause in the world outside, causation is now imagined as a constancy or error of thought which impels us to enrich the sense-data we call facts.

Within Mach's writing, epistemologies or theories of knowledge appear to have become questions of ontology, or conditions of being. Knowledge of the outside world becomes the constant illusions through which the body is impelled, as if by instinct, to enrich or supplement the sense-data by which consciousness becomes aware of its existence as self. The model of corporeality which is implicit within Mach's research methodology, the gestational model of being in the world, suggests the new questions which can be asked about the technologies of Value and productivity instituted within the various discipines given birth by 19th century mechanical and evolutionary knowledges. What are the conditions in which gestational beings apply the illusion of a body possessed by the ego to enrich their perception of the character of being in the world? What are the practices of supplementing a possessive embodiment? At stake in these questions of the subject's 'need for causation' is learning how to contest the limitations of contemporary forms of agency in which the subject is rarely constituted as autonomous in relation to activity. It is learning how to contest the identity of the slothful automaton. It is learning how to contest contemporary conceptions of agency in which the tendency to act and the release of that tendency are not within one's power.

Can we imagine another kind of personhood in whom earning capacity was a state of action, rather than inaction, or in which this 'tendency to action' could be self-started by virtue of some intrinsic property of the self, an ontology of productivity? Harre argues that we remain under the spell of a general causal model of action, in which the category of hypothetical mental acts, 'volitions', have been imported to make good the deficit in our experience in regard to mental events. Harre argues that to understand how we can conceive of ourselves as conscious beings we need to suppose that we are using a theory to organise our experience, a theory that introduces a unity of self as a theoretical concept rather than as an empirical discovery.[38] He argues that our conception of ourselves as agents can be understood as the employment of a theory, with the active and willing self as its prime theoretical concept. 'In possession of a theory that I am an agent capable of acting against the tide of my inclination, capable of getting myself up and going etc., I have the means for read-justing the many means-ends hierarchies which are involved in the preparation for action. And I have a way of explaining how my mental life (with others) appears to me the way it does.'[39] The problem is conceiving of such a theory when we inhabit a world we believe to be occupied by wound-up clocks and unwound-up clocks, by responsive machines and unresponsive, slothful machines.

Writing the characters of fiscal narratives

How do we write about that human condition of modernity which Foucault has called 'society's threshold of modernity',[40] in which one watches a predictable acceleration of western wealth and a predictable acceleration of famine elsewhere and one calls it economic development? How do we write about knowing the limits to this narrative, predicted as one of decay, which we are compelled to name as wealth? Foucault describes this condition as modern man being 'an animal whose politics places his exist-ence as a living being in question'. He described this threshold as having been reached 'when the life of the species is wagered on its own political strategies'.[41]

In volume one of his *History of Sexuality* Foucault set out his plan for writing about this human condition, it was to be 'a "history of bodies" and the manner in which what is most material and most vital in them has been invested'.[42] His plan for a history of bodies designated the manner in which life had been wagered as follows: 'this power over life evolved in two basic forms', one centred on the body as a machine, and the other on 'the species body', the body imbued with the mechanics of life by the techniques of statistical assessments and comprehensive measurements of the population. Sexuality was the name Foucault gave to the manner in which these forms of 'action' and 'normality' were deployed, and the name sex to the imaginative practices within which each person has access to identity. Foucault did not live to complete his project of writing that history of bodies in the post-17th century in which the western human condition acquired its character of wagering life, of using the techniques of statistical inference and probability theory to create predictions about the embodied norms with which living beings were compelled to provide confirmation with their identities and their lives. But in his plan he argued that:

> It is the agency of sex that we must break away from, if we aim—through a tactical reversal of the various mechanisms of sexuality—to counter the grips of power with claims of bodies, pleasures and knowledges, in their multiplicity and their possibility of resistance.[43]

I have used Foucault's plan here to write about the evolution of these forms—of the body as machine and the species body as calibrated—in the 19th century to learn how to 'counter the grips of power with claims of bodies'. My history of the calibrated body with its spirit or poetics of electromagnesis had the aim of understanding how the assumptions of the 'norm' in statistical thinking was able to invest the 'species body' with 'the mechanics of life', how we came to believe that the 'economy' had a life of its own. I am trying to understand how we came to compel human beings to acquire identities of nonproductivity as the condition of our proofs of progress, and how the imaginative characters of fiscal stories, the different forms of capital/fictional property, have acquired their human capacities for growth, generation and reproduction.

My problem is, how do you contest these deployments of sexuality when they are the narratives within which the modern subject learns to recognise the self? How can claims be made that bodies and their performances have other meanings without reinscribing the hierarchies of value which sexed identities take up in practice? My plan set out here is to name the coded calibrated body which serves as the proof of these deployments of sexuality—the discursive formations of fiscal energetics—as the taxpayer's body rather than as 'woman'.

From Irigaray's writing I have taken the next step in my methodology of entering the double bind of scientificity, my plan of writing, to be that of writing as the imaginative female characters of the masculinist texts on taxation, with the knowledges of a placental economy. These are the characters of fictitious property using female characteristics to explain their sexed relations with others, that is, the financial and juridical forms which give birth to new forms of money. These characters will differ from those female characters in Freud's stories whose images of themselves as a bodily-thing always required a professional interpreter. These female characters will carry the scientific credentials of Mach's sexed psychophysics and create stories in which humans are able to negotiate the prices paid for the fantasies of fictional property.

PART IV

Where does the body of legal discourse begin and end? Legal and non-legal knowledges

9

Black man, white woman, irresistible impulse: media, law and literature making the black murderer

Terry Threadgold

Fish is correct in insisting that law must simultaneously plunge into, and differentiate itself from, the realm of the extra-legal . . .

Law, however, is not an isolated practice, but rather one of a cluster of interrelated practices which need not be viewed exclusively as ends in themselves . . . To the extent that ethical, political and philosophical arguments have a genuine place within the practice of the law, however, that practice is not self-contained.
(Michel Rosenfeld in *Deconstruction and the Possibility of Justice*[1])

The hallucinating mind is in strict terms a mind that wanders, that 'lucinates', that goes astray. That is the source of common law, of unwritten law, it is the meandering of the legal mind, a temporal and geographic nomadism that snakes its path across the justificatory texts, the judgements, of the year books and the law reports. Here we can understand how the text is also the unwritten structure of everyday life, a reality which time treats badly and transmits very slowly over long periods, how reason itself becomes a mask 'worn by longstanding historical and political facts, the memory of which men [have] retained over centuries',[2] how the limits 'marked by reason' have nothing reasonable about them.

(Peter Goodrich and Yifat Hachamovitch in *Dangerous Supplements*[3])

Here is the question: Riviere's crime, in which the frontier between rationality and madness is hard to establish and which seems therefore to take its place in the sequence of crimes which had held the judicial stage in the 1820s—crimes disproportionate, excessive and incomprehensible, for they seemed to violate the natural and social order (parents killed, children killed, the

criminal feeding on his victim's flesh) while the criminals seemed to
have acted without apparent motive and to have been in possession
of their full intellectual faculties—Riviere's crime, then, seems to
have brought once again to the fore the dangerous question of the
coexistence of madness and rationality, of partial delusion and the
lucid interval.

(Michel Foucault ed., *I, Pierre Riviere, having slaughtered my
mother, my sister and my brother*[4])

I have quoted the above passages at length as a way of introducing
and framing the issues to be raised in this chapter. In their mutual
contradictions and intersections they signal and anticipate the
complexities and the legal and everyday fictions that surround the
Jimmy Governor murder case in Australia at the turn of the 19th
century. Narrative, hallucination, madness, rationality, history and
memory, truth, objectivity, gender, class and race are just some of
the issues at risk in the telling and multiple retellings of this story
within and outside the law, tellings that challenge and confront
the public face and presence of the law, and tellings that ultimately
deny the possibility of the category 'extra-legal' precisely because
the legal is always constructed and lived in the very space defined
as extra-legal—the space of what law defines as its 'others'.

I will take as my starting point Michel Foucault's *I, Pierre
Riviere, having slaughtered my mother, my sister and my brother
. . .* In this text, Foucault and others set out an agenda for the
exploration of the discursive construction of criminality: both the
making of the criminal self and the categorising of that self as
criminal, mad or deviant by the law and its agents. What this
work demonstrates are the inevitable and consistent intersections
between, on the one hand, the rationality and the contradictory
practices of the law, medicine and psychiatry, and the contradictory rationality and insanity of the self that is Pierre Riviere, and
on the other, the inevitable and consistent intersections between
the apparently implacable, scientific and neutral faces of the law,
medicine and psychiatry and their subjective, fictional, dialogic
and feminised 'others'—the institutions of the media, popular and
oral narrative culture and literature.

What is most interesting in all of this is the extent to which
all of these practices, the embodied realities, the talkings, and the
writings which are the traces we have of them, are limited and
constrained by what can be said and written and indeed meant
at a given point in time. Here I want to relate the Riviere case
to Foucault's work on the discourses of the social sciences where
he showed how official knowledges work as technologies or
instruments of 'normalisation', providing the disciplinary struc-

tures which produce populations with carefully controlled and limited notions of what the 'normal' or the 'true' might be at a given point in time. Any disciplinary structure such as the law, medicine or psychiatry participates in these processes, so that what is to count as 'truth' or 'knowledge'—the truth about a person's health or criminality or sanity—is always the result of the kinds of institutional and discursive practices which constitute a discipline on the exclusion of its others.[5] Expert knowledges thus discursively produce the objects of which they speak and simultaneously exclude those categories which cannot be accounted for within the established 'truth'. Such categories include knowledges and discourses like those of the madman, the pervert, the patient, the peasant—knowledges and discourses that cannot be heard by the established order, or that have been subjugated, made 'marginal' by official histories.

In the case study of Pierre Riviere, Foucault makes it clear that he regards it as an act of resistance to the dominant systems of knowledge, a critical activity in itself, to simply 'quote' these unruly positions, without commentary,[6] thus publishing and making visible what is otherwise located below the level of 'science'.[7] Thus we read Riviere's 'confession' along with a number of the original 19th century documents surrounding the case. There is no immediate commentary, but the documents dialogue effectively among themselves, juxtaposed so as to provide a study of the way techniques of normalisation, surveillance and punishment actually work. Riviere is a paradigm case in understanding how the modern criminal is produced.

He is a multiple murderer, with a history of apparently 'odd' behaviour, a peasant with little formal education who writes an apparently rational and 'educated' confession. In the course of the series of events which begin with the murder (or the murder/narrative—he writes that he had meant to write the narrative before the murder, that it was 'written in my head' before the murders), and proceed with his capture, the trial where he is found guilty and sentenced to death, the appeal where the sentence is commuted to life imprisonment, and his suicide in prison some years later, he is caught up in the contradictions, oppositions and 'indecisions'[8] between a number of expert discourses and practices. First there are the contradictory arguments of the medical and proto-psychiatric experts who find him mad or sane depending on whether it could be argued that a disease called 'monomania'—in which sufferers are mad for a short period and then completely recover their sanity—could be said to actually exist. If it did exist then was it possible to argue extenuating circumstances and thus to find the culprit not guilty of murder. These indecisions already

involve a second set in the form of two incompatible discourses
on punishment. These discourses evidence a temporal discontinuity
between the 18th and 19th centuries. Is a murderer to be exe-
cuted—the visible and public punishment of the body—or to be
sentenced to life imprisonment with the associated implications of
panoptic control[9] and the becoming object of the subject who is
then an object for scientific surveillance. But this is not yet the
limit of the indecisions. At the level of popular knowledge, the
witnesses contradicted each other. At the level of expert knowledge
so did the doctors—and the jury could not reach a decision.

Riviere committed these murders in 1835 at a time when
revolution and murder, official and illegal killings, were endemic.
At the same time as Riviere's trial for parricide was in progress,
a trial centring around attempted regicide was also in process and
being reported in the news. The parallels between the killing of
a parent and the killing of the symbolic father of the body politic
then entered the discursive fray, via the route of further indecisions
about the relative roles of the legislature (and the sovereign) and
the judiciary. The revolution had attached punishment solely to
the legislature. 'Extenuating circumstances' might have appeared
to be a reversion to the pre-revolutionary arbitrary discretion of
the judiciary. There were political indecisions here as well: the
judges could not deliver a verdict of 'extenuating circumstances'
in a case of parricide with its links to regicide without offending
the sovereign. They thus refused that verdict and then appealed
to the king for commutation. This is just one aspect of the
struggles for power that were enacted here in and around Riviere's
statement—his murder/narrative/confession. In the course of this
case psychiatric knowledge was introduced into the enforcement
of the law. The criminal madman, as a being harmful to the social
order, had to be condemned, 'but his status as madman took
precedence over his status as criminal'.[10] This paved the way for
the development of the theory of limited responsibility and the
introduction of all the degrees of insanity into the concept of
responsibility before the law. It made it possible for not only
psychiatry but all the social and human sciences to intervene in
judicial procedure and to reduce, as did the presence of the jury
as the representative of public opinion, the power of the judiciary.
Thus the domain of the 'extra-legal', at the level of expert
knowledges, and public opinion begins to enter the domain of the
legal. These complex processes constitute the discursive construction of the criminal.

Through all of these procedures the account of the crimes
which Riviere himself composed in prison continues to occupy a
kind of non-space. There is no space for it in the deliberations

and the discourses which surround it. 'The official discourses (law, psychiatry, medicine) simply do not know how to *treat,* in both senses, Riviere's memoir.'[11] One of the major problems is its indeterminacy, its genre, as narrative and/or confession, as diary, as plan of action even. Not the least of these imponderables, as Foucault has pointed out, is the way the murder and the murderer and the narrative/confession keep changing places.[12] The complexities of the relations between act, identity/subjectivity and discourse here are considerable: and they are not issues which the 'experts' in this case ever begin to *treat.* They persist in looking for a truth, for a certainty of knowledge in a discourse which has little to do with 'truth':

> It was this (Riviere's memoir) that had to furnish the proof, fill the gap, and make it possible to re-establish knowledge in a certainty regained.
> But what in fact happened? The subject who had fallen into a trap set a trap in turn; he behaved so as to raise the doctors' and lawyers' uncertainty to a sort of undecidable universal of madness instead of furnishing what was expected—the proof of the true and the false. In the event, the proof doubled back on itself as soon as they thought they had grasped it. One sentence is amply sufficient to demonstrate this: 'I was arrested with a bow and though I said I had made it in order to pass for mad, yet it was not exactly that.'[13]

What is paralysed by this discourse in which the question of true or false remains undecidable is the experts' will to truth.

Here I want to quote from Deborah Cameron and Elizabeth Frazer.[14] Speaking of their own attempts to discuss the question of murder, and anticipating criticism of the fact that their book is a text about texts about murder, not about some ultimate reality, they ask: 'What would constitute "the heart of the matter"?'—the absent ultimate reality. Their answer is that: 'The discourse by which sex-killing is made intelligible to us, whether it comes from the killer, a psychiatrist or *The Sun,* is not parasitic on some higher truth: it is the heart of the matter and the rest is silence'. That is, the accounts that people give of killers, or that killers give of themselves are not the 'truth'. They are constructions, and like all constructed texts, they depend on what Cameron and Frazer call 'the codes of the culture' to give them meaning. When a killer writes a confession, he cannot do it except within the limits of his own experience, within the limits of the discourses and texts to which he has had access. His understanding of the events he records, like his representation of them, is always mediated by that kind of coded understanding and discursive and intertextual limitation. Thus the 'truth' of the subjugated discourse, like that of the expert knowledge, is culturally, socially and historically specific, a cultural construction. It offers no blinding insight into the workings of the killer's mind. The explanations the killer provides are generic conventions which he has learnt in society to be associated with that kind of event and which others recognise as probable accounts of it.

It is within this kind of explanation that Riviere's confession/memoir finds its place. Foucault argues that it is a place in a particular discursive tradition and the knowledges that go with it—a tradition of 'narratives of crime', circulating as broadsheets and true confessions, in which the people, speech and rumour, local narrative and news and great events came to produce history:

> All these narratives spoke of a history in which there were no rulers, peopled with frantic and autonomous events, a history below the level of power, one which clashed with the law.
>
> Hence the relations of proximity, opposition, and reversibility set up by the fly sheets among the 'curious' news items, the 'extraordinary' facts, and the great events and personages of history. For the broadsheets narrated both contemporary crimes and episodes of the recent past; the battles of the Empire, the great days of the Revolution and the war in the Vendee, 1814, and the conquest of Algeria rubbed shoulders with murders . . . Murder establishes the ambiguity of the lawful and the unlawful.[15]

Thus it was that Riviere 'came to lodge his deed and his speech in a defined place in a certain type of discourse and a certain field of knowledge'.[16] That historical field 'was the condition which made this premeditated murder/memoir possible'.[17] The representations available to him enabled him to envisage his act of slaughter as meaningful and justifiable. 'They shaped the form of his killing and the way he understood it.'[18] Desire, text and action were inextricably linked because they were 'produced' by a particular discursive practice made up of Bible stories and history learned at school, murders recorded in fly-sheets and broadsheets, and confessional autobiographies, and his lived experience of the contemporary social order, shifts in 'what historians awkwardly call mentalities'.[19] 'He became aware that a snare lurked somewhere. What called itself order was a lie, or rather the existing order was the reverse of order. Pierre Riviere assumed the stance of a questioner of the straight and the crooked, the just and the unjust.'[20] This is precisely what Cameron and Frazer[21] demonstrate much more fully in their account of murderers as 'heroes' and 'deviants', taking up both kinds of discursive formation articulated in the Riviere case, the tradition of crime narrative and the expert knowledges of the normalising tradition. It is their conclusion with respect to the sex murderer as hero that I want to focus on here, since it links directly with the Riviere case and this change in 'mentalities' and leads into my discussion of the Jimmy Governor murders.

They explore the whole range of cultural representations of murder from Gothic models to 19th century broadsides to the emergence of detective fiction and its associations with the plea-sures of crime and horror stories such as Frankenstein,[22] pointing to the gradual emergence of a blurring of fact and fiction in the similarities between the generic characters of horror fiction and the murdering fiend of the tabloid press, and concluding with the development of sado-eroticism, the link between cruelty and dom-ination and the erotic, and the existentialist construction of fiends and libertines as rebels. They conclude that there seem to be two kinds of heroes, the fiend/beast/monster whose terrible desires and deeds remove him from the pale of society and reduce him to the status of animal, nature before the social contract, and the liber-tine or rebel, the 'outsider', whose desires are also outside social norms, but only because of the repressive and restrictive nature of society. In both versions the murderer is essentially a man in a state of nature—either a pre-social contract brutality and anar-chy or an idealisation of the state of nature. As they point out these two versions seem opposed but in fact are not so dissimilar. In placing the killer in a state of nature both versions explicitly 'deny that he could be in a "state of culture": that is a product of society not an outcast or a freak'.[23]

They argue that the state of nature arguments cannot be sustained when questions of gender and power are introduced in the context of social and cultural analysis. The culturally deter-mined nature of sexual murder emerges from its connections with cultural ideas of sexuality and gender. Man's 'beastliness' is a specifically late 19th century phenomenon. There have, they argue, to be reasons for this and they find them in a potential for sex murder that is profoundly embedded in Western culture and has been since the 18th century:

> The eroticising of domination, cruelty and death is by no means *natural*: it arose at a specific point in history. But it is also not confined to a few abnormal men: its imaginary forms are ubiquitous in the West, pervading both highbrow and popular culture, contributing to a taken-for-granted stereotype of masculine sexuality as intrinsically sadistic, intrinsically desiring to take the Other by force. In a culture which thus conflates sex, power and death, the sexual killer is hardly an exile.[24]

While the sex murderer that they deal with is explicitly one whose acts have a sexual or erotic aspect, there seem to me to be parallels with the murderers I am concerned with here who murder women without an apparent erotic or sexual motive. I say apparent because in both cases the implications of eroticism are very real—in the case of Riviere it is made explicit by the doctors for whom incest was associated with his fear of women[25] and it is constructed into the literary version of the Governor murders by Keneally for whom the murderer of women must be motivated by lust.

In many important ways then the Riviere case anticipates, contextualises and frames the Governor murders in Australia at the turn of the 19th century. It raises all the complex issues of discursivity, narrativity, subjectivity, memory and history that intersect with the law in the Governor case. What follows will focus on the early 'history' of the murders, but will allude to the textual and discursive transformations of that history which span almost a century and thus provide multiple sites for elaborating the critical and political agenda of Foucault's account of the making of a murderer in 17th century France. The aim will be to show how the law and its agents construct 'just' and 'equitable' judgements on the basis of discursive, corporeal and legal fictions, to relate the terrible acts of the murderer to his being in a 'state of culture' and to understand how the 'hallucinations'[26] of the common law are also inevitably 'in a state of culture' outside of which they cannot in fact exist at all.

In this context then the body of texts I will 'use as evidence' is not to be read as an empirical data corpus. It serves rather more the function of what Foucault called the archive in which the collection of texts, conversations, documents, are actually what represents the organisation of a discourse or set of discourses (their statements), a discursive formation. What they reveal are the conditions by which it is possible to 'know' something at a specific historical point and by which this knowledge changes. Foucault defines the archive as follows:

> I mean the set of rules which at a given period and for a definite society defined:
> 1) the limits and forms of *expressibility* . . .
> 2) the limits and forms of *conservation* . . .
> 3) the limits and forms of *memory* . . .
> 4) the limits and the forms of *reactivation* . . . [27]

In the case of the Governor murders these issues are directly related not only to gender but also to race. In this case the murderer was black and the women murdered were white and again the murderer is caught up in the contradictions and intersections of a number of sets of conflicting discourses and power relations in which the law is always and inevitably involved and which give the lie to any notion of linear progress. To be writing of these murders in the 1990s is inevitably to recognise the unruly and unseemly parallels between that other *fin de siecle* and this one. In 1988 Australia celebrated a bicentenary which symbolised a national identity and a homogeneity which were conceived at exactly the period when Jimmy Governor first behaved in ways that declared them to be dangerous and dominant fictions:

> The *fin de siecle* of the nineteenth century figures in British historiography not only as a crisis of empire and the rule of property, but also as a turning point between a society in which the 'New Woman' provoked a frisson of desire and dread, and the society that succeeded it, a society that considered individual rights so differently that it could within decades grant women the vote.[28]

It was, however, a society that failed to do the same thing for its Aboriginal peoples until many decades later, a society that in 1988 had still not come to terms with the 'human costs of unified constructions of national identity' and whose Aboriginal peoples again on that occasion demonstrated that: 'Assertions of national identity, unity and community are constructed by means of exclusions and repression.'[29]

'Australia's national identity has been built around explicit racial exclusions, both in terms of the limits imposed on Aboriginal peoples at home and the boundaries constructed against racial "others" from overseas. This process of exclusion is inseparable from the conceptualisation of white women as producers and guardians of a white nation.'[30] It is the resilience of these patterns of racist thought and behaviour and their complex intersections with an institutionalised sexism that the re-tellings and reactivations of the Governor stories across almost a century indicate most clearly. The public and published versions of the story effectively work to silence many other stories, some of which emerge around the margins of the dominant story in a number of contested and unpredictable ways. Recent feminist revisions of the history of the construction of the Australian nation and national identity have much to offer in providing archaeologies of the discourses that speak the murder story in the 1900s.[31] They demonstrate very convincingly just how much more varied and contested were the social and sexual and racial relations of the period than the public texts and narratives that are the traces of the Governor murders would indicate.

Of particular importance here are their discussions of institutionalised misogyny in the 'men's press' of the period and

its associations with the Bushman mythology,[32] and accounts of
the complexity of class relations between women in the domestic
sphere as depicted in the popular press[33] where the complex
'servant problem' of the 1990s was often assessed in 'a fundamen-
tally misogynistic way': 'Responsibility for the "problem" was
shifted to the "tyrannising" mistress, with the male household
head as mediator.'[34] Even more interesting are Castle and Pringle's
readings of political cartoons of the period depicting aspects of
the arguments for Federation and the 'birth' of the new nation.
They argue that at the time of Federation the cartoon images of,
for example, the Prime Minister dressed as a nurse, nurturing the
baby 'Commonwealth' are an indication that:

> No full-blown masculine image had emerged . . . to represent the
> spirit or identity of the new nation.[35] The masculine image is
> 'disguised' in women's clothing. The questions broached in these
> cartoons are not only concerned with the form of independence.
> They also bring into play sexual anxiety, and fears regarding the
> fitness for autonomy or self-sufficency of Australian manhood.[36]

All of these new histories are directly relevant to the question
of the representation and construction of masculinity and femininity in the period, issues which are central to the way the law
deals with, is able to 'read', and constructs the Jimmy Governor
case in 1900.

What is at issue in this murder story or stories—because there
is more than one version—is the way the telling of stories at all
levels in a social system becomes a huge machinery for the
construction of social realities, social and cultural institutions and
the people, men and women, black and white, who inhabit them
and make them in their turn. For they are made, not given, as
black, white, feminine, masculine and the law is but one of the
factors involved in this making. Exploring this involves a social
semiotics of the interactions between institutions, people, texts,
discourses and behaviours, between law and society, and an
understanding of the ways meanings are made and transmitted.
This begins to explain how apparently just, impartial and 'truthful'
institutions, like law, 'make' the worlds they think they merely
represent—and do it in talk and in writing—in discourse as social
process.

Jimmy Governor was a half-caste Aboriginal who married a
white woman, and worked, very much within the tradition of the
Lone Hand described by Lake[37] as part of the white Bush-
man/Mateship myth, as solitary fencer, shearer's hand, itinerant
farm worker—a tradition in which Jimmy Governor is clearly an
intruder. At a certain point in this history he murdered the wife

and children of his employer Mawbey, and their governess. The public version of the story—in the media and in the courtroom—is that the Mawbeys withheld supplies and rations—payment for the fencing he was employed to do—because members of Jimmy Governor's Aboriginal family had set up a 'black's camp' on the property. The Mawbeys reneged on the contract to pay with the argument that the job was not well enough done.

This part of the story is never prominent, however. It is overshadowed by a problem with women. In all the public accounts the real cause of the murders is attributed to the difficult domestic relations between the Mawbey women and their governess and Mrs Governor, the white wife of Jimmy Governor. These are both class and sexual relations. The women are said to have 'taunted her' because she had married a black man. Two crimes then are signalled here—both perpetrated by women. First, Ethel Governor, a white girl of doubtful parentage, has exchanged herself in marriage in quite improper and subversive ways. Second, the Mawbey women have engaged in typical 'tyrannical' behaviour towards their 'servant', have nagged and harassed in typical feminine fashion. Part of this construction is also related to Anne Summers' conceptualisation of Australian wives and mothers, particularly where the white mistress rules over 'blacks' and 'savages', as the moral guardians of society, as 'God's police'.[38] These women are perceived to have expressed and enacted a racism that is nowhere attributed to the white head of the Mawbey household, and are in the end responsible for their own murder. How you might ask? Ethel Governor too it seems has been nagging and hysterical, stirring up her already 'primitive' and problematic black (he is never referred to as half-caste) husband to take revenge on her behalf. Their moral guardianship over her, their nagging femininity, is the cause of her nagging in turn and of the murders.

The violence that is unleashed by her complaints—in the form of the first murders and then a number of subsequent killings—is easily explicable within the binary categories of the law, categories that were beginning to be established at the time of the Riviere case. When Jimmy Governor says in his statement to police: 'I got out of temper, and got hammering them, and lost control of myself. I do not remember anything after that', he categorises himself as irrational, subject to uncontrollable passion, and liable to a defence argument of diminished responsibility, manslaughter not murder, passion not premeditation. The possibilities of the adversarial arguments in the courtroom are constrained by the limits of a discourse that both silences and appropriates the stories of the everyday, the community and its others.

But it is more complex even than this. The Jimmy Governor story becomes a part of a much larger story, a media story, a story of the making of a nation, of masculinity, of subversive and unruly women and dangerous racial others, and of the need for masculine control and protection to resolve these issues. In this context the arguments and oppression of the courtroom at the Governor trial are inevitable. They are also partial and constructed and it is the nature of that construction, that making of the black criminal and his guilty white wife that I want to explore now.

Jimmy Governor first earns notoriety when the events of the murders are reported in the *Sydney Morning Herald* on July 23 1900. They are reported as a small paragraph in the Country News column. After the murders he and his wife and child and two male members of his Aboriginal family had 'gone bush'. Ethel Governor and the baby were left behind and taken into custody quite quickly. The older Aboriginal is also left and caught. Jimmy and a younger relative remain at large and at risk, committing further murders, for a number of months. The criminals are outlawed and bands of armed men take chase. Jimmy Governor is finally tried and sentenced to hanging in November. The media construction and representation of this 'escape' and the fear it creates in the countryside are extraordinarily interesting.

As the events escalate and the story develops it occupies more and more space in the daily newspapers. *The Sydney Mail* (November 1900) gives the story full-page spreads, with photographs and maps of the route followed by the Aboriginals and their pursuers. The story occupies half the columns in a full page of the *Herald*. It also occupies much of the space in the *Bulletin* and other local newspapers at the time. And this continues for three months. As the story develops it appropriates and intersects with other stories and is recontextualised by them. The writing of the story is framed by this context and the mutually intersecting stories construct another context and a set of reading positions for newspaper readers. Colin Mercer, writing of the function of newspapers in producing the nation as *habitus*—a 'specific way of being in the world'—at the time of the bicentennial celebrations, describes the way the various sub-genres involved in reporting that event operate 'to classify and delineate different phenomena, to enable certain forms of social identity and affiliation to be established and to establish in tangible forms the existence and arrangement of groups, classes and communities'.[39] He regards the newspaper as a 'civilising technique':

> . . . it is possible to follow some of the paths flagged by him
> (Elias) in the relationship between a regular material cultural form

like the newspaper and the elaboration of techniques for forming and mannering populations and citizens in the much more complex, extended and diverse national societies which emerged in the nineteenth century. Following this route, we can propose a concept of the nation itself not as a static structure, a container of dominant ideologies, a simple 'invention', or indeed a 'myth', but rather in terms of the rituals, daily practices and techniques, institutions, manners and customs which enable the nation to be thinkable, inhabitable, communicable and thereby governable.[40]

The newspaper is one such technique then and a crucial one in constructing the limits of what could be said and communicated about the Governor murders. The *Herald* format at this time is very different to the present one. There is a sense in which the story is 'reported' without any attempt at editorial synthesis, as if the snippets of information that form the titled parts of the story on the page had simply been collocated fairly randomly as they arrived in the newspaper office. Stories contradict one another on the same page. (The Fitzpatrick murders are a case in point. See Threadgold.[41]) Rumour, gossip and apparently factual accounts from 'experts' like the police or the law or the government—the final reports in the *Herald* are transcripts of the trial—are juxtaposed with individual narratives of the 'how I pursued the murderers' variety. The various sub-genres of reporting include the photo-essay, the historical narrative, politico-moral commentary and stories told by ordinary Australian men. This distinctive repertoire of images and narratives produces a characteristic construction and representation of the nation at the time of Federation. In this way private stories and the stories of the community and the everyday are included in an apparently heteroglossic report in which many voices seem to be heard and contestation and contradiction are entirely visible. There are important ways, however, in which the private and the heteroglossic, the heterogenous, are homogenised and rewritten in the narrative processes by which the private is made public knowledge.

The Jimmy Governor story is always accompanied in the papers of the day by a small group of other topical stories. There are stories of war, and of masculinity engaged in war—the Boxer rebellion in China and the Boer War in South Africa. These stories intersect with the myth of the Australian Bushman and the complexities of the discourse of property, sexuality and protection which emerges around the dangers to women and children that are always present in war. They are also explicitly racist in their treatment of the racial other. These stories begin to have explicit and important intertextual links with the Governor story as bands of armed Bushmen pursue the Governors, at first without success, a situation which demands some reconciliation of the conflicting stories of the indomitable nature of the Australian Bushman in Africa and the secret, tribal and primitive knowledges of the nomadic Aboriginal, the dangerous other, who eludes capture at home. Indeed, the story of the Aboriginal as nomad and expert bushman has to be mobilised to explain the white bushman's failure. Black trackers have to be called in to deal with the problem. And in this situation the populace has to be protected:

> Then there is another phase of the question which will likely escape attention. It is the reputation our bushmen now hold in the eyes of the outside world. That two men should be able to elude capture for over three months is what will not be readily understood by outsiders. But whilst mistakes have been made in the arrangements for capture, the nature of most of the country through which the Governors travelled was such that only blackfellows who knew the wild and perilous nature of the hills would have any chance of capturing the fugitives.[42]

The war at home against the senseless murder of women and children and the war abroad and its racial others begin to take on a very similar appearance. The visual and verbal genres, story and photograph, begin to parallel one another in the different geographical and newspaper spaces. Ranks of armed men in Africa look very like the photographs of the captors of Jimmy Governor, or even the ranks of men who form the jury which will judge him.

At the same time the woman suffrage question is constantly being debated, a story which constructs women very differently to the discourses of protection. This is juxtaposed in turn with stories on the question of the imminent federation of the Australian States and the choice of a site for the National Capital. Again, the genre of photograph which depicts the founding fathers of the nation is the same as that which depicts men at war saving the nation and men at home doing likewise. There is a very real sense in which the unruly women in the Governor story are intertextually implicated in and constructed by a constant reference to, deferral and fear of, female suffrage in the new nation. At the same time the Governor murders, like Australia's convict past, are a very real problem for imminent nationhood. In some way the story has to be made to be a narrative of masculine control and power, of national success, not failure. This I suggest is why women have to be seen to have caused their own murders and why institutionalised masculine white racism cannot be acknowledged. As Claudia Knapman demonstrates[43] this is unfortunately not an uncommon narrative. Women and non-whites had no voice of their own in our histories and narratives and were always constructed in terms of the stories that could be told, stories that were themselves constructed in terms of racial and gender ideologies. For her:

> This colonisation of historical explanation is the most significant of all the ways in which race and gender intersect. It is particularly obvious in the way in which a stereotype of the dependent and peripheral white woman has been brought into the action of the male colonising endeavour to 'explain' white racism and racial conflict.[44]

The media narrative, carried on in a variety of specific sites over a period of months is a narrative of masculine protection and the mobilisation of masculinity against the irresistable passion of the primitive and the irrational, women and the racial other. It is a reassuring story which attempts to contain and eradicate (by hanging) and quickly (before Federation and the public ceremonies which must argue for unity and identity) and by innuendo (women out of place are the cause of this unrest) those elements of its own masculinity which it cannot speak and will not acknowledge. In fact Jimmy Governor was arrested just three weeks after Federation. But just as in the case of the political cartoons surrounding Federation (discussed above) this masculinity is extremely problematic, a masculinity indeed '"disguised" in women's clothing'[45] in the case of this media and legal narrative.

I want here to quote from just three stories which surround early reports of the Governor murders and are juxtaposed with these on one page of the *Herald* in order to illustrate some of the points I have been making:

> From China the news contradicts itself day by day. It is not more than a week since the world was filled with horror at the news of the slaughter of Europeans in Peking. Only on Saturday last we received detailed accounts of the stripping and a hacking of European women in the streets and the ruthless massacre of children. Shortly before that there was a circumstantial story of that last stand of the refugees at the legations, when white women and children were pistolled by their defenders at the last extremity to prevent their falling alive into the hands of their Chinese Assailants. It would now appear, if the latest of these reports is to be believed, that all this is officially denied.[46]

Here is the discourse of protection in full force—women and children as property, sexuality and death and the fear of the racial other. Here protection is murder. This has uneasy and troubling connections with Cameron and Frazer's account of murders by

husbands, and suicide murders, where the notion that the woman
and/or her children are extensions of the male self, his property—
'if I go she goes'—is very common.[47] What is even worse, as they
point out, is the extraordinary judicial attitudes that emerge in
trials following such murders where statements like: 'I regard this
as a sad case. I am satisfied you were deeply devoted to your
wife'[48] are not uncommon. That this discourse of protection by
murder was common and often associated with racism is also
illustrated by its appearance in the newspaper *Boomerang*, in a
story published in twelve weekly parts in 1888. The story was
called 'The Race War' and is about white Australian fears of
Chinese immigration. In it a man speaking to the father of a girl
he wants to marry repeats the discourse we have noted above:
'I'd sooner kill her with my own hands than have her live to raise
a brood of coloured curs.' Her father replies that he knows: 'the
fate of a white girl among those leprous minded Asiatics'. (Quoted
by Robin McLachlan, Charles Sturt University, in a lecture entitled
The Past Invents the Future.) As if this were not sufficient the
second quote from the *Herald* goes like this:

> The burghers who after submission went away to join the raiders
> left their wives and families at Pretoria, to be maintained there by
> the British . . . These undesirable inhabitants were now ordered to
> join their husbands so that the capital may be relieved of their
> presence—dangerous as well as expensive. When they are
> encumbered with their wives and families the Boers will not be so
> eager in their guerilla warfare.[49]

Foreign women and children it seems do not warrant the kind of
'protection' given to one's own, but the consequences are probably
similar. Juxtaposed with these two reports is the following:

> So far as the objections to womanhood suffrage are concerned
> which base themselves on the unfitness of women to vote, they are
> answerable in the same way. Fitness comes with exercise, and once
> the privilege of franchise is asked for, there is no valid abstract
> reason against its being granted. The remarkable fact about the
> situation as regards womanhood suffrage however is that so far no
> representative majority of women has asked for the franchise.[50]

The representation of the 'unfit' woman voter stands curiously
and yet entirely appropriately beside the women in need of
protection and the fear of the racial other in the examples above.
Women must be kept in their place, and that place is not the
public space of politics and voting. What we have here is a
representation of femininity and masculinity which permeates the
newspaper reports of the Governor murders and the accounts of
the trial with which they conclude. In all of them sexuality and

race are inextricably intertwined. In all of them women and people of colour are marginalised, silenced and oppressed. In all of them the masculinity of the black murderer is an issue. In all of them the controlling and protective masculinity which represents, constructs, reports, judges and condemns is problematic in the extreme. In all of them there are traces of the institutionalised racism which would produce the White Australia Policy and a nation that in 1988 would still be struggling with the issues signalled here. One is reminded of Cameron and Frazer's[51] comment that in a society where death, sexuality and property are so inextricably linked, and here one could add racial hatred and fear, the sex murderer, the black murderer of white women, are hardly 'exiles'. There is a fine line between the violence perpetrated by a Jimmy Governor on the white race and the violence that is legalised and socially ratified in war against foreign women and children and in a crime scenario where the criminal is 'outlawed', outside the law, and therefore able to be murdered with impunity. The masculinity that is at stake here is indeed not 'outside the social and the cultural', deviant, abnormal, but absolutely 'in the social and the culture', culturally, socially constructed, and the men of law are no exception.

I want to turn briefly to another set of discursive or narrative constructions of femininity and black masculinity before I look briefly at the summations in the Governor trial as reported in the *Sydney Morning Herald* in November 1900. It is the construction of Ethel and Jimmy Governor that concerns me here. The newspapers do not concern themselves with her. It is only when the case comes to trial that she is constructed as the ultimate cause of her husband's violence. The law then is directly implicated in producing this explanation as the conclusion of the media narrative. It is only when the transcripts of the court proceedings become available for publication that the narrative of nation and masculinity can conclude with the accusation of the feminine, a conclusion produced and constructed by the ultimate in masculine and paternal protection, the law and the state.

In the public versions of the Governor stories there are a limited number of narrative explanations of Ethel Governor. It is important to recall here that the story circulates and escalates well beyond the confines of the newspaper and legal narratives in 1900. In the 1950s, contextualisd by debate over the White Australia Policy, Frank Clune's documentary *Jimmy Governor*[52] was published. In the 1970s the issue of Aboriginal rights, including finally the issue of Aboriginal suffrage, contextualise and reactivate the story in Keneally's novel, *The Chant of Jimmie Blacksmith*.[53] The film version of the novel was directed by Fred Schepisi and screened in 1978. The novel and the film in turn reactivate a series of newspaper accounts of the events of the murders in 1900. The closing of Dubbo and Wollar gaols during this period, and the transforming of the former into a tourist museum, has a similar effect. New versions of old stories appear in the press and a new anonymous, ballad, 'The Breelong Blacks', which had been in circulation in pamphlet form ever since the murders, is reprinted in the booklet produced to commemorate the closing of Dubbo Gaol.[54] This ballad again tells a version of the story that is different from the public constructions of the events. In 1990 my own interest in these events led to contact with the family of Kieran Fitzpatrick, one of those murdered by the Governors in 1900. Family papers and photographs, including a letter written by S.G. Ellis,[55] a hawker who knew the Mawbey property at the time of the murders, provided a further set of variations on the public story. An interview with a family member whose memory of the events, constructed through oral family narrative and newspaper clippings, as well as the novel and the film, also offered a very different version of the story to that available through the legal and media construction of the events. In 1994 I taught these materials in a first year course at Monash. One of my first year students who had helped in her final year of school with the editing of a Koori students' magazine provided me with a narrative of the events written last year by a Year 9 Koori girl student.

The story obviously continues to circulate among black and white families and it continues to bear the marks in both places of the versions of events that constituted the public and national narrative in 1900, a sexist and racist narrative told by men. In all of these versions, pre- and post- the actual trial of Jimmy Governor, the law remains implicated. It remains implicated through its judicial construction of the black murderer, his irresistable passion to kill, and his guilty white wife.

Ethel Governor is a problem. Why would a white woman marry a blackfellow? One explanation is class. As Clune puts it: 'an ignorant young woman who had taken an irrevocable step so far down the social scale that, in the opinion of the scornful, she could sink no lower'.[56] Her father was a miner and she was pregnant and sixteen when she and Jimmy married. This was a girl who was 'no better than she should be'. Frank Clune's 1959 story goes like this:

> Probably she was a waif, in domestic service in the township, or at a farmhouse, earning the wage of five shillings a week and keep that was usual at that time for young domestic servants or nursemaids, and with little romance in her life. Jimmy Governor

was handsome, athletic, honest, sober, a steady worker, a fine
horseman. Why shouldn't she fall in love with him?[57]

Clune's story is sympathetic, a Mills and Boon romance version
of events. But there are already contradictions which emerge in
his account of Jimmy: 'Why shouldn't he marry a white girl? Their
children would be three-quarters white, and legitimate. Why
not?'[58] And then: 'Jimmy Governor had done the right thing by
a white girl he had seduced. He had made an honest woman of
her, and had given her child his name'.[59] Was she the victim of
her own irresistible passion for the black man, or a victim of his
desire to ally himself with the white race, his seduction? In the
Keneally novel and in the film she is represented as a slut, a girl
who sleeps around. The stereotype of the white woman's irresistable lust after black flesh is also mobilised. A popular misogynistic
version of these complexities is to be found in 'The Ballad of the
Breelong Blacks':

> Now Mawbey he had no right
> In touching those posts at all.
> No doubt he thought he was cunning:
> But it stuck in the Darkies' gall.
> And there is that brazen faced woman,
> I'm alluding to Governor's wife.
> Who prompted them on with the murder.
> She ought to be jailed for life.
> For the lies and the yarns she told Jimmy,
> Of the things that the Mawbeys said,
> That for living her life with the blacks,
> Both Jimmy and her should be dead.
> That's how she worked up a row,
> A scheme that was worked some time:
> And if ever the truth gets known,
> She coaxed Underwood into the crime.

She is even depicted as taking part in the actual murders:

> But they were seen by Governor's wife,
> 'Look Jimmy, there go the girls!'
> Were the words that vixen said.
> The criminal ran them down.
> With his Bondi killed them dead.

Even Clune has her nagging hysterically, constructing her words
from the transcripts of Governor's account at his trial:

> Ethel's voice was shrill, scolding him. 'They rub it in. You let them
> insult me, and they do what they like with you!' . . .
> 'No', said Jimmy. 'I'll put a stop to it. . . . I'll tell them what I

think of him and his missus and that giggling schoolteacher. I'll get even with them.'[60]

Clune is also instructive in elaborating on the details of the relationship between Ethel, Mrs Mawbey and Miss Kerz. The schoolteacher he says is jealous of this much younger woman who is already married and a mother. The mother cannot encourage this sixteen year old while her own daughters must be discouraged from imagining that mixed race marriages are either acceptable or possible. All the elements in Hamilton's[61] account of relations among women in mistress/servant relations are present here. All of these representations of Ethel are constructed by men. Ethel's own version of these events is not something we can know. That it might, however, have been very different is suggested in the hawker's letter[62] sent to a member of the Fitzpatrick family, again a story told by a man. He represents her as working alongside her husband of whom 'she was very fond', and confirms that the Mawbey women 'sneered' at her, and that she became 'spiteful towards them and gradually embittered the blacks towards the women at the homestead'. His account of her marriage, however, is very different:

> Mrs Governor told me the history of their courtship and of how many white girls she beat to him and what a heroine she thought herself when she became legally married to him in the Church of England at Gulgong. She fully believed in the sanctity of their marriage. They took it as part of their tribal laws and were just as sincere about it.[63]

This is not, I think, another of those stories of white women lusting after black flesh. It is a story of women and courtship and of the desirability of a good-looking man, and of feminine competition and victory. In this story Ethel has some agency, some control. She also seems to have acted independently after she had left the camp on the night of the murder to go to Dubbo when she gave a warning that the murders were to occur: 'She said she was Jimmy Governor's wife and that the blacks were going to murder the Mawbeys that night. McDonald thought she was queer, but did not treat her seriously, but Percy McDonald investigated in the morning.'[64]

None of this, however, is ever part of the trial proceedings. What is part of them is her role in inciting her husband to murder, a story on which the defence counsel builds his arguments of diminished responsibility and around which he constructs the murder as a crime of passion. The adversarial nature of the courtroom requires that the prosecution argue the opposite, premeditated murder. This binarism which plays itself out in the panoptic context of cross-examination and summation in the courtroom appears to revolve around Ethel Governor's hysteria and arguments about a tomahawk. Why would one have one if not to use it? But there are traces here of another set of arguments and another binarism that revolve around Jimmy Governor's ancestry, his blackness and his whiteness, the same contradictory elements that weave their way through the representations of Ethel Governor.

The defence arguments construct Jimmy as black, a man who, because black cannot help himself: 'a man who by his environment and nature had not learned to control himself as other men had'. Miss Kerz sneered at him and 'that was the turning point; when those words were spoken to him the sudden passion rose and that was the last of self-control. The savage heart, tainted with the thirst of blood, burst through reason and one of the foulest crimes was committed.'[65] The defence argument is about femininity and its fatal effects when it acts through a primitive black man, 'a better man than most blacks'.[66]

This argument depends on Ethel Governor's evidence and yet there is some doubt about Ethel Governor's complicity with the defence story at the trial. Jimmy Governor testifies that his wife had complained to him about the Mawbeys and what they had said to her, and this is in all versions of the story, but when she is cross-examined she effectively denies it until the defence counsel reminds her of the story she is supposed to be telling. There is a sense in which she seems not to understand any of the procedures in which she is involved, or in which for reasons of her own she subverts them. Told that she does not have to give evidence against her husband, and asked whether she understands, she replies: 'I am not well enough educated to understand', and proceeds to give the evidence. Cross-examined by the defence it is as though she has been trained, rehearsed, to follow the defence argument and forgets the script, or her own voice is heard briefly and then silenced:

> I was living in Gulgong with my mother before I married Jimmy. He was very fond of me. He was particularly 'touchy' about his colour. He did not like to be called a blackfellow. It is true I had to put up with a great many taunts because of my marriage. Some people said I ought to be shot for marrying a blackfellow. Mrs Mawbey and Miss Kerz never said anything to me about Jimmy. They said it was a wonder a nice girl like me would throw myself away on a blackfellow. They only said that once to me. It did not make me unhappy, nor did I grow unhappy at Breelong because of the taunts. It made no difference between me and my husband.

At this point the defence lawyer prompts her to remember the story she is supposed to be telling:

> Mr. Boyce: I do not mean that. I mean did it make a difference to your own private happiness.
> Witness: Yes it did. Once in the camp I went down on my knees and prayed: 'O Lord! Take me away from here; I cannot stand what these people are saying about me'.[67]

It is these lines, probably the words of the defence lawyer, not Ethel Governor, which go on record as her position at the trial. It has to be remembered here I think that this is a seventeen year old single mother whose own story is not only never heard but not even particularly relevant to the adversarial arguments in this courtroom.

The prosecution case is not interested in her. The argument here is that: 'The case of a blackfellow could not be regarded in any different light from that of a white man, no matter how his habits of life differed.'[68] This is an interesting and profoundly ironic statement of equality, but one whose ironies parallel the paradoxical arguments in Clune, much later, that Jimmy Governor's violence and 'irresistable passion' was a result of his white pride:

> If he had the aristocratic blood of the haughty Grosvenors and the fiery Fitzgeralds in him, inherited from the scions of those two noble families, who had demanded 'droit de seigneur' from aboriginal damsels, then it is no wonder that he would avenge insult, regardless of consequences.[69]

Indeed, it is taunts about his prowess as a bushranger, delivered by his Aboriginal companions, which the prosecution adduces as the reason for his premeditated attack on white women and children. It is the questioning of his masculinity that results in his determination to take revenge. What I am suggesting here is that premeditation is associated with whiteness and blind passion with blackness. It is the stories that can be told about race and racial conflict, with all their binary contradictions and racist and sexist limitations, that structure the legal arguments.

The judge's summation participates in that gentleman's agreement which Keneally's novel will make explicit much later: the agreement to dispatch these matters as quickly and quietly as possible in a country that has just become a nation:

> The sweetness of it carried him through a swift trial in December.
> In the dock he told how innocent Jackie and Mort and Gilda were.
> Then Australia became a fact.
> It was unsuitable, too indicative of what had been suppressed in

the country's making, to hang two blackmen in the Federation's
early days.
Press cartoonists sketched the nascent motherland. She was young,
with shoulders like a boy, and a firm mouth . . .
She rather resembled Miss Graf.
Easter came and filled centre ring at the Showground . . .
People laughed in their state of grace, the old crimes done, all
convict chains a rusted fable in the brazen Arcady and under the
roar of buskers in temperate April 1901.
And the other viciousness? The rape of primitives?—it was done
and past report.[70]

The judge assures the defence that he has done his duty by his
client, that his conduct of the case has been admirable. He tells
a lengthy tale of the horror that passed through the community
when the murders were committed, and of the 'weeks or months'
of excitement that followed. He then makes the usual and gener-
ically proper address to the jury which asks them to view the case,
despite all this, 'apart from their prejudices', to try the case 'on
the sworn evidence presented to them', and to consider nothing
outside of that.

It is the impossibility of this injunction, with its belief in the
myth of objectivity and rationality, despite its own complicity with
the subjective and very public memories that the 'thrill of horror
that passed through the whole community' have constructed for
the judge as well as the jury and the prosecuting and defending
counsel, with which I want to conclude. Legal processes and legal
agents are people and they cannot be immune to the networks of
meanings and beliefs which they live in the rituals and practices
of daily life. The law cannot be and must not construct itself as
separate from these processes. It is essential to any concept of
justice that the semiotics, the gender and racial bias, the struggles
over meaning and for power, and the narrativity of all legal
process be understood. This was not a story of unruly women
and innocent white men. It was a story about institutionalised
racism and sexism, a story about the way those things are constructed through the textuality of everyday life, a story about the
way the law participates in these processes and a story which the
law in Australia in 1900 could not speak or read, any more than
the law in 17th century France could speak or read its own
complicity in the production of a Pierre Riviere:

Law is a material presence, a visual structure of everyday life, a
heritable form of repetition which comes to constitute in a very
real sense part of the nature of things. For a semiotics of law this
point is crucial . . . Its traces are legible in all the surfaces of daily

life: precisely because it is experienced as a system of images, not a system of rules, law represses, repeats and institutes life.

A semiotics of common law must thus pursue the tradition through its images, through the forms in which it works its way into the nervature of everyday life . . . Law is in that sense nothing other than its image, its textuality and its rhetoric . . . It is only because . . . life represses law by repeating law, forgets law by repeating law, that law makes itself felt in the living body, in the element of everyday life, in the gravity of the normal.[71]

10 The dangerous individual and the social body

Rosanne Kennedy*

It seems to me that the possibility exists for fiction to function in truth, for a fictional discourse to induce effects of truth and for bringing it about that a true discourse engenders or 'manufactures' something that does not as yet exist, that is, 'fictions it'.

Michel Foucault, Power/Knowledge[1]

Popular, medical and legal knowledge

A recent article in the *Australian* about a sensational American murder trial suggests the perhaps surprising extent to which popular knowledge, today constituted largely by the media and entertainment industries, is authoritative in official arenas such as the courtroom. By popular knowledge, I mean the knowledge that ordinary people would acquire in their everyday lives, as opposed to specialised knowledge that results from academic study and training. I mean popular in the sense in which my desktop dictionary, *The American Heritage*, defines it: 'Of, representing, or carried on by the common people or the people at large; Fit for reflecting the taste and intelligence of the people . . . Accepted by or prevalent among the people . . . Suited to or within the means of ordinary people; Originating among the people.'

To return to the murder trial. A few years ago, two wealthy young men from Beverley Hills murdered their parents. They stood to inherit US$14 million. While awaiting trial, they steadfastly maintained their innocence, until someone overheard the younger brother 'confess' to his psychiatrist. The psychiatrist's tape of the confession was subpoenaed, and the young men are now on trial. If convicted, they could receive the death penalty. To everyone's surprise, they are pleading self-defence, claiming that their father sexually abused them during childhood and adolescence. Although there is little evidence to support their allegations 'neither had ever mentioned the abuse to their psychiatrists or anyone else', the sons have gained considerable sympathy with the public. Call-in viewers watching the trial on a cable channel, *Courtroom TV*, have overwhelmingly supported them. Their convincing performances on the witness stand, and the ability to stick to the same story under days of cross-examination, have been taken by some as a sign of truth.

It would be impossible for the brothers to gain support for their defence were it not for the fact that a popular discourse of sexual abuse constituted by talk shows, newspaper and magazine articles, television dramas, popular novels and films has produced, in the last half-dozen years, a hysteria of accusations, denials, exposures and recantations. The discourse of sexual abuse incites moral outrage and necessitates that the victim be given the benefit of the doubt, regardless of whether there is independent evidence. Consequently, this discourse today functions as a condition of possibility for a defence in a legal trial, and for the inevitable psychiatric testimony that will be brought forward by both sides to support or refute the defence. The point I would like to stress is that popular knowledge is characterised by the circulation and in-mixing of discourses. It exemplifies what the feminist philosopher Susan Bordo refers to as the 'postmodern conversation' typical of liberal talk shows, where all discourses are levelled because everyone has a right to their own beliefs, and everyone's beliefs are equally valid.[2] Within the frame of the television screen, psychiatric and legal discourse are on a par with the discourse of call-in television viewers: all are contributors to the post modern conversation. In short, the field of popular knowledge, despite its lack of professional credentials, functions as an authoritative discourse in relation to the objects and domains it produces and addresses. It has the authority, for instance, to legitimise, and thus to force the law and psychology to take seriously, despite the lack of evidence, sexual abuse as a defence to premeditated murder.

Yet, when we leave the realm of popular knowledge, and enter the professional institutions of psychiatry, law and the university, an entirely different scenario emerges. Here, medical and legal discourses are viewed as rational, specialised fields of knowledge which have nothing to do with the debased world of popular culture. This view is manifested, for instance, in the debate over the jury in insanity cases. In trials raising an insanity defence, psychiatric experts are brought in to provide scientific knowledge of mental phenomena of which the jury is assumed to be ignorant. The expert witness is meant to furnish the judge or jury with the necessary scientific criteria for testing the accuracy of their conclusions.[3] However, over the past few decades, legal and medical reformers have argued that juries disregard the expert testimony of psychiatrists, in favour of popular conceptions of insanity. Summarising the findings of Rita Simon's major study of juries in insanity trials, Thomas Maeder exemplifies this criticism:

> In Simon's experiments, recordings were made of the jurors'
> deliberations, and she found that they were quite fully aware that
> they were not supposed merely to rubber-stamp the experts'
> diagnosis, but were to reach their own opinions about the
> defendant's insanity. Their conclusions hinged upon a view of
> mental illness that was rather naive from a modern psychiatric
> point of view, and even, perhaps, from the perspective of a
> nineteenth-century alienist, but which was in fairly close accord
> with popular conceptions of madmen and responsibility.[4]

There are two aspects of Maeder's statement that merit attention. First, it posits an opposition between modern psychiatric knowledge of 'mental illness' and popular knowledge of 'madmen and responsibility'. The opposition is hierarchical in that scientific knowledge constitutes the standard by which popular knowledge is judged to be 'naive'. Second, it assumes that the jury is the locus or site of popular knowledge, and thereby implies that psychiatric discourse is formed independently of popular views of madness.

Today, this sort of opposition is immediately suspect, but what exactly is at stake? To those not professionally invested in the debate over the insanity defence, the answer would appear to be, not much. Either the defendant will be sent to prison or to a mental hospital; either they will be in the normalising grip of the psychiatric institution or the disciplinary grip of the penal machine. What is really at issue, however, is not typically discussed in the literature. That is, that the opposition encourages us to continue to think of popular, medical and legal knowledge as discrete fields that have nothing to do with each other, although we know from everyday life that they have everything to do with each other. It attributes impossibly antiquated ideas to popular knowledge, negates its power and authority, and dismisses it as a serious field of investigation and research, rather than ask what constitutes it, how it functions, and what effects it has. It measures discourses according to a criteria of truth, that is, as representations of reality, rather than as modalities of power.

In *The Postmodern Condition*, Jean Francois Lyotard's distinction between scientific and popular language games exposes the limits of a rationality which hierarchises discourses based on criteria of truth. He argues that although popular knowledge is not a language game of truth, it does the important work of constituting the social bond. Thus, his method provides a way of distinguishing between scientific and popular knowledge without dismissing the popular as uneducated, backward or naive.

Lyotard argues that scientific knowledge and popular knowledge are different types of language games. A scientific language game is not self-legitimating; it must use argument and evidence to verify its statements. It is 'exclusively denotative': the validity of scientific statements is determined on the basis of criteria of truth to a referent.[5] Consequently, we expect the sender to speak the truth about the referent. To speak the truth means that they should be able to provide proof of what they say, and that they should be able to refute any opposing or contradictory statements concerning the same referent.[6]

Although scientific knowledge dominates contemporary Western cultures, Lyotard contends that knowledge cannot be reduced to science. Knowledge is a matter of competence that goes beyond the determination of truth. To have knowledge means to have technical efficiency, and to be able to make good ethical judgements and good evaluations.[7] Lyotard refers to the language game of competence as 'popular' or 'narrative knowledge'. Unlike scientific knowledge, popular knowledge is legitimated by what it does rather than through proof and argument. Narrative knowledge cements the social bond by, for instance, circulating narratives among the members of a community, and thus establishing norms of conduct and criteria for determining what constitutes good judgements.

Lyotard's analysis of language games shows that the question of truth is irrelevant to the function of popular knowledge. Popular knowledge constitutes the social bond regardless of its truth content. For instance, advertising, which is constitutive of popular knowledge in advanced capitalist culture, functions to define ideals of masculinity and femininity that are operative, although it would be odd to say that these ideals are 'true'. It would be more correct to say they produce masculinity and femininity as true gender identities. If we take Lyotard's analysis seriously, the realm of popular knowledge cannot simply be dismissed as uneducated, irrelevant, or as mere entertainment. Rather, we have to ask: what kind of authority does popular knowledge constitute? How is it operative for social institutions and practices? Is popular knowledge opposed to official knowledge, as some theorists argue? Or is it a part of a carceral whole, as certain readings of Foucault would suggest? What kinds of power/knowledge projects does popular knowledge make possible and legitimate, and how?

In what follows, I address these questions by analysing two canonical films in the popular discourse of madness, Alfred Hitchcock's *Psycho* and Martin Scorsese's *Taxi Driver*. I then consider an American trial in which *Taxi Driver* functions as evidence of insanity. I use my analysis of these texts to map, in a provisional way, the circulation of discourses of the dangerous individual, both within the field of popular knowledge constituted by the media and entertainment industries, and between the field of popular knowledge and the field of specialised knowledge such as the courtroom. Two Foucauldian texts from the 1970s, 'The Dangerous Individual' and *I, Pierre Riviere*, provide a methodological basis for this project.

The madman and the psychiatrist

In 'The Dangerous Individual', published in the late 1970s, Foucault argues that the gradual psychiatrisation of criminal law had produced, by the end of the 19th century, a shift from the crime to the criminal, so that today the crime primarily signifies the presence of a 'dangerous element' in the social body.[8] Psychiatry gained prominence in the early 19th century by promising to control dangers inherent in the social body, which was no longer imagined as a mere juridical-political metaphor, but as a 'biological reality' requiring medical intervention.[9] Although he makes only a few suggestive remarks about the role of popular knowledge, Foucault's analysis provides a model for my project by showing how, by the end of the century, the 'summonings and interactions' between law and psychiatry had produced a concept of the dangerous individual, which today continues to legitimate medical and legal regulation of individuals perceived to be dangerous.

Foucault contends that the concept of 'homicidal mania' provided the basis for psychiatric intervention into the justice system in the early 19th century. 'Homicidal mania' referred to a type of insanity that was alleged to manifest itself only in violent crime, which lacked any apparent motivation or personal gain.[10] The great unmotivated crime was a problem for law because, in the 19th century, the exercise of power implied 'reasoned technology applied to individuals'.[11] Punishment could no longer simply incarcerate; it now had to reform, and to reform, it had to be adapted to the individual, to his motives, inner will, instincts. For a punishment to be properly designed, it was necessary to know the criminal's mind, to know why he did what he did. The concept of 'homicidal mania' named insanity as a cause for serious crimes which lacked motivation; it posited a cause for that which lacked a cause. Since homicidal mania could not be detected by laypersons until it erupted in a criminal act, everyone was potentially at risk, either of harbouring a hidden insanity or of being the victim of it. Only a trained psychiatrist could detect signs of homicidal mania. However, what was really at stake for psychiatry in its intervention into law was justifying its own agenda of therapeutic confinement for the mentally ill. To justify confinement, psychiatry had to show that 'madness, by its nature, and even in its most discrete manifestations, was haunted by the absolute danger, death'.[12] Homicidal mania allowed psychiatry to establish the link between insanity and death. Foucault observes, however, that the kinship between madness and death 'was not scientifically established but rather symbolically represented in the figure of homicidal mania'.[13]

By 1870, psychiatry had abandoned the concept of homicidal mania, but only at the cost of a more generalised psychiatric intervention. This transformation was linked to a new way of posing the problem of legal responsibility. In the past, psychiatry only intervened in cases of violent crime which lacked motivation. Now, psychiatry raised questions of causality right across the range of infractions. This led to the impossible conundrum that still plagues criminal law: 'if an act is determined by a causal nexus, can it be considered to be free?'.[14] The psychiatrisation of crime, so that any criminal was now treated as potentially pathological, produced a shift, in the course of the century, from the crime to the criminal. Before the intervention of psychiatry '[c]riminal law knew only two terms, the offense and the penalty. The new criminology recognizes three, the crime, the criminal and the means of repression'.[15]

Foucault argues that this shift 'from the crime to the criminal, from homicidal mania to the psychiatrisation of all crime' is accompanied by the demand for a new kind of discourse. Now that the justice system is no longer satisfied with determining the author of crime, but solicits an explanation as well, it is no longer enough for the accused simply to confess.

Beyond admission there must be confession, self-examination, explanation of oneself, revelation of what one is . . . The magistrates and the jurors, the lawyers too, and the department of the public prosecutor, cannot really play their role unless they are provided with another type of discourse, the one given by the accused about himself, or the one which he makes possible for others, through his confessions, memories, intimate disclosures, etc.[16]

Foucault lists a number of conditions of possibility for the shift from the crime to the criminal. These include the development of a police network; the failure of the penitentiary system; the emergence of an image of an enemy of society who could be 'a revolutionary or a murderer'; and a corresponding 'literature of criminality' which developed in a wide range of popular media.[17] However, he says virtually nothing about the fields of knowledge in which these concepts, all of which he maintains emerged in the latter half of the 19th century, were elaborated, nor what role they played in the production of a concept of the dangerous individual. There would seem to be a potentially interesting link between 'an image of an enemy of society', the 'literature of criminality', and the discourse of the criminal. Although Foucault says little about these potential links, he has made this area available for further research by providing us with concepts to map links between these fields of knowledge.

Despite his silence concerning the role of popular knowledge in the constitution of the concept of the dangerous individual, Foucault concludes with an important methodological point:

> this transformation [from the crime to the criminal] took place not only from medicine towards law, as through the pressure of rational knowledge on older prescriptive systems; but . . . it also operated through a perpetual mechanism of summoning and of interacting between medical or psychological knowledge and the judicial institution. It was not the latter which yielded. A set of objects and of concepts was born at their boundaries and from their interchanges.[18]

In *I, Pierre Riviere, having slaughtered my mother, my sister, and my brother*, Foucault takes some steps towards elaborating the function of the discursive field constituted by popular memoirs and narratives of crime. He shows how the same discourse, in this case Riviere's murder/memoir, when taken up by different language games, has entirely different meanings and effects. In 'Tales of Murder', a short essay at the end of the collection, Foucault distinguishes the fields of knowledge in which Riviere's murder/discourse was situated, the discursive rules it encountered, and the effects it produced. Foucault contends that Riviere lodged his deed/discourse in a field of historical and popular knowledge by using certain historical markers in his memoir. By referring to

Biblical history and events in the fly-sheets, Riviere vested his murder/narrative in an historical field of popular knowledge, which was in turn 'the condition which made this premeditated murder/memoir possible'.[19] In the field of popular knowledge, Riviere achieves infamy, and gives voice to his life and to the life of peasants. Foucault claims that after the Revolution, peasants were battling for the right to kill and be killed and the right to speak and narrate: 'It was in the background of this underground battle that Pierre Riviere enrolled his narrative/murder, and it was through it that he provided the communication between it and the history of sacrificial and glorious murders, or rather, with his own hand accomplished a historical murder.'[20]

But when his murder/memoir was taken up by the institution of criminal justice, it confronted a different game, the game of truth. Not only did Riviere's discourse not have the same status, but 'the discourses were not the same type of event and did not produce the same effects. Riviere was the accused; the point at issue, therefore was whether he really was the author of the crime.'[21] In the game of truth played by law and medicine, his discourse became the basis for determining whether he was sane or insane, responsible or not.

Foucault justifies his publication of Pierre Riviere's memoir on methodological grounds; the documents were meant to be the basis for drawing a map of 'the combats' between popular, medical and legal discourse, for reconstructing 'confrontations and battles' and determining how those discourses interact.[22] However, rather than map intersections, Foucault privileges the popular, claiming that when Riviere's murder/narrative, which was 'profoundly committed to the rule of popular knowledge', was taken up by the language games of law and psychiatry, 'there was applied a question derived elsewhere and administered by others'.[23] In what follows, I will show some of the ways in which the literature of criminality constitutes an authoritative field of knowledge, and will consider what effects are produced when it is taken up by official knowledge.

Hinckley's deed in the field of the historical and the everyday

On 30 March 1981 John Hinckley, Jr, shot President Reagan, wounding him and three others. The act was captured on camera, and was repeatedly screened on television. By choosing Reagan as his target, Hinckley effectively situated his act in the field of the historical. He secured himself a place in a tradition of presidential assassins, and gave meaning to a life that was judged a failure by every other standard. Interviewed after the shooting, Hinckley acknowledged the desire for fame as one of his motives, and said that he had accomplished everything he had intended.[24]

After Hinckley was arrested, a letter he had left in his hotel room, addressed to Jodie Foster, was discovered. He professed his love for her and hoped, with this 'historical deed', to gain her respect and love'.[25] Shooting a president who had been a movie star, for the love of a movie star, Hinckley lodged himself in the fields of popular knowledge and of fiction. Later, when psychiatrists interviewed him, the full extent of Hinckley's fusion of the real and the imaginary was further revealed by his obsession with *Taxi Driver,* in which Jodie Foster played a twelve-year-old 'rescued' from prostitution by a taxi driver. He became obsessed with Foster after seeing the film, and patterned his dress and actions on Travis Bickle, the 'hero' of the film. Hinckley's deliberate adoption of Travis Bickle as a model, together with his careful study of presidential assassinations, indicates his deliberate attempt to '[accomplish] his crime at the level of a certain discursive practice and of the knowledge bound up with it', 'the discursive practice constituted by a popular media discourse of infamous crimes'.[26] Yet the very deliberateness of his act became, in the trial, the basis for a debate about his sanity. What could a Hollywood motion picture about a man who plays out his murderous fantasies and is rewarded by becoming a local hero contribute to a psychiatric diagnosis of madness? How did *Taxi Driver* function as medico-legal evidence of insanity? What could a fictional film 'prove', since it does not claim to constitute 'knowledge' of insanity? Or if it does produce knowledge, what kind of knowledge is it?

Cleansing the social body: comments on *Psycho* and *Taxi Driver*

Before examining how *Taxi Driver* was operative in the trial, I first want to place it in the context of a popular discourse of the dangerous individual, which today is the mainstay of a massive entertainment industry. This discourse includes not only Hollywood motion pictures, but the whole range of detective and crime fiction, television dramas, talk shows, *Courtroom TV*, journalistic and literary accounts of crime and criminals, and published trial transcripts. The literature of criminality would today include canonical 'true' narratives such as *In Cold Blood, The Executioner's Song,* and *The Killing of Bonnie Garland.* But it would also include fictional narratives such as *Psycho, Taxi Driver, Silence of the Lambs* and *Henry: Portrait of a Serial Killer.* Hitchcock's

Psycho, now a classic, is my first example of a popular discourse of the dangerous individual. Film theorists have written extensively on *Psycho*; here my aim is not to consider its filmic inventiveness, but to consider it as a canonical text in a popular knowledge of criminal madness. Due to space constraints, I will focus primarily on the ending, and will assume the reader's familiarity with the film.

Norman Bates and Marion Crane meet when, just fifteen miles from her destination, she stays the night at his lonesome highway hotel. On the run to her lover after having stolen $40 000 from her employer, Marion's criminality is overtly signified by her theft, by her bad girl habit of meeting her lover in cheap hotels, and by her visible fear and guilt; her criminality is written all over her face. Norman, on the other hand, looks innocent enough; he's clean-cut, friendly, white, your all-American male. The ordinariness of his appearance is reinforced by a profile shot which exploits the resemblance between him and Marion's lover, Sam Loomis. Norman's 'normality' is undermined, however, by intermittent signs of peculiarity. His hobby is taxidermy, which suggests that he is well acquainted with death and corpses. A voyeur, he peeps through a hole in the wall to watch Marion undress. And he becomes aggravated whenever madness is mentioned. When Marion casually suggests that Norman should put his mother 'someplace' and get on with his own life, he fiercely accuses her of implying that he should send 'mother' to a madhouse.

In many ways, Norman meets the 19th century alienists criteria of a homicidal maniac as elaborated by Foucault: he commits a serious violent crime; it takes place in a domestic setting; and Norman lacks any visible signs of madness.[27] The only difference is that Norman's crime is motivated by delusions about his mother, whereas homicidal mania was meant to explain crimes lacking any motivation. Norman signifies crime lurking where we do not expect it, in the domestic sphere. The murder takes place in the semi-domestic setting of the motel room, and is motivated by his relationship with his mother. However, there is a sign that all is not right in the social body: the 'domestic settings' are not quite domestic. Marion makes love to Sam by day in a hotel, rather than at night in bed at home; Norman lives 'alone' in what appears to be a haunted house, without family or friends. As Slavoj Zizeck comments, Marion is Norman's other half: '[Marion's] American alienation (financial insecurity, fear of the police, desperate pursuit of a piece of happiness, in short, the hysteria of everyday capitalist life) is confronted with its psychotic reverse: the nightmarish world of pathological crime'.[28]

The final shock of the film comes when Lila and Sam discover the secret in Norman's closet: his mother's skeleton, which he has been harbouring for the past ten years. But it is the penultimate scene, in which the psychiatrist enters to explain Norman's mind, that is important to my discussion of the popular representation of psychiatric knowledge. The scene itself is marked off from the rest of film by its artificial and affected character. The local sheriff and his deputies, together with Marion's lover, Sam and her sister, Lila, sit in the sheriff's office, still uncertain of the whereabouts of Marion and Detective Arbogast, but suspecting the worst. Having examined Norman, the psychiatrist, taking up the position of the pedagogue, lectures his captive audience on Norman's mental disorder. Even though he has just told Sam and Lila that Norman has murdered Marion, they do not react emotionally; instead, they listen attentively to the psychiatrist's 'explanation', as if, in the face of death, reason preceded emotion. Yes, Norman did kill Marion, but it was really Norman's mother who did it. Ever since his father's death, Norman has been 'dangerously disturbed'. He and his mother lived in an unhealthily close relationship (incest is implied), and when she fell in love with a man, Norman murdered them both in a jealous rage. For years his mind has been split between Norman and his mother. The mother-half killed Marion out of jealousy because Norman was attracted to her. Revealed as the murderer of four people, Norman is immediately implicated in two other missing persons cases.

In *Psycho*, the law is revealed to be ineffectual. It bows to the superior knowledge of the psychiatrist, who takes over the function of the law, by diagnosing Norman as a 'dangerous individual' and placing him securely in the camp of the mad, and thus, in the grip of the therapeutic machine. The psychiatrist's explanation produces narrative closure, and ties madness to the rule of truth. Up until he enters, we do not have a comprehensible account of Norman's life. We only know that his mother died ten years earlier, but that he claims she is still alive, demanding and jealous. In the fruit cellar, we discover that Norman has been dressing up as his mother, but we do not know why. The psychiatrist functions to 'account' for Norman, in both senses of the word: he provides a narrative account of Norman's life which in turn makes Norman accountable, though not responsible, for his actions. Lyotard argues that narrative accounts that take the form of a life story become the basis for a culture's determination of norms of competence and conduct:

[P]opular stories . . . recount what could be called positive or negative apprenticeships (Bildungen): in other words, the successes

or failures greeting the hero's undertakings. These successes or
failures either bestow legitimacy upon social institutions (the
function of myths), or present positive or negative models (the
successful or unsuccessful hero) of integration into established
institutions (legends and tales). Thus, the narratives allow the
society in which they are told, on the one hand to define its
criteria of competence and, on the other, to evaluate according to
those criteria what is performed or can be performed within it.[29]

On Lyotard's analysis of the function of a biography, it is not
surprising that the psychiatrist's account brings Norman within
the sphere of the law of science/narrative. By subjecting Norman
to a psychiatric exam, the psychiatrist individualises Norman and
thus turns him into an object of power. Foucault explains how
the exam 'in this case the psychiatric exam' turns the individual
into an object by making him a 'case':

> The examination, surrounded by all its documentary techniques,
> makes each individual a 'case': a case which at one and the same
> time constitutes an object for a branch of knowledge and a hold
> for a branch of power. The case is no longer, as in casuistry or
> jurisprudence, a set of circumstances defining an act and capable
> of modifying the application of a rule; it is the individual as he
> may be described, judged, measured, compared with others, in his
> very individuality; and it is also the individual who has to be
> trained or corrected, classified, normalized, excluded, etc.[30]

If *Psycho* constitutes 'a collective fear of danger', a function
Foucault attributes to the literature of criminality, at least Norman's behaviour can be explained. According to the psychiatrist,
Norman really is mad. Psychiatry restores order to the social body
both by explaining Norman's motive for murdering his mother,
her lover, and Marion, and by 'laying the psychiatric groundwork'
which will assure that Bates spends the rest of his life in a mental
hospital.

Up until the end of the film, *Psycho* reinforces the link between
madness and death. Norman, the madman, kills Marion and
Arbogast, and maintains his mother's corpse. In the final scene,
in which Bates is sitting in a detention room, the link is made
even more explicitly. He is now, the psychiatrist has explained,
completely taken over by his mother. The identification with his
mother is made in three ways: he is wrapped in a blanket, as he
had wrapped his mother's skeleton in a blanket; he talks in her
voice, saying she should have put him away years ago, as they
will do now; and as the scene fades, we glimpse, just for an
instant, a skull superimposed on Bates's eerily grinning face. The

skull visually links insanity to death, reminding the viewer that insanity 'harbors the absolute danger, death'.

What do these comments on *Psycho* suggest about the function of a popular discourse of the dangerous individual in terms of a medical agenda of therapeutic confinement? Firstly, by treating Norman as a 'case', *Psycho* has participated in producing 'domains of objects and rituals of truth' that support a disciplinary apparatus. *Psycho* undermines the opposition between the scientific and the popular by revealing that popular culture carries out the project of a technical knowledge system of psychiatry, and that fiction as well as psychiatry is a site of discipline. Secondly, it constitutes ideologies of normality and criminality, sanity and madness, psychopathology and sociopathology, that in turn constitute the norms by which we judge the conduct of ourselves and others. Using Lyotard's concept of popular knowledge, we could say that *Psycho* defines a field of competence. Thirdly, *Psycho* ties madness to the rule of truth; the psychiatrist functions to assure us that Norman is mad, and that his actions are the product of a force beyond himself, thereby participating in the shift from the crime to the criminal.

Whereas *Psycho* functions both to constitute a collective fear of danger, and to offer us security by cleansing the social body, Martin Scorsese's *Taxi Driver* does not conclude in such a predictable way. If *Psycho* can be viewed as representative of an era when psychiatry only intervened to explain the rare, truly pathological crime, *Taxi Driver* represents the shift to an era in which everyone is suspected of being mad. In short, it can be viewed as a post modern rewriting of *Psycho*. The main character, Travis Bickle, is an alienated, white, working-class male, a Vietnam veteran and a night time taxi driver in New York City. Unlike Norman Bates, he does not function on the other side of law; rather, he takes the law into his own hands and goes where the law does not.

Taxi Driver opens to the strains of sinister music; we watch Bickle apply for a job as a taxi driver, to cure his insomnia. He takes all beats, goes everywhere, sees everything. He complains about the filth and scum of the city, referring to the people who come out at night, the hookers, pimps, druggies, transvestites. He wants to clean up the city. He meets a blonde woman, Betsy, whom he describes as 'an angel' and who works for a presidential candidate. After Bickle takes her to a porn film, she rejects him. In response, he begins stalking the candidate, with the intention of assassinating him. He buys several guns, works out, goes to target practice, shaves his head into a mohawk, and finally attempts to assassinate the candidate but a security guard sees him reach into his jacket, and he runs off at the last minute. He then decides to 'rescue' a twelve-year-old prostitute, Iris, whom he has befriended. Frustrated after his failed attempt at assassination, he goes to the brothel and guns down her pimp-boyfriend, the hotel owner, and a client. Later the local newspapers declare him a hero for killing 'gangsters' and Iris's parents write and thank him for sending their daughter home. An ironic ending.

In *Psycho*, madness and criminality were localised in Norman Bates, officially designated as mad. Bickle, however, is not diagnosed. We do not know what he is suffering from, or if he is suffering from anything other than being an alienated subject in late capitalism, against the law of exchange in a society in which exchange relations dominate all. He is potentially everyman pushed over the edge, not exactly normal but not necessarily crazy in a clinical sense. The main difference between Norman and Bickle is that Bickle reasons about his condition; he says he is planning to do something 'real bad'. Norman simply occupies the personality of Norman or, alternatively, of his mother. However, he never reasons about being his mother, for that would be faking and would call into question the 'truth' of his madness. Norman really is mad, and true madness does not reason. The fact that Bickle reasons leads us to question his sanity; perhaps he is just frustrated rather than mad.

The ending of *Taxi Driver*, in which Bickle is rewarded for his brutal murders, is a subversive fantasy. The world of New York City in the 1970s is far removed from the small, white, middle-American town of the 1950s, in which the Bates Hotel is located. Bickle, a marginalised white male, takes over the function of the police and psychiatrist, eliminating danger from the social body. He restores the nuclear family by returning Iris to her family. Whereas *Psycho* legitimates the project of psychiatric intervention, *Taxi Driver* does not. Bickle, identified as a dangerous individual, remains at large in the social body. But in *Taxi Driver*, the social body itself is a dangerous body; it has multiple dangerous elements. The elements are signified in terms of race, class and sexuality; it is the blacks, the ethnics, the whores, gays and transvestites that Bickle, in his white heterosexual panic, identifies as 'filth'. *Taxi Driver* neatly reveals the thin blue line between legal killing and murder: Bickle was a soldier, paid to kill Vietnamese civilians as well as the official enemy. How dangerous he is depends not upon whether he kills, but whom he targets. The illegal killing of the presidential candidate would target Bickle as an enemy of the people. Yet he becomes a hero for murdering social 'undesirables', such as the black underclass male robber we see him murder in cold blood. Rewarded for his vigilante activities, he remains within the social body. Has he been cleansed or is he still dangerous? In *Taxi Driver*, the social body is a white, heterosexual body; it is not entirely surprising that the disenfranchised white male has inherited the project of cleansing the social body, but through violent elimination rather than therapy or reform.

Hinckley and the medico-legal machinery

In the early summer of 1982 Hinckley was tried and pleaded insanity. As is customary in insanity trials, both the prosecution and the defence introduced psychiatrists to give expert testimony on Hinckley's state of mind at the time of the shooting. All of the psychiatrists diagnosed Hinckley on the basis of the same material: interviews with him; the shooting and the events surrounding it; a selection of Hinckley's stories, letters, poems, songs, tape recorded monologues and conversations, and *Taxi Driver*, which Hinckley had seen more than fifteen times. However, the defence and prosecution drew different inferences concerning the nature and severity of Hinckley's disorder. The defence argued that he was psychotic; they maintained that the evidence showed that he had withdrawn into his own 'inner world' and that his 'anchors' to reality had slipped away.[31] The prosecution's experts agreed that Hinckley was disturbed, but they thought he was suffering from garden variety personality disorders rather than anything more serious.

Roger Alderman opened the trial for the prosecution with a videotape which showed Hinckley stalking Carter in 1980; it was followed by a videotape of Hinckley shooting Reagan in 1981.[32] Whereas Alderman started by establishing the crime, Vincent Fuller, leading the defence, began by providing an account of Hinckley's life. From the start of the trial, Fuller played up Hinckley's obsession with Jodie Foster and his identification with Travis Bickle as evidence of his inability to form normal relationships, and of his retreat from reality. During the trial, the prosecution focused the jury's attention on Hinckley's crime, arguing that his actions showed deliberation and planning, and that he was not acting impulsively or irrationally. The defence, on the other hand, gave much more weight to the 'discourse of the criminal', and used Hinckley songs, poems, tape recordings, short stories and other writings to provide a portrait of a disturbed young man.

Although only a small amount of testimony during the six week trial explicitly referred to *Taxi Driver*, the film functioned as both a frame and a touchstone. Fuller described it in his opening speech, and it was the last piece of evidence admitted in the case for the defence, when it was screened for the jurors and the court. Throughout the trial, the prosecution, the defence, and the psychiatric witnesses repeatedly returned to the film, as they debated the nature of Hinckley's obsession with Foster, and his identification with Bickle. The defence psychiatrists argued that Hinckley took Bickle as a role model for his own behaviour: he dressed like Bickle, made up a fictional girlfriend to match Bickle's Betsy, bought a gun, stalked a president, became obsessed with Foster and, when rejected, decided to 'rescue' her from Yale, as Bickle had rescued Iris (Foster) from prostitution. It would be easy enough to see how *Taxi Driver* could constitute evidence of psychosis if the defence was arguing that Hinckley really thought he was Travis Bickle, as someone suffering from delusions might think he is Napoleon or Jesus Christ. Could he conform his conduct to the requirements of the law? No because he had lost his last anchors to reality and it was this driven quality of his inner state that was foremost in determining [his] actions. But when pressed on this question, defence psychiatrist Dr William T. Carpenter repeatedly rejected that interpretation:

Q. Did he think he was Travis Bickle on October 2nd in Dayton?
A. He had important aspects of Travis Bickle as part of his makeup through this identification process.
Q. Not my question, not my question.
A. He did not think, literally believe that he was Travis Bickle. What he was doing was finding himself with many attributes of Travis Bickle.

Then the judge intervened to clarify the witness's answer:

The court: Doctor, on this date in question did [Hinckley] consider, did he think that he was Travis Bickle?
The witness: No. He experiences himself living out things from the Travis Bickle scenario. He did not literally believe himself to be Travis Bickle.[33]

On another occasion when Hinckley was arrested for carrying guns in the Nashville airport, the prosecution asked whether, when he was arrested, he gave the name Travis Bickle. The witness replied that he gave his own name.[34]

Declining to argue that Hinckley was so deluded that he thought he was Bickle, the defence's main strategy was to argue by analogy rather than by direct inference. Experts for the defence repeatedly asserted that Hinckley was 'like' Bickle, that Hinckley 'identified' with Bickle, that he took on 'parallels' of the Bickle scenario. For instance, a leading defence witness, Dr Carpenter, argued that after Hinckley failed to make a 'successful encounter' with Jodie Foster when he visited Yale, '[h]e was now trying to get himself back into a frame of mind where he felt more competent, more able, more effective in life [and he] found himself doing this by taking on the Travis Bickle parallel'.[35] Using phrases such as 'he found himself', Carpenter stressed Hinckley's passivity, as if he had no control over his actions. The prosecution, on the other hand, stressed the active nature of Hinckley's 'choices', which, according to the prosecution's expert witness, Dr Dietz, included 'long-standing interest in fame and assassinations . . . study of the publicity associated with various crimes . . . extensive study of assassinations . . . choice of Travis Bickle as a major role model . . . [and] multiple writings about assassination plans'.[36]

In the closing argument, Fuller repeated the strategy of pressing home similarities and identifications between Hinckley and Bickle. He countered the prosecution's assertion that Hinckley was 'an ordinary American put under a microscope' with the claim that the defendant 'is unique in this sense: He lived a solitary life. He was a prisoner of himself for at least seven years before this tragedy . . .'. In his loneliness, Fuller argued, Hinckley saw *Taxi Driver* '. . . and he made identification, sympathized with Travis Bickle . . . John Hinckley saw him as a loner, as he, Hinckley, was a loner. Isolated. Angry at what he saw in the outside world. Unable to establish any relations in that world that he saw'.[37] Comparing a picture of Hinckley with a gun to his head to a scene from *Taxi Driver*, Fuller pointed out that the photo was '[m]uch in the likeness of the character Travis Bickle'.[38]

Why did the defence repeatedly draw analogies between the defendant and the fictional character? What was to be gained? The analogy allowed the jury to draw certain inferences about Hinckley's mental state without the defence explicitly putting dubious arguments into open play where they could be questioned and exposed by the prosecution. Firstly, the defence implied that it was irrational for Hinckley to respond to the frustrations in his life by borrowing ideas, plots and personality from a fictional movie. This implication supported the defence's argument that Hinckley's identification with Bickle and his obsession with Foster were evidence that he lived in a fantasy world and had lost touch with reality. To this line of reasoning, the prosecution objected that there was nothing abnormal about identifying with a film character; people do it all the time. In fact, the prosecution treated Hinckley's obsession with Foster as a sign of his 'ordinariness', his status as an 'All-American Boy'. In addition to the inference that it was a sign of madness to borrow life strategies from a movie, it could be inferred from the anology that Hinckley was mad because he identified with a character who was mad. Although the state of Bickle's mind was not discussed during the trial, the film itself puts Bickle's sanity into question. He certainly does not come across as a 'normal guy'. But if the defence was implying that Hinckley became mad in the course of simulating Bickle's character, then it is peculiar that they took Bickle, a fictional character, as a medical standard of what constitutes madness. On the whole, the analogy between Hinckley and Bickle functioned to support the defence's claim that Hinckley was driven by his fantasies, and had lost touch with reality.

Regardless of its inability to prove anything, *Taxi Driver* performed several important functions in the trial, and served the defence well in validating Hinckley's insanity defence. One of the problems for the defence was how to humanise Hinckley, how to make him sympathetic to a working class jury of eleven blacks and one white. Importantly, *Taxi Driver* distanced Hinckley from his white upper-class privilege by identifying him with a working class man. By stressing Hinckley's identification with Bickle, the defence was able to legitimate Hinckley's conception of himself as marginalised and alienated. *Taxi Driver* strongly suggested that alienation is a condition of everyday life, and that it is understandable that someone could become crazy in a world like contemporary America. In addition, *Taxi Driver* gave a narrative structure and a logic to Hinckley's apparently random and bizarre actions; it allowed the defence to tell a story about Hinckley. Perhaps most importantly, it functioned to displace responsiblity from Hinckley onto the film and the fictional character Bickle. By identifying *Taxi Driver* as the source of Hinckley's obsessions and ideas, it made Hinckley look as if he were not the author of his actions; they came from elsewhere.

The question of whether Hinckley could be 'faking' came up repeatedly in the trial, but it was usually masked in psychiatric discussions of delusion, ideas of reference and manipulativeness. The prosecution argued that Hinckley manipulated the truth when it suited him, whereas the defence argued that these alleged manipulations were signs of delusion. Surprisingly, however, the defence was aided in its refutations of manipulation by *Taxi Driver*. We can see how *Taxi Driver* functioned to validate Hinckley's claim of insanity by substituting *Psycho* for it. If the defence claimed that Hinckley identified with Norman Bates, and adopted him as a model, what implications would that have? One might get ideas about how to murder from *Psycho*, but it would seem odd, if not impossible, to identify with Norman's state of mind. Why? Because Norman's insanity is non-transferable; it results from the specific domestic situation in which he grew up. He is, in a sense, essentially mad, which is signified by the fact that he does not reason about his madnesss. If Hinckley were alleged to have modelled himself on Bates, we would have to conclude that Hinckley was faking, because in taking Bates as a model, he would be reasoning about his madness. Bickle's 'madness', on the other hand, seems to be a response to the frustrations of being a subject of late consumer capitalism. If he is sick, it is a sickness that affects a significant proportion of the population. One could not have Bates as a model without choosing him as a model, because one could not identify with Norman's state of mind in the same way that one could identify with Bickle's frustrations and sense of alienation. By modelling himself on Bickle, whose own state of mind is uncertain but not essentially mad, Hinckley raised the spectre of simulation: was he really mad or was he faking? In 'Simulacra and Simulations', Jean Baudrillard considers the implications of faking and simulating for the truth status of medicine. Someone who fakes an illness does so without taking on any of the symptoms, whereas someone who simulates an illness produces in themselves some of the symptoms. He argues that '. . . feigning or dissimulating leaves the reality principle intact: the difference is always clear, it is only masked; whereas simulation threatens the difference between "true" and "false", between "real" and "imaginary". Since the simulator produces "true" symptoms, is he or she ill or not? The simulator cannot be treated objectively either as ill, or as not ill'.[39] Whereas faking can be routed out, simulation challenges the truth-status of medicine, which only knows how to treat 'true' illnesses.[40] Baudrillard argues that 'all lunatics are simulators', and simulation subverts the distinction between true and false on which medical knowledge depends.

To return to the question I raised at the beginning of this chapter, how is popular knowledge authoritative in the court-room? How is it a condition of possibility for medical knowledge? Did it, in the case of Hinckley, undermine or support the scientificity of medical knowledge? Whereas Pierre Riviere enrolled his murder/narrative in a historical field of popular knowledge by writing a memoir, Hinckley situated his crime in a field of popular knowledge by inserting himself into a pre-existing fictional narrative. By 'imitating' Travis Bickle, Hinckley located himself within the specific narrative of *Taxi Driver*, and within the general field of popular narratives of the dangerous individual. By choosing Bickle as a model, Hinckley brought *Taxi Driver* 'a popular discourse of criminality/madness' into the official sphere of the court. Rather than aiding the court to decide, however, *Taxi*

Driver and the other evidence of Hinckley's state of mind exposed the undecidability of insanity. Hinckley's trial exposed the limits of the 'scientificity' of medical knowledge. The science of medical knowledge depends upon the speech of the individual under observation, but the very thing in question is the value of that speech, speech that in this case has been formed according to the rules of a popular field of discourse. To quote from an essay on *I, Pierre Riviere*, '[g]iven a certain concept of madness, the question of true or false remains undecidable; what is paralyzed is not so much the sick man's will as the doctor's and lawyer's will to truth'.[41] Yet, despite the exposure of the limits of psychiatric knowledge, the defence nonetheless won the trial: Hinckley was acquitted by reason of insanity. The verdict caused a national outrage and resulted in major reforms and limitations to the insanity defence. In light of the undecidability of psychiatric knowledge in the trial, it seems reasonable to suppose that popular knowledge, and particularly *Taxi Driver*, contributed substantially to the defence's success.

PART V

Response from feminist legal theory

11 Do (only) women have bodies?

Frances Olsen

As Pheng Cheah and David Fraser point out in their introduction to this book, 'the body of the law' is an ambiguous phrase. As well as the determinate corpus of legal codes, statutes and common law decisions, the body of the law also refers to all the other bodies with respect to which law may be said to be in the relationship denoted by 'of the law'—including the body recognised by law, the body the law constructs, and the body inscribed by the law. It turns out that this body the law constructs, inscribes, and so forth, is as indeterminate as Critical Legal Studies (CLS) has shown the corpus of statutes, codes and common law decisions to be. Just as Critical Race Theorists question why CLS focuses on the ideological role of rights rather than, say, racism, feminists might ask why so many male theorists focus on the indeterminacy of law rather than, say, sexual inscription. This book is a useful start in that direction.

'Thinking through' has a similar ambiguity. Conventionally, thinking through a topic is a mental process that is seen to have a sequentiality to it: one starts at the beginning and thinks through the topic to a resolution at the end. But it also means an ongoing process of thinking in a particular manner—through the medium of the body of the law. The same kind of ambiguity as that detected by Jane Gallop in her landmark book, *Thinking Through the Body*, between thinking through the body to dominate it and thinking through the body as a means of transcending the mind-body dichotomy, is also at work in the concerns addressed in this present book.[1] Certainly the hierarchical separation between the

mind and body and the association of women with the body has
long been a mainstay of male devaluation of women. Women as
a group would seem to have a greater stake than men as a group
in the re-embodiment of the world of ideas.

With so many delightful ambiguities to play with, I could not
resist the invitation to write an epilogue to this book. But it is
no simple task to write an epilogue to a book parts of which one
does not understand. Of course, when anyone first begins trying
to think through the body of the law, it may be inevitable that
much will not be clear. For example, I find the Introduction's talk
of the 'disembodied bodies of legal subjects' puzzling. That the
whole quote reads 'somehow disembodied bodies of legal subjects'
really doesn't help, except to reassure the reader that it is not a
printing error. Similarly, Rosalyn Diprose talks of the problems in
legislation governing the sale or gift of body-property, 'particularly
when the body involved is sexed'. I don't know what it would
mean for a body *not* to be sexed, especially a human body such
as she seems to be referring to. It seems to me that even the bodies
of single-sex species can more accurately be considered single-
sexed than not sexed. Moreover, many feminists have shown that
non-biological bodies, such as the corpus of the law, may properly
be considered gendered or sexed.

This is the first book of its kind as far as I know, ambitious
and worthwhile. It seeks to revise the ostensibly obsolete epistemological framework of academic legal knowledge, challenging
the mind-body distinction and reconceptualising corporeality as
active and productive. The essays attempt to rethink the role of
the body in the foundation, maintenance and regulation of legal
systems and social consensus. A further goal of the book is to
explore the implications of embodiment for issues of legal responsibility and justice, questioning the central role played by abstract
rationality and individual autonomy in conventional analyses of
these notions. This is an ambitious and worthwhile project. The
proper question is what one gets out of this book, what one can
make of it, not those parts that leave one unable either to agree
or disagree. What have these essays contributed to the project of
thinking through the body of the law?

In one of the alternative understandings, 'through' suggests a
transparency of the law. Transparency also carries with it an
ambiguity: one could mean either transparent as opposed to visible
or transparent as opposed to opaque. The law is often transparent
in the sense of invisible when it operates in the so-called private
sphere. Many people believe that much of the oppression of
women at home and in the family is due to society, not to law.
Perhaps we can think through the body of the law to reduce its

transparency and to expose the role law has played and continues to play in such oppression.[2] While the law may be too transparent in this bad sense, it may also be not transparent enough in the good sense. The law is often opaque in the sense of being a block beyond which people cannot see or an obtuse mystery people cannot understand. Perhaps by thinking through it, we can make the corpus of the law more understandable.

So too with the body constructed by the law; we may think through this body to reduce its transparency or to reduce its opacity. The mind-body dichotomy allocates mind to men, body to women. Men often seem not to have bodies at all. To transcend the mind-body dichotomy and to overcome the privileging of mind over body, it may be necessary to understand the body as a complex construction of legal and non-legal discourse or social processes and not as any simple material substance, or an object external to the law.

This epilogue draws on insights from feminist theory to suggest some of the difficulties inherent in the project of trying to embody law, and it concludes that the project of this book is particularly important to feminist theory. The epilogue takes a more skeptical view of the book's claim to contribute to, much less to resolve, the equality-difference debate within feminism. I argue that the equality-difference debate is more context-dependent than often recognised and use David Fraser's discussion of anti-Semitism and the Holocaust to emphasize the importance of context more generally. The third portion of this epilogue examines this book's contribution to the feminist debate over sexuality. I examine Rosalyn Diprose's essay and place it in the context of the developing field of transgender theory. After arguing that there may be as great a tendency to exaggerate as to underestimate the difficulty of changing the status quo, the epilogue concludes with a brief narrative illustrating the pervasive role of law in affecting options and behaviour.

Feminism and bodies

The project of embodying law and gaining insights therefrom is difficult in part because of the complex situation of bodies. They are problematic when they are women's, but simple and acceptable when they are men's. For some years it has been common ground among feminist legal theorists that one problem with Anglo-American law is that the subject of juridical thinking is a male subject, masquerading as universal. Just as the subject of juridical thinking is male, the unproblematic body is also male, again passing itself off as universal. When bodies are addressed in an unproblematic way, the body does not get pregnant, it has a constant body temperature that may vary a bit from one part of the day to another but does not shift by half a degree or a degree on a regular cycle during the month, and it never menstruates. Women do not appear to have bodies at all.

It seems rather unjust that men and even the law can have a body without creating a scandal, yet women's bodies have for years worked against them. Generally, the male perspective presents itself as disembodied, universal and true. It is disembodied—with bodies left to the ladies. Men also make the female body the object of their gaze, an object of their discourse, and their property right. Feminist legal theorists have appropriated much of Simone de Beauvoir's critique of the masculine subject. The Cartesian disavowal and disparagement of embodiment and the effective relegation of the body to the female sphere reverberates with the cultural association of men with mind and women with body. Men associate women with sex and body. For many, the mind-body dualism associates men with freedom, while women are considered to be trapped in their bodies. One would think that only women have bodies. Or, if men have bodies, women are bodies. Men control their bodies to enjoy freedom, women are controlled and limited by their bodies. There is an important quote from Simone de Beauvoir:

> [f]rom puberty to menopause woman is the theatre of a play that unfolds within her and in which she is not personally concerned. Anglo-Saxons call menstruation 'the Curse'; in truth the menstrual cycle is a burden, and a useless one from the point of view of the individual . . . Woman, like man, is her body; but her body is something other than herself.[3]

Women are said to be embodied and to be inferior on the basis of that embodiment. Bodies present such a problem for them that it often seems that women can be treated as equals only by renouncing their bodies. A disavowal of the body is also one typical response to sexual abuse—a psychological clitoridectomy. Moreover, women's association with the bodily and the justification of women's oppression on the basis of their body makes it easy too for women to want to reject their bodies. Women can defend embodiment as such, but they then seem to be doing so because of their own particular embodiment as women. Alternatively, when women reject the particular association of women with embodiment and point out that their embodiment is actually much like men's, they seem to be renouncing much of the specificity of women's embodiment. How does one reject the meaning ascribed to a body without rejecting the body itself?

The meaning of the female body is often reduced to reproduction—a major arena of human activity with respect to which men might be considered to be situated in an inferior position. As Luce Irigaray puts it, children are the fruit of female, not male labour.[4] Women's bodies may also be reduced to sexual pleasure (a field in which men might seem to have similarly situated bodies, but they usually do not quite look at it that way). Generally, the male subject has not yet accepted Irigaray's invitation to redefine himself as a body—with a view to exchanges between sexed subjects.[5] Menstruation and maternity are burdens to women because society chooses to make them so.

Many of the views that continue to affect the lives of most men and women in Western society derive from Kant and Hegel. Immanuel Kant's negative view of the body is strikingly illustrated in a quote cited by Roxanne Mykitiuk: 'Who is so fond of this body that he would drag it about with him through all eternity if he could get on without it.'[6] An important aspect of Hegel's views is described by Catriona Mackenzie:

> Hegel's notion of transcendence of the natural invokes a distinction between production and reproduction, in the terms of which reproduction is seen as a merely natural process, requiring nothing on the part of the individual and involving neither creativity nor rationality. Reproduction is immersion in species-being; it is an unreflective process with no specific aim except the unconscious one of perpetuating the species. Production, on the other hand, is seen as an attempt to create value which does not merely reproduce the given conditions of existence, but transforms them. It is a reflective, rational, man-made process which involves the transformation of nature, the ultimate aim of which is truth, knowledge, self-understanding. In addition, the two terms of this distinction are in a sense in contradiction in that they are seen to occupy two mutually exclusive theoretical spaces.[7]

A similar, conventional view was elegantly stated by Simone de Beauvoir:

> Giving birth and suckling are not activities, they are natural functions; no project is involved; and that is why woman found in them no reason for lofty affirmation of her existence—she submitted passively to her biological fate.[8]

The view of many thinkers is that men—even slaves—engage in creative activity when they make products by applying their labour and intelligence to matter. Within this tradition, women are usually closely linked to reproduction, which is thought to be

work of lesser value, natural rather than creative. It is important
both to show that women do more than reproduce *and* to revalue
women's reproduction. Reproduction involves choice and work
and is, in fact, a project. It is not a woman's only project and
not exactly a project in which men cannot participate, but still a
project that privileges women and female metaphors.

Arguably, men's production could come to be seen as something that does more than satisfy natural needs only with the
development of surplus value. As people have become plentiful
enough and survival likely enough, the same situation has developed regarding women's reproductive activity. The major
transformation of society may turn out not to be the creation of
surplus value as such, as some Marxists have believed, but rather
the reduction in infant mortality and the concomitant development
of birth control and abortion. Contraception and abortion
challenge the male view of reproduction as a natural process,
requiring neither creativity nor rationality on the part of women.
Women's role in reproduction is thus transformed, which perhaps
helps to explain why so much ideological struggle between the
sexes in our society takes place in these arenas of contraception
and abortion.

There is an awkward period when women cease to be valued
for reproductive necessity and before they assert themselves suc-
cessfully to establish the basis for new treatment and conditions.
One can compare this to the awkward period in capitalism when
the conditions of production seemed to lead to economic crisis
and loss of profits.

As we throw the female body into question, let us also throw
into question the idealised body of men—subject to rational
control by the intellect and will (at least if women are kept out
of sight). Men think they control their bodies (except erect
penises). Anti-abortion regulations and forced intercourse are
areas where society or men try to reduce women's control over
their bodies. (As one feminist has said of men, they can't control
their own bodies, but they want to control ours!)

Throughout most of human history, one of the major distinctions in the role of men and women in reproduction has been that
a woman regularly puts her life in jeopardy to bring forth children.
In some parts of the world complications of pregnancy are still a
leading cause of death. In this regard, consider the oddness of the
following quote from Simone de Beauvoir about male hunting
parties:

> The warrior put his life in jeopardy to elevate the prestige of the
> horde, the clan to which he belonged. And in this he proved

dramatically that life is not the supreme value for man, but on the contrary that it should be made to serve ends more important than itself. The worst curse that was laid upon woman was that she should be excluded from these forays. For it is not in giving life but in risking life that man is raised above the animal; that is why superiority has been accorded in humanity not to the sex that brings forth but to that which kills.[9]

An important understanding of de Beauvoir, to which I will return later, is Judith Butler's assertion that she tried to overcome the mind-body dualism but got caught up within it because she underestimated the difficulty of bringing about change. 'The theory of embodiment informing Beauvoir's analysis is clearly limited by the uncritical reproduction of the Cartesian distinction between freedom and the body.'[10] The issue of the body and its relation to the mind is an important ongoing topic in feminist theory, and this book contributes to that question.

The sameness-difference debate and contexts

It is more problematic whether the effort to think through the body of the law contributes to any clearer understanding or resolution of the so-called sameness-difference debate in feminist legal theory. The sameness-difference debate is often simplistically understood to be based on the natural bodily differences between men and women, and what society should do about these differences. Equality is seen to be based on sameness—treating women as well as men when they conform to a male model. Differences should be recognised, it is often argued, but doing so runs the risk of the conservative use of difference and of essentialist exclusion of women of colour and other women who do not fit the model of woman (white, able-bodied, middle-class) that underlies most concepts of women being different from men. Paul Patton's essay discussing the *Mabo* decision correctly focuses the issue as 'what differences are recognised and what normative structure is applied to such recognition'.

In fact, all claims of unequal treatment and discrimination are based on perceived differences. It is a claim of discrimination, not random decision-making or arbitrariness. (In this regard, it is interesting to note that in the 1971 United States decision in *Reed v. Reed*, before sex or gender was recognised as a constitutionally-problematic category, the United States Supreme Court's conclusion that the Utah preference for male over female executors was unconstitutional was based on the Court's assertion that it had no rational basis. It was arbitrary, though not random.)[11]

With antidiscrimination law, we are always talking about some particular difference, such as between men and women.

The recent decision of the United States Supreme Court purporting to apply strict scrutiny to any distinction based on race discrimination illustrates the problem.[12] The Court's approach threatens to dissolve race-discrimination law insofar as the state cannot effectively bar discrimination if it is itself foreclosed from recognising race. The point of feminist struggles should not be the affirmation of women's differences, but rather the affirmation of women. One way to understand claims of formal inequality of treatment between men and women is that it represents a (rare) strong indication of the subordination of women—that when women act like men, they are still not treated as well as men. The current thrust of equal protection for women legitimates departures from rigid female gender identities—allowing what would once have been considered cross-dressing and so forth. Some would criticise the law for basing protection for women too much upon women's departure from gendered ways of being and argue thus that the law protects women, not femininity. But the distinction between protecting femininity and coercing women to be feminine is a slight one, especially under conditions of male domination. No one would defend the double standard on the basis that it gives women lots of choices: they can be a virgin or a whore; they can be the Virgin Mary or Mary Magdalene.

The issue between sameness and difference depends entirely upon context. Women can be oppressed by same treatment and they can be oppressed by different treatment. In some contexts differences should be deemphasised; in other contexts it would make no sense to do so. The same is true of many discussions.

For example, Fraser's essay criticises CLS for not dealing with Auschwitz, or the Nazi genocide. Yet it seems to me that the essay itself illustrates the difficulties of trying to do so and indirectly presents reasons why many people might hesitate to address the issue. So much depends upon context.

Americans criticising the war in Vietnam often suggested that the United States' behaviour in Vietnam was all too much like the behaviour of the Nazi Wehrmacht in Eastern Europe. This strong rhetoric had a significant degree of accuracy. Yet, when conservative German historians tried to relativise the Nazi genocide and to argue, for example, that the Communists' behaviour was essentially as bad as that of the Nazis, it quite properly caused the uproar that came to be known as the *Historikerstreit*. Fraser's focus on European anti-Semitism is important and it seems to me largely correct, yet it also feeds into the German apologist position. Some conservatives, like an awkward adolescent seducer, try one line after another to get people to downplay the horrors of Nazism and forget the damage done by Hitler and his followers.

I feel uncertain about what Fraser intends to be saying and feel concerned about how well his focus on innocent Jewish victims resonates with the latest conservative line in Germany. German conservatives have long tried to present themselves as the greatest victims of Nazism, with a certain confusion between conditions during the war and supposed injustices inflicted upon the defeated Germans. More recently, at the 50th anniversary commemorations of various end-of-war activities, the ruling Christian Democratic Union (CDU) politicians kept emphasising the 'total innocence' of the victims of the genocide, who were killed solely because of the group into which they were born. To some listeners, this may sound like real regret and acceptance of responsibility—the more innocent the victims the more outrageous the murders. Yet it also tries to create a sharp distinction between 'innocent victims' and 'those who did *something* that contributed to their deaths', thus setting the stage for isolating and excusing the brutal suppression of dissent and the massive murders carried out against opponents of Nazism. It also obliterates the political dimension of the murder of Jews. It was not just that they were accused of being the Christ-killers—although that played a far greater role than most Christians are willing to admit these days—but also that the Germans viewed the Jews as the backbone of the radical movement in Germany and throughout Europe. Nazis drew some distinction between their political opponents and Jews as a whole, but their opposition to Jews was political as well as racial or religious and they frequently seemed to use 'Jew' and 'Bolshevik' interchangeably.

The CDU government officials say or certainly imply that the Nazi persecution in Gestapo headquarters, concentration camps and death camps was irrational. Thus, they actively leave out the brutal suppression and persecution of the opponents of Nazism and refuse to consider whether brutal suppression of opposition was a basic element essential to the maintenance of power and popular support. The CDU government officials also try to obscure the relationship the Nazis saw between the Jews and left-wing radicals. And now if we can add that anti-Semitism is (a) common throughout Europe and/or (b) an odd obsession of Hitler's, then we can continue the work begun by the Nuremberg trials and place all responsibility for the concentration and extermination camps upon Hitler personally, separate from the regime of which the camps were an integral part. Soon, the only thing wrong with the Nazi times will be this strange obsession of Hitler's and that they lost the war.

The Nuremberg trials had the effect of privatising the guilt for the war crimes—these individuals did these terrible things, not the vast majority (who let it happen in their name and many of whom benefited or expected to benefit from the Nazi regime). Compare this with the privatisation of the 1995 bombing in Oklahoma when it was found to have been done by right-wingers. When they had speculated that the bombing was done by Muslims or Arabs, Americans were quite ready to blame all Muslims or Arabs, or at least any Muslim or Arab who advocated what the West refers to as terrorism. The whole group would have been considered implicated. Efforts to suggest any responsibility of the radical right in the United States for the Oklahoma bombing have met with considerable resistance from the press and politicians.

The feminist debate over sexuality

As a whole, the chapters in this book are very concerned with contexts, and the book deals with several important ones. Among the most noteworthy, and the one I focus on here, is the feminist debate over sexuality. The ongoing debate between so-called anti-sex and so-called pro-sex feminists is referred to in the Introduction and addressed at some length in the chapter by Rosalyn Diprose.

In her provocative chapter, Diprose seems to suggest three radical conclusions that bear on the feminist pro- and anti-sex debate. First, drawing on Merleau-Ponty's notion that the distinction between self and other develops through the objectification of one's body by another, she argues that 'the emergence of a body we can call our own occurs, not prior to but through the "alienation" of corporeality', and thus that 'the difference between consent and coercion is at best indeterminate'. Later, she suggests that if what were at stake in surrogacy or rape were 'a woman's control over her body or her informed consent', then 'no self-respecting woman could have sexual relations or children'. Finally, she argues that the widespread assumption that maternity or female sexuality is 'proper to the woman's body' and that the giving away of what is proper to the woman's body must result from coercion (which she says 'accounts for the widespread resistance to "non-commercial voluntary" surrogacy') 'risks reducing all heterosexual sex to rape (or it at least requires that explicit consent be given for every sexual encounter)'. Lest this be mistaken to be an endorsement of the so-called anti-sex position, I would direct the reader to a footnote in which Diprose asserts:

> While to many this determination may be better for women than
> the reverse, it tends to trivialise and hide rape. And/or it leads to
> the ludicrous situation exemplified by a manual on sexual conduct
> at Antioch College, Ohio, which suggests . . . that 'verbal consent
> should be obtained with every new level of physical and/or sexual
> contact or conduct in any given interaction, regardless of who
> initiates it' and that 'the request for consent must be specific to
> each act'.

Why this creative effort to shift the burden of miscommunication
should be considered 'ludicrous' by so many people is beyond
me—especially given the damage to women of the high level of
real and feigned misunderstanding that presently exists. When a
sexual encounter is actually mutual, and often even when it is not
really, no-one will care whether these rules were followed; they
amount to the precept, when in doubt, ask. Maintaining the status
quo is always easier than trying to change it significantly. The
only reason that the informal norms of sexual behaviour that
prevail at most colleges do not seem far more ludicrous and
offensive than the Antioch College norms is that these conventional norms do not need to be explicitly spelled out in a manual.

A more complicated reason that the 'explicit verbal consent'
norm might seem ludicrous would relate to Diprose's first assertion that 'the difference between consent and coercion is at best
indeterminate'. Anyone who thinks Antioch's manual solves the
whole problem of coercion and consent would of course be
mistaken. Yet the explicitness of the manual may give that impression.

However much we may now condemn as unjust the laws that
provided immunity to rapists who could claim that their victim
had consented on bases having nothing to do with consent, it was
these laws that formed the background against which were created
the informal rules and norms that continue to exist. Some of these
bases that have nothing to do with consent are that the woman
who was raped was 'not of chaste character', or that she was a
Negro woman, or that she was married to the perpetrator, or that
she worked as a prostitute. Other bases upon which a woman
would have been found to have 'consented' are that she dated the
rapist, that she let him into her home or went into his, or that
she allowed any significant physical contact to take place. Basically, rape laws treated a woman as having consented to sexual
intercourse if she did not effectively resist sexual advances the
man saw or chose to treat as foreplay—a prelude to intercourse.
Enacting formal rules that favour women and that counteract
these assumptions of consent may be the most effective way to
change the norms. The 'rules' in the Antioch manual are a

statement of the conditions under which a claim of consent will
be accepted or not accepted and the circumstances in which a
claim of non-consent might not be listened to. Obviously, the
norms need not be followed by those confident enough of consent
to run the risk.

Since it is predominantly women who claim lack of consent to
sexual contact, any limits on what counts as lack of consent tend
to favour men over women. In contrast, imagine how things would
seem if there were a legal norm that whenever a couple has sexual
intercourse, it implies consent to a commitment to share finan-
cially and emotionally with one another. In our society it would
be more men than women who would object that such a sharing
was not really their intention. If we made it difficult or impossible
for a party to claim he or she had not consented to such broad
sharing, this would generally favour women over men. In fact, we
go the other way. Only under very limited situations of marriage
or living together for extended periods of time does law imply the
promise of on-going sharing and commitment that a good number
of women may assume (and a promise that might be reasonable,
given the strong social bonding that may result from a sexual
relationship).

The chapter by Diprose also illustrates the splitting of the
subject. The notion of the splitting of the concept of mother is
exemplified in the rare cases in which reproduction is carried out
through in-vitro fertilisation and implanting a fertilised egg in the
womb of some other person. In this case, the notion of mother
loses the illusion of certainty and the child could be said to have
two biological mothers—a genetic mother and a gestational
mother—as well as possible other parents, such as a social mother,
a genetic father and a social father. Similarly, in the relatively rare
cases in which sex is easily debatable, with a failure of a clear
lining up of hormonal, anatomical, genetic and other indicators
of sex (as for example in cases of so-called hermaphrodites), the
notion of sex loses the illusion of certainty it has sometimes been
thought to have.

In both cases, there is a hierarchical preference for the simple
alignment. Alternative reproduction is resorted to in those cases
in which a person is unable to have a simple confluence of genetic,
gestational and social motherhood. 'Surrogacy' cases have almost
always involved women who are physically unable to conceive or
carry a pregnancy to term. Even artificial insemination through
donor sperm generally takes place only when there is no male
partner or the male partner is unable to produce sperm. Only a
serious genetic problem in a husband would lead a couple to
choose artificial insemination by a third party if they were able

to have a child genetically related to them both. It is even uncertain that an identical twin who was exposed to some pollutant that could cause problems with his sperm would readily resort to the presumably identical sperm of his identical brother.

In the case of sex, the proud parents of a newborn would probably not be considered especially blessed if the answer to the common question, 'Is it a boy or a girl?' were to be 'a little bit of each', unless twins or some other multiple birth were intended to be conveyed. Yet the binary division between men and women has become increasingly problematic as transgendered people have become perhaps more visible and certainly more vocal. Not only is there the split between physical sex, social gender and the object choice of sexual desire, but the seemingly physical fact of sex has been recognised to be less determinate than once thought. People dispute whether sex should be seen as an anatomical concept, a genetic one, or a hormonal one. Judith Butler is no doubt right that sex is a social and discursive concept rather than a pre-social 'fact' and the division between sex and gender is not actually sustainable in any simple way.[13]

It can be quite valuable to focus our attention as Diprose does on those relatively rare cases in which issues that seem clear become clearly ambiguous. For example, it is usually considered clear who a child's mother is. There have always been rare cases in which for one reason or another from the moment a child was born, or even before birth, it was clear that some other person was going to act as mother to the child and this other person might be considered to be the mother. Two things have changed to make this a more common occurrence. First, for a variety of reasons involving the maladjustment in the timing of career paths and optimal child-bearing years on one hand and environmental pollution on the other, there may be more instances than before in which a woman is unable to give birth to a child but wants very much to be a mother and raise a child. Second, developments in reproductive technology make it possible to extract eggs and embryos from one woman and deposit them into another woman. Thus, now in addition to any number of social or intending mothers, a child may have a genetic mother and a separate gestational mother. Either or neither (though rarely both) may intend to be the social mother.

Suppose A's egg is fertilised and is made into a baby by B in B's womb. Has A donated an egg to B or has B provided a service for A? Since we 'award' custody—use power against the bodies of the adults and the child as well as grant legitimacy to the feelings of one or another—we think we have to decide the issue—and generally look to intent at some earlier time.

Yet, suppose one or both parties change their mind, perhaps several times. A may see B as a 'surrogate'. Then, if during the pregnancy A's spouse decides he does not want a child and coerces A to seek to get out of her contract, B might say fine, I'll be happy to keep the child. Then if A breaks up with her husband and she and B decide before birth to raise the child together, surely they must both be considered mothers.

If, and as the techniques for the extraction of eggs, in-vitro fertilisation, and embryo transfer become less expensive and otherwise materially problematic, it could be that female couples who wish to raise a child together might choose to divide the biological parenthood between them by using the egg of one partner and the gestational capacity and work of the other. (Potentially there could be a third biological mother in whose body fertilisation or conception took place, though in practice no reason has been found for transferring an egg for purposes of fertilisation into the body of a woman who does not intend to carry a pregnancy to term.)

Similar issues could arise in cases involving (other) bodily parts. Supposing that organ transplants got to the point where someone who was brain-dead could donate his entire body to someone whose brain, but nothing else, worked well. Has she received a(n) (almost) full-body transplant or has he received a brain transplant? Although there would be no custody problem, as there might be in a surrogacy or egg donation case, there could be any number of other problems. Should the surviving person be legally responsible for action taken by the brain-dead person—for example, can a paternity action be brought against her (or him)? Should the surviving person retain ownership right over inventions patented by the person who received the (almost) full-body transplant?

Conclusions

The feminist critique of sexuality argues persuasively that male domination and female submission are built into our conventional notions of what is sexually appealing or arousing and that many of the character traits valued as feminine are at least in part the result of subordination and sexual abuse of women. These recognitions highlight the difficulty as well as the importance of social change and raise important questions for women and for men of good will. First, how can an individual live an ethical life in such an imperfect world? Can one nevertheless find pleasures and sexual happiness within this world? Second, how can men be persuaded to change the system if they benefit from it? How much might some women lose from changing the system? Feminists have long pondered whether recognising the damaging linkage between eroticism and inequality means women cannot enjoy 'having sex' without collaborating in their own oppression. The male version of this concern is whether a man can enjoy women's sexiness or whether, in taking pleasure in sexuality, he is collaborating with the abusive gender system and thereby partly responsible for the sexual abuse of women. At stake, according to some men, is their 'possibility of self-respect'.[14]

At a symposium held at Humboldt University, Berlin, to mark the 50th anniversary of the end of the war in Germany, a Polish speaker addressed the issue of the forced resettlement in Germany of the German populations living in various places outside Germany before World War II, a topic that has been gaining in popularity in the period since German Unification. Many Germans have been making nostalgic trips back to the areas from which they or their parents were expelled, arguing the injustice of the expulsion, especially to those individual Germans who did not themselves encourage the Nazi invasion of the countries in which Germans were living. Some Germans talk of trying to reclaim property confiscated in 1945. The Polish speaker attempted to draw a line separating guilt from responsibility. He asserted, 'I do not feel guilty for expelling Germans from the territory from which they were expelled after World War II. But I do feel responsible for it and for the consequences that follow from it.'

Perhaps such an attitude—separating guilt from responsibility—is appropriate for people to adopt with respect to the oppression of women. Men who get a charge out of pornography or out of abuse of women do not need to feel guilty for their feelings. But one would like men to accept responsibility for their feelings, which would mean investigating fairly the consequences of their actions and trying as far as possible to undo any damage.

The oppressiveness of abuse and the limits it places upon women's activities are greater than most men imagine. Women are always in the position of having to evaluate the sexual interests of men. Street violence against women in the United States undermines women's freedom so much that women might rationally decide to reject the limitations and take the risk of rape or premature death. But it is not as easy as this. The choice to ignore something cannot always be made, as in the story of the person so concerned not to notice the odd nose of a visitor that upon her arrival he greeted her as 'Mrs Nose'. Once we recognise the pervasiveness of abuse, we can no longer relax and feel the breeze and let our mind wander as we walk down a dark street.

Although it is useful to recognise the depth and pervasiveness of male dominance, such a focus can also be demobilising and depressing, as well as incorrect. The difficulty of change is often exaggerated. A slight warming in the world atmosphere might eventually melt the polar icecaps, although the change could go virtually unnoticed until suddenly there were flooding everywhere. Remember the advice the debtor Mr Micawber gave to David Copperfield: 'Annual income twenty pounds, annual expenditure nineteen six, result happiness. Annual income twenty pounds, annual expenditure twenty pounds nought and six, result misery.'[15] The State of California is slowly washing away into the Pacific Ocean—on occasion there is a sharp rupture—but basically it cannot be noticed most of the time.

Yet I do not mean to suggest that change is easy. Women are oppressed, women's actions are valued lower than men's actions, and the production of meaning in society seems to be dominated by men. Simone de Beauvoir, like liberal feminists, may have underestimated the pervasiveness of male domination and have mistakenly believed that women could simply claim subject status for themselves and be extended the rights that men enjoy. Whatever women touch seems to turn to mud: when women enter a profession, it is feminised and devalued. In contrast, when a man enters a kitchen, he becomes a chef. When a man parents a child, he becomes super-dad. Perhaps this distinction is nowhere so obvious as in child custody decisions where women are expected to do 100 per cent and lose credit for every minute they fail to devote to their child, while few expectations are placed on men— who are given credit for every minute they spend with their child, whether or not they pay attention to or even spare much space for the child.

Like the Gestalt picture that can look like a stemmed glass or like two people talking to one another, it could all shift from the one picture to another.[16] I argue that there are at least two rather complete and full pictures of the world, filled with details that overlap but are none-the-less in total conflict and seem unable to coexist with one another. At the moment, the male-formed picture is dominant, but if that were to change, there is a female picture waiting in the wings. It is a picture most women are familiar with to one extent or another and which many women have experienced validated in short glimpses.

Men can quickly change what seem to be entrenched habits whenever it serves their interests to do so, whenever the gig is up. Although male domination may seem like the Bozo that always bounces back up, a more realistic metaphor for the persistent tendency of women's efforts at power to topple over again and again is provided by Christopher Columbus' egg that stands on end quite handily once you smash flat the end of it.

It might just be that the gig is up. For example, women know maternity is creative and a project in which they have a privileged position. However willing women once may have been to accept that pregnancy happened to them and to give a child for adoption if they could not raise it themselves, increasingly women recognise that pregnancy is a choice and that creating and birthing a child is work. Women are less willing to remain pregnant against their wishes and less willing to give up a child, which they increasingly recognise as the product of their work. Law plays important roles in this recognition.

Nor should one forget that the Hollywood blacklist was a bluff. People thought there was big money behind it, but there really was not: one good challenge and it collapsed. Empires rise and fall. When monarchies tumbled, they began falling all over one another, each seemingly faster than the last. Change in Central and Eastern Europe proceeded with breathtaking speed. The erotisation of domination and subordination could suddenly become stale and boring—repetitious and without meaning—worse than 'last night's popovers'.[17]

Laws affect the resources available to individuals as well as directly affecting their behaviour. An experience many years ago of a very explicit choice regarding resistance and danger may illuminate the pervasive role of law in governing bodies. In the summer of 1967, a friend, Linda, and I got into a dangerous situation hitchhiking. As dusk approached we found ourselves in an isolated part of what was then Yugoslavia near the border with Albania with two men—the owner of the car, who wanted to seduce at least one of us, and a younger man who seemed to want to rape one or both of us and who seemed to me capable of murder. Our best chance for safety seemed to lie in using this conflict of interest between them. Because neither of them understood much more English than we understood Serbo-Croatian, Linda and I were able to consult with one another quite explicitly about our choices regarding resistance and danger. The owner of the car wanted to force himself on me, but he apparently also wanted to experience himself as having obtained my consent. Because there were two of us whose fate would be determined jointly and language differences allowed it, Linda and I discussed explicitly the decision process women often make by themselves under dangerous or potentially dangerous circumstances. As the situation gradually escalated, we continued to consult to make a joint decision. Linda just wanted to stop the abuse; I feared they might wind up killing us. They tried to separate us; we tried to stay together. They tried to maintain a united front; we tried to divide them. At one point when we were separated, the younger man hit Linda, taking a clear turn toward forcible rape. She was able to rejoin me and we had a quick talk. We agreed that I would get the licence number of the car and be sure the owner knew I had it and we would talk about police. In doing this, I felt we were increasing the possibility of avoiding rape but also radically increasing the possibility that if we were raped we would also be killed. It turned out that the owner had put a cloth over the licence plate, so I began removing the cloth. At this point he decided to drive the car off the road to a more concealed place. The younger man could not be sure that he was not being left behind (outnumbered by women?) and ran alongside the car, giving Linda and me a chance to escape.

We took off running across the fields as fast as we could and got a reasonably good head start. Linda thought the men were following us but was not sure. When a dog began barking we realised there was a house a few hundred yards ahead and Linda wanted to veer off to avoid it. Again, we had a decision to make. I wanted to approach the house—assuming the chances were good it would be a family or some other safer situation. I urged that we at least stay close enough that it might discourage the men from pursuing us or otherwise offer some protection. Linda feared we might be worse off, so we tried to avoid contact with the tiny house while staying close enough to it that we could approach if the two men renewed their attack on us. Women are always making such calculations, casing out situations, judging which men present a lesser risk. The law against rape was not sufficient protection, but it gave us some bargaining power and increased our room for manoeuvre. Similarly, the law against murder probably increased the chances of our survival. Both laws increased our ability to travel through Yugoslavia by slightly decreasing the risk of doing so. In the end, an adult son from the house investigated the disturbance and understood enough of our situation to offer protection, and Linda and I got a good night's sleep safely ensconced on thick rugs on the floor, surrounded by his younger brothers and sisters.

Millions of women have been faced with sexual abuse of one kind or another and have made similar calculations and decisions. Every improvement in the law may increase the resources available, decrease abuse and increase the possibility of women's picture of the world gaining legitimacy.

Endnotes

Introduction

1 See Duncan Kennedy and Karl Klare, 'A Bibliography of Critical Legal Studies', *Yale Law Journal*, vol. 94, 1984, p. 461

2 See Richard Delgado and Jean Stefancic, 'Critical Race Theory: An Annotated Bibliography', *Virginia Law Review*, vol. 79, 1993, p. 461

3 Friedrich Nietzsche, *On the Genealogy of Morals/Ecce Hons*, trans. N. Kaufman, Vintage Books, New York, 1969

4 On Deleuze, see *Gilles Deleuze and the Theater of Philosophy*, eds Constantin Boundas and Dorothea Olkowski, Routledge, New York, 1993. On Foucault, see Judith Butler, *Bodies That Matter*, New York: Routledge, (1993). See also Elizabeth Grosz, *Volatile Bodies: Towards a Corporeal Feminism*, Bloomington, Indiana U.P. (1994)

5 See generally, Jacques Perrida, *Writing and Difference*, trans. A. Bass, University of Chicago Press, Chicago, 1978

6 See Vincent Descombes, *Modern French Philosophy*, Cambridge: Cambridge University Press, (1980)

7 See Drucilla Cornell, 'Gender, Sex and Equivalent Rights', in Judith Butler and Joan Scott (eds), *Feminists Theorize and the Political*, New York: Routledge (1992); *Beyond Accommodation: Ethical Feminism, Deconstruction and the Law*, New York, Routledge, (1991); *Transformations: Recollections, Imagination and Sexual Difference*, New York; Routledge (1993)

8 See Mary Joe Frug, *Postmodern Legal Feminism*, New York: Routledge, (1992). See also Gary Peller, 'The Metaphysics of American Law', *California Law Review*, vol. 73, p. 1152 (1985)

Chapter 1   The body of the law

1   St Thomas Aquinas, *Treatise on Law—Summa Theologica: Questions 90–97*, Gateway Edition, Illinois, 1969

2   Thus, even though John Austin analyses positive law in terms of coercive force which is never entirely rational because it is arbitrary, he classifies positive law and Divine law as species of the genus 'law' defined in terms of command and obedience. These terms necessarily carry a reserve of rationality insofar as they signify the peculiar status of man as *homo erectus*, suspended between animality and God. See John Austin, 'A positivist conception of law', from *The Province of Jurisprudence Determined*, in Joel Feinberg and Hyman Gross eds *Philosophy of Law* (4th Ed), Wadsworth Publishing, California, 1991, pp. 27–38

3   H.L.A. Hart, *The Concept of Law* , Clarendon Press, Oxford, 1961, esp. Chs V–VI

4   Hegel, *Philosophy of Right*, T.M. Knox trans. Clarendon Press, Oxford, 1967, para 210–229, pp. 134–145

5   Cf. Zillah Eisenstein, *The Female Body and the Law*, University of California Press, California, 1988, p. 45: 'The prevailing discourse about law privileges the so-called objectivity of scientific method, views nature as definitive, and assumes a superior rationality . . . However varied the theories concerning law are—be they legal positivism, formalism, or realism—they do not exist outside the dominant discourse'

6   See Genevieve Lloyd, *The Man of Reason: 'Male' and 'Female' in Western Philosophy*, (2nd Ed) Minnesota University Press, Minneapolis, 1993

7   See in particular, 'The necessity of sexuate rights' and 'How to define sexuate rights' both in Margaret Whitford ed. *The Irigaray Reader*, Blackwells, London, 1991

8   For accounts of the polemics within and between Critical Legal Studies, feminist legal theory and Critical Race Theory, see, for instance, Mark Tushnet, 'Critical Legal Studies: a political history', *Yale Law Journal* vol. 100, 1991, pp. 1515–1544; Frances Olsen, 'Feminism and Critical Legal Theory: an American perspective', International Journal of the Sociology of Law, vol. 18, 1990, pp. 199–215; Deborah Rhode, 'Feminist Critical Theories', *Stanford Law Review*, vol. 42, 1990, pp. 617–638; Mari Matsuda, 'Looking to the bottom: Critical Legal Studies and reparations', *Harvard Civil Rights and Civil Liberties Law Review*, vol. 22, 1987, pp. 323–399; Randall Kennedy, 'Racial critiques of legal academia', *Harvard Law Review*, vol. 102, 1989, pp. 1745–1819; Marlee Kline, 'Race, racism and Feminist Legal Theory', *Harvard Women's Law Journal*, vol. 12, 1989, pp. 115–150

9   See Martha Minow, 'The Supreme Court 1986 term—foreword: justice engendered', *Harvard Law Review*, vol. 101, 1987, pp. 10–95, at p. 95: 'Justice is engendered when judges admit the limitations of their own viewpoints, when judges reach beyond those limits by trying

to see from contrasting perspectives, and when people seek to exercise power to nurture differences, not to assign and control them. Rather than securing an illusory universality and objectivity, law is a medium through which particular people can engage in the continuous work of making justice'

10 Cf. Phyllis Goldfarb, 'From the worlds of "Others": minority and feminist responses to Critical Legal Studies', *New England Law Review*, vol. 26, 1992, pp. 683–710

11 Z. Eisenstein, *The Female Body and the Law*, p. 109

12 ibid., pp. 64–65

13 ibid., pp. 76–77

14 ibid., p. 2

15 ibid., pp. 2–3: '[J]ust as biological constitution is never irrelevant to the definition of individual identity, so gender is never completely distanced from biology. Biology is, in part, gendered—which is, in part, culture; and gender is in part, biological—which is also in part cultural . . . Recognizing that gender differences exist is a way of acknowledging that biology exists but gender differences need not be reduced to or determined by biology . . . In contrast, the supposition of engendered sex "difference" . . . establishes gender on the basis of biology . . . Rejecting the engendered form of "difference" allows us, consequently to refocus our attention on the particularities that exist within female bodies and women's lives'

16 ibid., p. 29

17 ibid., p. 85: 'Sex "difference" is someplace between the real and the ideal because the body exists but always through its signs. There are differences between male and female bodies, but the "difference" of sex is not found just in the body. It is also in the discussion and language that interpret the body and the social arrangements surrounding it. "Difference" is therefore articulated and reproduced through the body as flesh and "sign": the language of sex "difference" may not be all *true*, but it is *real*.'

18 See Lon Fuller, 'Positivism and fidelity to law—a reply to Professor Hart', in Feinberg and Gross, eds. *Philosophy of Law*, pp. 82–104

19 Eisenstein, ibid., pp. 93, 97

20 On this question of rethinking the concept of mind in terms of the permutations and surface inscriptions of the body, see E. Grosz, *Volatile Bodies: Toward a Corporeal Feminism*, Indiana UP, Bloomington, 1994

21 Robert M. Cover, 'Violence and the word', *The Yale Law Journal*, vol. 95, 1986, pp. 1601–1629

22 Thus, Max Weber suggests that 'law exists when there is a probability that an order will be upheld by a specific staff of men who will use physical or psychical compulsion with the intention of obtaining conformity with the order, or of inflicting sanctions for infringement of it', in *From Max Weber—Essays in Sociology*, eds. H.H. Gerth and C. Wright Mills, Routledge, New York, 1991, at p. 180. Ronald Dworkin also subscribes to this definition of law in *Law's Empire*, Fontana Press, London, 1986

23 Robert Cover, 'Violence and the word', pp. 1617–8
24 See also Robert M. Cover, 'The Supreme Court 1982 term—foreword: *Nomos* and narrative', *Harvard Law Review*, vol. 97, 1983, pp. 4–68
25 Robert Cover, 'Violence and the word', p. 1604
26 ibid., p. 1611, fn. 25
27 This differentiates Cover's position from that of Stanley Fish who derives legal violence from the historical use of force without consideration for this prior level of transcendental violence. See Fish's reading of Hart in 'Force', Ch. 21 of *Doing What Comes Naturally—Change, Rhetoric and the Practice of Theory in Literary and Legal Studies*, Duke University Press, Durham, 1989, pp. 503–24
28 Robert Cover, 'Violence and the word', pp. 1604–5
29 ibid., p. 1629: '[I]f we truly attend to legal interpretation as it is practiced in the field of fear, pain and death, we find that the principal impediment to the achievement of common and coherent meaning is a necessary limit, intrinsic to the activity. Judges, officials, resisters, martyrs, wardens, convicts, may or may not share common texts; they may or may not share a common vocabulary, a common cultural store of gestures and rituals; they may not share a common philosophical vocabulary. There will be in the immense human panorama a continuum of degrees of commonality in all of the above. But as long as legal interpretation is constitutive of violent behavior as well as of meaning, as long as people are committed to using or resisting the social organizations of violence in making their interpretations real, there will always be a tragic limit to the common meaning that can be achieved'
30 See Scott Lash, 'Genealogy and the body: Foucault/Deleuze/Nietzsche', *Theory, Culture and Society*, vol. 2.2, 1984, pp. 1–8, at 3–5, who makes this claim even more strongly
31 Friedrich Nietzsche, *The Will to Power*, Walter Kauffman trans., Vintage Books, New York, 1968, pp. 348–9
32 ibid,. p. 270
33 Nietzsche, *On the Genealogy of Morals/Ecce Homo*, W. Kaufman (trans.), Vintage Books, New York, 1969, p. 33
34 Nietzsche, *The Will to Power*, p. 274: 'Consciousness is present only to the extent that consciousness is useful. It cannot be doubted that all sense perceptions are permeated with value judgements'
35 Nietzsche, *On the Genealogy of Morals*, pp. 84–5
36 ibid., p. 61
37 ibid., p. 61
38 ibid., p. 64
39 ibid., pp. 64–5
40 ibid. pp. 65–7
41 ibid., p. 68
42 Robert Cover, 'Violence and the word', p. 1629
43 See Michel de Certeau, 'Des outils pour ecrire le corps', *Traverses*, vol. 14/15, 1979; 'Tools for body writing', trans. Paul Foss and Meaghan Morris, *Intervention*, vol. 21/22, 1988, pp. 7–11, at pp. 4–5

44 ibid., p. 8
45 Nitya Duclos, 'Lessons of difference: feminist theory on cultural diversity', *Buffalo Law Review*, vol. 38, 1990, pp. 325–381, at p. 359
46 See Michel Foucault, *Discipline and Punish—the Birth of the Prison*, trans. Alan Sheridan, Penguin, Harmondsworth, 1977
47 ibid., p. 194
48 ibid., p. 138
49 Michel Foucault, 'Clarifications on the question of power' in *Foucault Live—Interviews 1966–84*, Semiotexte, New York, 1989, pp. 179–192, at pp. 183–184
50 Michel Foucault, *The History of Sexuality. Volume 1: An Introduction*, trans. Robert Hurley, Pantheon, New York, 1978, pp. 92–3: 'Power must be understood . . . as the multiplicity of force relations immanent in the sphere in which they operate and which constitute their own organization; as the process which, through ceaseless struggles and confrontations, transforms, strengthens or reverses them; as the support these force relations find in one another, thus forming a chain or a system, or on the contrary, the disjunctions and contradictions which isolate them from one another; and lastly, as the strategies in which they take effect, whose general design or institutional crystallization is embodied in the state apparatus, in the formulation of the law, in the various social hegemonies . . . Power is everywhere; not because it embraces everything, but because it comes from everywhere. And "Power", insofar as it is permanent, repetitious, inert, and self-reproducing, is simply the overall effect that emerges from all these mobilities, the concatenation that rests on each of them and seeks in turn to arrest their movement. One needs to be nominalistic, no doubt: power is not an institution, and not a structure; neither is it a certain strength we are endowed with; it is the name that one attributes to a complex strategical situation in a particular society'
51 Foucault, *Discipline and Punish*, p. 156
52 ibid., p. 28
53 Foucault, *The History of Sexuality*, p. 95
54 ibid., p. 96
55 Robert Cover, 'Violence and the word', p. 1629
56 Cf. Austin Sarat and Thomas Kearns, 'A journey through forgetting: toward a jurisprudence of violence' in *The Fate of Law*, Ann Arbor, The University of Michigan Press, 1991, pp. 209–273, at 269: 'Force is disdainful of reason; it pushes it aside; it takes it over completely . . . [R]eason and force have no way to share control of human agency . . . [L]aw's violence does not sit well—indeed, it wars with—the conception of human agency that is built into, and held out to us, by a jurisprudence of rules'
57 Austin Sarat and Thomas Kearns, 'Making peace with violence: Robert Cover on law and legal theory' in Sarat and Kearns eds, *Law's Violence*, Ann Arbor, The University of Michigan Press, 1992, pp. 211–250, at 242

58 Drucilla Cornell, 'The good, the right and the possibility of legal interpretation', Chapter 4, *The Philosophy of the Limit*, Routledge, New York, 1992, pp. 91–115, at p. 95

59 Jacques Derrida, *Of Grammatology*, Johns Hopkins UP, Baltimore, 1976, pp. 139–40: 'There is no ethics without the presence *of the other* but also, and consequently, without absence, dissimulation, detour, *differance*, writing. The arche-writing is the origin of morality as of immorality. The non-ethical opening of ethics. A violent opening'

60 Jacques Derrida, 'Mochlos; or, the conflict of faculties' in Richard Rand ed., *Logomachia: The Conflict of Faculties*, University of Nebraska Press, Lincoln, 1992, pp. 3–34, at p. 11: 'One can doubtless imagine dissolving responsibility's value by relativising, secondarising or deriving the effect of subjectivity, consciousness and intentionality; one can doubtless decenter the subject, as is easily said, without retesting the bond between, on the one hand, responsibility, and on the other, freedom of subjective consciousness or purity of intentionality . . . Conversely, would it not be more interesting, though difficult and perhaps impossible, to think of responsibility—a summons, that is, requiring a response—as no longer passing, in the last instance, through an ego, an "I think", an intention, an ideal of decidability? Would it not be more "responsible" to try pondering the ground . . . on which the juridico-egological values of responsibility were determined, attained, imposed?'

61 Derrida, 'Force of law: the "mystical foundation of authority"', *Cardozo Law Review*, vol. 11, 1990, pp. 919–1045, at p. 971: 'That justice exceeds law and calculation, that the unpresentable exceeds the determinable cannot and should not serve as an alibi for staying out of juridico-political battles, within an institution or a state or between one institution or state and others. Left to itself, the incalculable and giving (*donatrice*) idea of justice is always very close to the bad, even to the worst for it can always be reappropriated by the most perverse calculation . . . And so incalculable justice requires us to calculate'. For a fuller discussion of the implications of Derrida's argument see, of course, Drucilla Cornell, *The Philosophy of the Limit*. See also John D. Caputo, 'Hyperbolic justice: deconstruction, myth and politics', *Research in Phenomenology*, vol. XXI, 1991, pp. 3–20

62 Jacques Derrida, 'The politics of friendship', *Journal of Philosophy*, vol. 85, 1988, pp. 632–644, at p. 641

63 Drucilla Cornell, 'The philosophy of the limit, systems theory and feminist legal reform', *New England Law Review*, vol. 26, Spring 1992, pp. 783–804, at p. 80

64 Dennis E. Curtis and Judith Resnik, 'Images of justice', *The Yale Law Journal*, vol. 96, 1987, pp. 1727–1772, at 1758–9

Chapter 2 Spinoza, law and responsibility

* I would like to thank Paul Patton and Genevieve Lloyd for their helpful comments on this chapter and many conversations on these issues. This chapter first appeared in my collection of essays *Imaginary Bodies: Ethics, Power and Corporeality*, Routledge, New York and London, 1996

1   G. Deleuze *Spinoza: Practical Philosophy*, trans. Robert Hurley, City Lights Books, San Francisco, 1988, p. 126, emphasis added
2   *A Political Treatise*, p. 292. There are several translations of Spinoza's works. The best is *The Collected Works of Spinoza*, trans. E. Curley, Princeton University Press, New Jersey, 1985. Unfortunately only Volume I has appeared to date. References to the *Ethics* and *Treatise on the Emendation of the Intellect* will be to Curley's editon. References to *A Theologico-Political Treatise* and *A Political Treatise* will be from *Works of Spinoza*, Vol II, trans. R. H. M. Elwes, Dover Publications, New York, 1951. I have used both editions for Spinoza's correspondence
3   *The Passions of the Soul*, Article VI, in *The Philosophical Works of Descartes*, Vol. I, trans. E. S. Haldane and G. R. T. Ross, Cambridge University Press, 1970, p. 333
4   See Descartes' letter to Princess Elisabeth in A. Kenny ed, *Descartes: Philosophical Letters*, Clarendon Press, Oxford, 1970, p. 141
5   *Ethics*, Part II, Lemma 7, Scholium
6   *Ethics*, Part II, Postulates on the Body, IV
7   *Ethics*, Part II, Propositions 11 & 13
8   H. Jonas, 'Spinoza and the theory of organism' in M. Grene, *Spinoza: A Collection of Critical Essays*, University of Notre Dame Press, Notre Dame, Indiana, 1979, p. 271
9   *Ethics*, Part III, Proposition 2
10 *Ethics*, Part V, Preface
11 *Ethics*, Part II, Proposition 49; see also Letter II to Oldenburgh, where Spinoza writes: 'will is merely an entity of the reason.' in Elwes, p. 279
12 *Ethics*, Part III Preface
13 G. Deleuze, *Spinoza: Practical Philosophy*, City Lights Books, San Francisco, 1988, p. 102
14 *Ethics*, Part II, Proposition 13, Scholium
15 Spinoza defines joy as the '. . . passage from a lesser to a greater perfection.' *Ethics*, Part. III, Definition of the Affects, II
16 Spinoza defines sadness as the '. . . passage from a greater to a lesser perfection.' Definition of the Affects, III
17 G. Deleuze, *Expressionism in Philosophy: Spinoza*, Zone Books, New York, 1990, p. 280
18 From *Discourse on Method*, quoted in J. Blom, *Descartes: His Moral Philosophy and Psychology*, Harvester Press, Sussex, 1978, p. 43
19 *A Political Treatise*, p. 313
20 ibid., p. 294. See also, p. 297; and *Ethics*, Part IV, Appendix, VII & IX

21 *A Political Treatise*, p. 297
22 *A Theologico-Political Treatise*, p. 208
23 *A Political Treatise*, p. 299
24 For an excellent and systematic account of Spinoza's views on law
    see: G. Belaief, *Spinoza's Philosophy of Law*, Mouton, The Hague,
    1971. I will not discuss ceremonial law here as it is not relevant to
    the issues at hand. However, see Belaief, Part II, B, pp. 38–41
25 *Ethics*, Part II
26 *A Theologico-Political Treatise*, p. 44
27 The example which Spinoza most commonly employs to illustrate the
    nature of this confusion is the 'story of the first man': Adam's
    'disobedience' to the 'command' not to eat of the tree of the knowl-
    edge of good and evil. (Curiously, Eve is never mentioned in this
    connection.) Spinoza uses this example in the famous 'letters on evil'
    to Blijenbergh; and again, in *A Theologico-Political Treatise*, p. 62f.;
    and in the *Ethics* Part IV, Proposition 68. In Letter 19 to Blijenbergh,
    Spinoza writes: 'The prohibition to Adam, then, consisted only in
    this: God revealed to Adam that eating of that tree caused death, just
    as he also reveals to us through the natural intellect that poison is
    deadly to us.', in Curley, p. 360. On these letters see: G. Deleuze,
    Spinoza: Practical Philosophy, City Lights, 1988, pp. 30–43, and
    G. Deleuze, *Expressionism in Philosophy: Spinoza*, Zone Books,
    New York, 1990, pp. 247–48
28 G. Belaief, *Spinoza's Philosophy of Law*, Mouton, The Hague, 1971,
    pp. 41–42
29 As Spinoza writes, in *A Political Treatise*, '. . . liberty . . . does not
    take away the necessity of acting, but supposes it', pp. 295–96
30 *A Theologico-Political Treatise*, p. 58, p. 59
31 The notion of an arbitrary will is consistently rejected at all levels of
    Spinoza's thought: God or Nature is not separate from that which it
    wills, human being does not will separately from its various under-
    standings, and the sovereign can not will laws separately from its
    understanding of what the civil body must affirm in order to persevere
    in its existence
32 H. Cairns, *Legal Philosophy from Plato to Hegel*, John Hopkins,
    Baltimore, 1949, p. 289. See also, G. Belaief, *Spinoza's Philosophy
    of Law*, Mouton, The Hague, 1971, pp. 25–26
33 *A Political Treatise*, p. 310
34 G. Belaief, *Spinoza's Philosophy of Law*, Mouton, The Hague, 1971,
    p. 25, capitals in original
35 G. Belaief, *Spinoza's Philosophy of Law*, Mouton, The Hague, 1971,
    p. 52. See also, A. Negri, *The Savage Anomaly*, trans. Michael Hardt,
    University of Minnesota Press, Minneapolis, 1991, where he insists
    on the distinction in Spinoza's texts between *potentia* and *potestas*—a
    distinction usually lost in English translations, though not in French
    and Italian—in terms of 'constitution' versus 'command'
36 *A Political Treatise*, p. 311
37 ibid., p. 312

38 G. Belaief, *Spinoza's Philosophy of Law,* Mouton, The Hague, 1971, p. 104
39 ibid., p. 106
40 ibid., p. 77
41 ibid., p. 83
42 Spinoza makes his views on this clear in *A Theologico-Political Treatise* where he writes that people are distinguishable '. . . by the difference of their language, their customs and their laws; while from the two last—ie. customs and laws,—it may arise that they have a peculiar disposition, a peculiar manner of life, and peculiar prejudices.' p. 232
43 Y. Yovel in *Spinoza and Other Heretics: The Adventures of Immanence,* Princeton University Press, New Jersey, 1989, draws attention to this point in the following terms: 'What to do about the multitude is the general problem underlying [*A Theologico-Political Treatise*] and spelled out in both its parts. The general answer is to reshape the cognitive and emotive power governing the multitude—what Spinoza calls *imaginatio*—as an external imitation of *ratio,* using obedience to authority in order to enforce and institutionalise the results.' p. 14. However, because Yovel fails to grant any notion of historical growth—either intensive or extensive—to Spinoza's notion of reason, he fails to see that *A Theologico-Political Treatise* concerns itself with that which the *Ethics* assumes: the *development* of a rational community
44 See *Ethics*, Part IV, Proposition 67, Demonstration
45 As Spinoza observes in *A Political Treatise,* '. . . rewards of virtue are granted to slaves, not freemen', p. 382
46 This question is the specific focus of my paper 'Lust, love and freedom of soul (in a political frame)' in my book *Imaginary Bodies and their Practices: Gender, Body, Desire,* Routledge, London and New York, forthcoming
47 *A Theologico-Political Treatise*, pp. 258–59; see also *Emendation of the Intellect*, paras 14 & 15
48 Y. Yovel, *Spinoza and Other Heretics: The Adventures of Immanence,* Princeton University Press, New Jersey, 1989, p. 6
49 ibid., p. 177
50 For example, that proposed by A. MacIntyre in *After Virtue: A Study in Moral Theory*, Duckworth, London, 1985, second edition. Note the role of his notion of a practice and the centrality of practices to tradition and virtue; for example, p. 220, pp. 239–40, p. 273. Iris Marion Young offers a cogent account of the oppressive aspects of communitarianism, especially for women, in *Justice and the Politics of Difference*, Princeton University Press, New Jersey, 1990
51 This failure to address structural causes of crime is very apparent in the 'Massie case' in which Darrow defended a man and his mother-in-law in a murder case where the husband shot one of the men allegedly involved in a particularly brutal gang rape of his wife. The case is complex and deserves more careful treatment than I can offer here, but it is important to note that the woman who is raped is all

but 'invisible' in Darrow's long defence speech. Further, in a postscript to the case, Darrow is credited with talking the 'family' (presumably, this included the wife?) out of pressing charges against the other men allegedly involved in the gang rape. See *Attorney for the Damned*, ed. A. Weinberg, MacDonald, London, 1957

52 Letter 25 to Oldenburg, in Elwes, p. 306
53 Letter 42 to Tschirnhausen, in Elwes, p. 392
54 As reported in *Sydney Morning Herald*, 30 October 1993
55 ibid.
56 See C. Pateman, *The Sexual Contract*, Polity Press, Cambridge, 1988 for an excellent and controversial reading of the marriage contract
57 *Ethics*, Part IV, Appendix, XIV—XVI
58 S. Freud 'The Ego and the Id' in *The Standard Edition of the Complete Psychological Works of Sigmund Freud*, trans. J. Strachey, London, Hogarth Press, 1978, Vol. XIX, p. 45
59 S. Freud 'Notes upon a case of obsessional neurosis', ibid., p. 176
60 On this phenomenon, see B. Massumi 'Everywhere you want to be: introduction to fear', in *The Politics of Everyday Fear,* (ed) B. Massumi, University of Minnesota Press, Minneapolis, 1993, pp. 4–5

Chapter 3   Mabo, difference and the body of the law

* I am grateful for helpful comments by Moira Gatens and Karin Emerton on earlier drafts of this chapter. This case is reported in 107 ALR 1 and 66 ALJR 408. All references in this paper are to page numbers in the ALR text published in book form as *The Mabo Decision,* with a commentary by R.H. Bartlett, Butterworths, Sydney, 1993

1 ibid., p. 82
2 Ibid., p. 27
3 ibid., p. 27
4 ibid., pp. 16, 27. See *Attorney-General v Brown* (1847) 1 Legge 312. Other cases in this series include *Cooper v Stuart* (1889) 14 App Cas 286; *Williams v Attorney-General (NSW),* (1913) 16 CLR 404; *Randwick Corp v Rutledge* (1959) 102 CLR 54; *New South Wales v Commonwealth,* (1975) 135 CLR 337
5 *The Mabo Decision,* p. 18
6 *Milirrpum v Nabalco Pty Ltd,* (1971) 17 FLR, 141–294
7 *The Mabo Decision,* p. 41
8 ibid., pp. 31, 34
9 ibid., p. 33
10 ibid., p. 34
11 F. Brennan, '*Mabo* and the Racial Discrimination Act', *The Sydney Law Review*, vol. 15, no. 2, p. 220
12 With regard to Australian history, see especially Henry Reynolds, *The Other Side of the Frontier*, Penguin, Ringwood, Vic., 1983 and *The Law of the Land*, Penguin, Ringwood, Vic., 1987
13 F. Nietzsche, 'On the uses and disadvantages of history for life', in

Untimely Meditations, translated by R.J. Hollingdale, Cambridge University Press, Cambridge, 1983, p. 60

14 Gilles Deleuze suggests that societies may be regarded as particular solutions to the fundamental problem of sociability in *Difference and Repetition*, translated by Paul Patton, Athlone Press, London, 1994, pp. 186, 206–8

15 *The Mabo Decision*, p. 41. See also Barbara Hocking 'Aboriginal law does now run in Australia', *The Sydney Law Review*, vol. 15, no. 2, 1993, p. 197

16 17 FLR, pp. 272–3

17 Joan W. Scott, 'Deconstructing equality versus difference: or, the uses of poststructuralist theory for feminism', *Feminist Studies*, vol. 14, no. 1, 1988, p. 44

18 Iris Marion Young spells out the case for such group specific rights in the context of defending an emancipatory politics of difference, in *Justice and the Politics of Difference*, Princeton University Press, Princeton NJ, 1990, pp. 163–191

19 M.J. Detmold, 'Law and difference: reflections on *Mabo*'s case', *The Sydney Law Review*, vol. 15, no. 2, 1993, pp. 159, 164

20 R.H. Bartlett, '*Mabo*: another triumph for the common law', *The Sydney Law Review*, vol. 15, no. 2, 1993, p. 178

21 G.A. Moens, 'Mabo and political policy-making by the High Court', *Mabo: A Judicial Revolution*, eds M.A. Stephenson and S. Ratnapala, University of Queensland Press, Brisbane, 1993, pp. 48–62

22 Gilles Deleuze and Felix Guattari *A Thousand Plateaus*, trans. Brian Massumi, University of Minnesota Press, Minneapolis, 1987, p. 9

23 R.H. Bartlett, '*Mabo*: another triumph for the common law', p. 179

24 *The Mabo Decision*, p. 28

25 ibid., pp. 18, 29

26 ibid., p. 19

27 *Dietrich v The Queen*, (1992) cited in F. Brennan, '*Mabo* and the Racial Discrimination Act', *The Sydney Law Review*, vol. 15, no. 2, 1993, p. 221

28 *The Mabo Decision*, p. 33

29 ibid., p. 32

30 8 Wheat 543 (1832). Other US Supreme Court cases in which the concept of native title was affirmed include *Worcester v Georgia*, 6 Pet 515 (1832); *United States v Cook*, 86 US 591 (1873); *Cramer v United States*, 261 US 219 (1922)

31 Cited in R.H. Bartlett, '*Mabo*: another triumph for the common law', p. 182

32 In *Trident General Insurance Co v McNiece Pty Ltd* (1988) 165 CLR 107, a case in which the High Court overturned the common law rule of privity of contract, Mason CJ and Wilson J asserted that 'Regardless of the layers of sediment which may have accumulated, we consider that it is the responsibility of this Court to reconsider in appropriate cases common law rules which operate unsatisfactorily and unjustly'. Cited in D. Solomon, *The Political Impact of the High Court*, Allen & Unwin, Sydney, 1992, pp. 187–8

33 *The Mabo Decision*, p. 65

34 ibid., p. 144

35 *Amodu Tijani v Secretary, Southern Nigeria* (1921) 2 AC 399. The judgement in *Amodu Tijani* referred to Canadian cases which recognised a native title to traditional homelands on the part of Indian tribes, including *St Catherine's Milling and Lumber Co v R* (1888) 14 App Cas 46; *Attorney-General for Quebec v Attorney-General for Canada* [1921] 1 AC 401. The approach adopted in this case was subsequently endorsed in *Adeyinka Oyekan v Musendiku Adele* (1957) 1 WLR at 880; [1957] 2 All ER, at 788

36 *The Mabo Decision*, pp. 35, 62, 152

37 ibid., p. 51

38 ibid., p. 42

39 These remarks were made in discussion at the *Martung Upah Indigenous Conference*, organised by the Aboriginal and Islander Commission of The Australian Council of Churches, Wesley College, University of Sydney, 5–11 December 1993

40 M.J. Detmold, 'Law and difference: reflections on *Mabo*'s case', p. 166

41 Hugh Morgan is Managing Director of Western Mining Corporation and the author of several speeches critical of the *Mabo* judgement: see his 'Mabo and Australia's future', *Quadrant*, no. 302, December, 1993, pp. 63–7. Geoffrey Blainey is an historian who has also criticised the High Court decision and the Government's response in speeches reported in the press: see the *Sydney Morning Herald*, 10 November 1993. Michael Mansell is a lawyer with the Tasmanian Aboriginal Legal Service: see his 'The Court gives an inch but takes another mile', *Aboriginal Law Bulletin*, vol. 2, no. 57, 1993, pp. 4–6; 'Australians and Aborigines and the *Mabo* decision: just who needs whom the most?', *The Sydney Law Review*, vol. 15, no. 2, 1993, pp. 168–77

42 Jacques Derrida, *Dissemination*, translated by Barbara Johnson, University of Chicago Press, Chicago, 1981, pp. 63–171

43 Council for Aboriginal Reconciliation, *Making Things Right: Reconciliation After the High Court's Decision on Native Title*, A.J. Law, Commonwealth Government Printer, Canberra, 1993, p. 7

44 The Hon. P. J. Keating, 'The H.V. Evatt Lecture—new visions for Australia', unpublished typescript, Evatt Foundation, Sydney, 1993, p. 6

45 Noel Pearson, the *Australian*, 8 June 1993. Similar remarks occur in the *First Report 1993* of the Aboriginal and Torres Strait Islander Social Justice Commission, AGPS, Canberra 1993, pp. 26–30. The Commissioner, Michael Dodson, argues that the 'denial, loss or impairment of hunting, fishing and harvesting rights amounts to a denial, loss or impairment of the opportunity to maintain and participate in the enjoyment and exercise of indigenous cultural life and to transmit culture from one generation to another'. As such, it is 'a denial of human rights'. See *First Report 1993*, p. 29

46 See S. Gray, 'Wheeling, dealing and deconstruction: Aboriginal art

and the land post-*Mabo*', *Aboriginal Law Bulletin*, vol. 3, no. 63, 1993, pp. 10–2; and K. Puri, 'Copyright protection for Australian Aborigines in the light of Mabo, *Mabo: A Judicial Revolution*, eds M.A. Stephenson and S. Ratnapala, pp. 132–64
47   *The Mabo Decision*, pp. 51, 58
48   ICJ 1975, 12
49   *The Mabo Decision*, p. 28
50   Garth Nettheim, 'The consent of the natives: *Mabo* and indigenous political rights', *The Sydney Law Review*, vol. 15, no. 2, 1993, p. 228
51   Noel Pearson, 'Reconciliation: to be or not to be—separate Aboriginal nationhood or Aboriginal self-determination and self-government within the Australian nation?', *Aboriginal Law Bulletin*, vol. 3, no. 61, 1993, p. 15

Chapter 4   Law before Auschwitz

1   S. Gilman, *The Jew's Body*, Routledge, New York and London, 1991
2   A. Dundes, ed, *The Blood Libel Legend*, University of Wisconsin Press, Madison, 1991
3   J. P. Sartre, *Réflexions sur la question juive*, Gallimard, Paris, 1954
4   S. J. Gould, *The Mismeasure of Man*, W. W. Norton & Co, New York, 1981; R. Proctor, *Racial Hygiene*, Harvard University Press, Cambridge and London, 1988
5   A. Bein, 'The Jewish parasite', *Leo Baeck Institute Year Book*, vol. 9, 1964, p. 3
6   P. Pulzer, *The Rise of Political Anti-Semitism in Germany and Austria*, (rev. ed.), Harvard University Press, 1988
7   J. Thompson, *Studies in the Theory of Ideology*, University of California Press, Berkeley and Los Angeles, 1984, pp. 205–231
8   M. Burleigh and W. Wipperman, *The Racial State: Germany 1933–1945*, Cambridge University Press, Cambridge and New York, 1994
9   I. Müller, *Hitler's Justice*, Harvard University Press, Cambridge, 1991, pp. 90–119
10   U. Adam, 'Persecution of Jews: bureaucracy and authority in the totalitarian state', *Leo Baeck Institute Year Book*, vol. 23, 1978, p. 139; U. Büttner, 'The Persecution of Christian Jewish Families in the Third Reich', *Leo Baeck Institute Year Book*, vol. 34, 1989, p. 267;
11   J. Noakes, 'The development of Nazi policy towards the German Jewish "Mischlinge" 1933–1945', *Leo Baeck Institute Year Book*, vol. 34, 1989, p. 291
12   R. Proctor, *Racial Hygiene* pp. 95–117
13   ibid., pp. 177–222
14   Y. Arad, *Belzec, Sobibor, Treblinka: The Operation Reinhard Death Camps*, Indiana University Press, Bloomington and Indianapolis, 1987
15   J. Ringelheim, 'The unethical and the unspeakable: women and the Holocaust', *Simon Wiesenthal Center Annual*, vol. 1, 1984, p. 69;

'Women and the Holocaust: A Reconsideration of Research', *Signs*, vol. 10, 1985, p. 741

16 J. Halberstam, 'From Kant to Auschwitz', *Social Theory and Practice*, vol. 14, 1989, pp. 41, 51

17 *Buck v Bell*, 274 U. S. 200 (1927)

18 Müller, *Hitler's Justice*, p. 95

19 F. Gény, *Méthode d'Interprétation et Sources en Droit Privé*, Louisiana State Law Institute trans., Baton Rouge, 1963; F. Walton, *The Scope and Interpretation of the Civil Code of Lower Canada*, M. Tancelin ed., Butterworths, Toronto, 1980

20 P. Friedman, 'The Jewish badge and the yellow star in the Nazi era', *Historia Judaica*, vol. 17, 1955, p. 41

21 E. Kedourie, 'Introduction', *Spain and the Jews* (E. Kedourie, ed.), Thames and Hudson, London and New York, 1992, pp. 8–32; M. Garber, *Vested Interests*, Routledge, New York and London, 1992, pp. 224–233

22 J. Améry, *At Minds's Limits*, Schocken Books New York, 1990, pp. 82–101

23 J.F. Lyotard, *Heidegger and 'the Jews'*, University of Minnesota Press, 1990

24 Améry, *At Minds's Limits*, p. 89

25 J. Habermas, *The Theory of Communicative Action Vol. 1: Reason and the Rationalization of Society*, Beacon Press, Boston, 1984

26 J. Schlegel, 'Notes towards an intimate opinionated and affectionate history of the conference on Critical Legal Studies', *Stanford Law Review*, vol. 36, 1984, p. 391; G. Peller, 'The metaphysics of American law', *California Law Review*, vol. 73, 1985, p. 1151

27 S. Cohen, 'Human rights and crimes of the state: the culture of denial', *Australian and New Zealand Journal of Criminology*, vol. 26, 1993, p. 97, but see A. Freeman and E. Mensch, 'The politics of virtue', *Georgia Law Review*, vol. 25, 1991, p. 923, and N. Christie, *Crime Control As Industry*, Routledge, London and New York, 1993

28 J. Derrida, 'Force of law: the mystical foundation of authority', *Cardozo Law Review*, vol. 11, 1990, p. 919

29 J.-F. Lyotard, *The Postmodern Explained to Children*, Power Publications, Sydney, 1992, pp. 30 & 31

30 Lyotard, *Heidegger and 'the Jews'*, P. Lacoue-Labarthe, *Heidegger, Art and Politics*, Basil Blackwell Ltd., Oxford and Cambridge, Mass., 1990

31 J. F. Lyotard, *The Différend*, University of Minnesota Press, Minneapolis, 1988

32 ibid., p. 8

33 Lyotard, *Heidegger and 'the Jews'*, p. 25

34 G. Wellers, 'The existence of gas chambers: the number of victims and the Korherr Report' in *The Holocaust and the Neo-Nazi Mythomania*, S. Klarsfeld ed., The Beate Klarsfeld Foundation, New York, 1978, p. 106

35 M. Amis, *Time's Arrow*, Penguin, London & New York 1991

36 Halberstam, 'From Kant to Auschwitz'

37 Z. Bauman, *Modernity and the Holocaust*, Cornell University Press, Ithaca, 1991, p. 89
38 Reich Entailed Farm Law, 1933
39 P. Lacoue-Labarthe & J.L. Nancy, 'The Nazi myth', *Critical Inquiry*, vol. 16, 1990, p. 291
40 Lyotard, *Heidegger and 'the Jews'*, p. 70
41 Derrida, 'Force of Law', p. 1040
42 ibid., p. 1011
43 J. Derrida, *Of Spirit: Heidegger and the Question*, University of Chicago Press, Chicago and London, 1989
44 Derrida, 'Force of law', p. 1035
45 ibid., p. 1042

Chapter 5 Of pleasure and property

* A longer version of this chapter first appeared in *Diacritics*; E. Povinelli, 'Sexual Savages/Sexual Sovereignty: Australian Colonial Texts and the Postcolonial Politics of Nationalism', *Diacritics*, Spring/Summer 1994, vol. 24, nos 1–2

1 W. Tench, *Narrative of the Expedition to Botany Bay with an Account of New South Wales*, Swords, London, 1789, p. 24
2 ibid
3 ibid, p. 25. Tench's use of a lower class (criminal) boy's bottom to substitute for a face of greeting can be aligned with what Allan White has described as the 'plundering of ethnographic material' at the very moment that an indigenous European tradition of carnival is being repressed. See A. White, 'Bourgeoisie Hysteria and the Carnivalesque', in *Politics and Poetics of Transgression*, eds P. Stallybrass & A. White, Cornell Univerity Press, Ithaca, NY, 1986, p. 171
4 Such as A. Phillip, *The Voyage of Governor Phillip to Botany Bay with an Account of the Establishment of Port Jackson and Norfolk Island*, John Stockdale, London, 1789; J. Collins, *An Account of the English Colony in New South Wales*, Strahan, London, 1802; G. Barrington, *A Voyage to New South Wales with a Description of the Country, the Manners, Customs, Religion, etc. of the Natives in the Vicinity of Botany Bay*, Stewart, Philadelphia, 1800; W. Tench, *Narrative of the Expedition to Botany Bay with an Account of New South Wales*, Swords, London, 1789; J. Hunter, *An Historical Journal of the Transactions at Port Jackson and Norfolk Island*, John Stockdale, London, 1793; and J. Grant, *The Narrative of a Voyage of Discovery Performed in His Majesty's Vessel The Lady Nelson, of Sixty Tons Burthen with Sliding Keels in the Years 1800, 1801, and 1802 to New South Wales*, Roworth, London, 1803
5 I discuss these discursive and narrative constructions in E. Povinelli, 'Sexual savages/sexual sovereignty'
6 S. Amussen, *An Ordered Society: Gender and Class in Early Modern England*, Basil Blackwell, New York, 1988; R. Hyam, *Empire and*

242 THINKING THROUGH THE BODY OF THE LAW

Sexuality: The British Experience, St. Martin's Press, New York, 1990; G. Mosse, *Nationalism and Sexuality: Respectability and Abnormal Sexuality in Modern Europe*, H. Fertige, New York, 1985

7 'Opinion of Brennan J.', *Eddie Mabo v The State of Queensland*, F.C. 92/014, 3 June 1992, p. 27

8 See G. Mosse, *Nationalism and Sexuality: Respectability and Abnormal Sexuality in Modern Europe*; A. Parker, M. Russo, D. Sommer, & P. Yaeger, eds, *Nationalisms and Sexualities*, Routledge, New York, 1992

9 See N. Peterson, 'Aboriginal land rights in the Northern Territory of Australia', in *Politics and History in Band Societies*, eds E. Leacock & R. Lee, Cambridge, Cambridge University Press, 1982, pp. 441–462; E. Wilmsen, ed, *We Are Here: Politics of Aboriginal Land Tenure*, University of California Press, Berkeley, 1989; ed, A. An-Na'im, *Human Rights in Cross-Cultural Perspectives*, University of Pennsylvania Press, Philadelphia, 1992

10 N. Williams, *The Yolngu and their Land*, Stanford University Press, Stanford, 1986

11 'Opinion of Brennan J.', pp. 44, 53

12 *Mabo, The High Court Decision on Native Title*, Commonwealth Government Printer, Canberra, 1993, 1

13 'Justice at last for an invisible people', *Manchester Guardian Weekly*, 31 October 1993

14 'Editorial', the *Australian*, 3 September 1993

15 'Opinion of Brennan J.', p. 27

16 *Mabo, The High Court Decision on Native Title*, p. 2

17 *Sydney Morning Herald*, 1 December 1993, quotes Keating as saying, 'Anyone who puts this bill asunder will wear the stain on their soul forever' and 'There is no dirty compromise here. I think it was a very haughty and proper process and one which has brought forward an historic piece of legislation good not just in Australian national terms but good in world terms'

18 See M. Morris, *The Pirate's Fiancee: Feminism Reading Postmodernism*, Verso, London, 1988; D. Hebdige, 'After the Masses', in *New Times: The Changing Face of Politics in the 1990s*, eds S. Hall & M. Jacques, Verso, London, 1991

19 An essay discussing Australia's changing 'identity' as it shifts away from Western Europe and the United States to Asia and the Pacific closes with the paragraph, 'Even as it addresses human rights abroad, Australia is as vulnerable as the United States to criticism of its own human rights and social problems (the treatment of the Aboriginal people, for instance).' 'Australia confronts an identity crisis', *New York Times*, 20 March 1994

20 See N. Williams, *The Yolngu and their Land*

21 H. McRae, G. Nettheim, and L. Beacroft, *Aboriginal Legal Issues*, Law Book Company Ltd, Sydney, 1991, pp. 151–2

22 ibid., pp. 152–4

23 ibid., p. 154; see also B. Trigger, *Whitefella Comin': Aboriginal*

Responses to Colonialism in Northern Australia, Cambridge University Press, Cambridge, 1992
24 'Opinion of Brennan J.' p. 59
25 M. Gumbert, 'Paradigm lost: anthropological models and their effect on Aboriginal land rights', *Oceania*, vol. 52, 1981, pp. 103–123; S. Weaver, 'Struggles of the nation-state to define Aboriginal ethnicity: Canada and Australia', in *Minorities and Mother Country Imagery*, ed G. L. Gold, Social and Economic Papers No. 13, Institute of Social and Economic Research, Memorial University of Newfoundland, Newfoundland, 1984, pp. 182–210; K. Maddock, *Your Land is Our Land, Aboriginal Land Rights*, Penguin, Ringwood, 1983
26 L.R. Hiatt, 'Traditional land tenure and contemporary land claims', in *Aboriginal Landowners: Contemporary Issues in the Determination of Traditional Aboriginal Land Ownership*, ed. L.R. Hiatt, University of Sydney, Sydney, 1984, p. 25
27 See especially, R.M. Berndt & C. H. Berndt, *The World of the First Australians*, Ure Smith, Sydney, 1964; A. Radcliffe-Brown, 'The social Organization of Aboriginal tribes', *Oceania*, vol. 1, 1930–31, pp. 34–63; W.E.H. Stanner, 'Aboriginal territorial organisation: estate, range, domain, and regime', *Oceania*, vol. 36, 1965, pp. 1–26
28 F. Merlan, 'Land, language and social identity in Aboriginal Australia', *Mankind*, vol. 13, no. 2, 1981, p. 135
29 Other authors have noted that the 'orthodox model' fails to account for the 'demographic and political dynamics of Aboriginal land-holding groups' (see I. Keen, 'A question of interpretation: the definiton of 'traditional Aboriginal owners' in the Aboriginal Land Rights (N.T.) Act', in *Aboriginal Landowners, Contemporary Issues in the Determination of Traditional Aboriginal Land Ownership*, ed L.R. Hiatt, University of Sydney, Sydney, 1984, pp. 24–45; M. Gumbert, 'Paradigm lost'; L.R. Hiatt, 'Traditional land tenure and contemporary land claims', pp. 11–23), for non-cognatic methods of affiliation to sites such as conception (A. Hamilton, 'Descended from father, belonging to country: rights to land in the Australian Western Desert', in *Politics and History in Band Societies*, eds E. Leacock & R. Lee, Cambridge University Press, Cambridge, 1982, pp. 85–108; F. Myers, *Pintupi Country, Pintupi Self: Sentiment, Place and Person Among the Western Desert Aborigines*, Smithsonian Institute Press, Washington, D.C., 1986), or for 'the practical relationships between land-using local groups and the larger social system' (ibid, p. 20)
30 See F. Myers, 'Burning the truck and holding the country: Pintupi forms of property and identity', in *We Are Here, Politics of Aboriginal Land Tenure*, ed E. Wilmsen, University of California Press, Berkeley, 1989, pp. 15–42, for an insightful account of Aboriginal notions of 'property'
31 A. Montagu, *Coming into Being Among the Australian Aborigines*, Routledge, London, 1937
32 F. Merlan, 'Australian Aboriginal conception beliefs revisited', *Man*, vol. 21, 1986, pp. 474–493

33 L. Solan, *The Language of Judges*, University of Chicago Press, Chicago, 1993

34 F. Merlan, 'The limits of cultural constructionism: the case of Coronation Hill', *Oceania*, vol. 61, 1991, p. 351

35 'Opinion of Brennan J.', p. 47

36 ibid., p. 48

37 ibid., p. 49

38 See K. Theweleit, *Male Fantasies*, University of Minnesota Press, Minneapolis, 1987. Brennan's own thinking on traditions vacillates significantly. For instance he also claims 'It is immaterial that the laws and customs have undergone *some change* since the Crown acquired sovereignty provided the *general nature of the connection between the indigenous people and the land remains*', 'Opinion of Brennan J.', p. 59, [my emphases]

39 'Opinion of Deane J. and Gaudron J.', *Eddie Mabo v The State of Queensland*, F.C. 92/014, 3 June 1992, p. 101

40 *Mabo, The High Court Decision on Native Title*, pp. 14–15

41 See J. Clifford, *The Predicament of Culture: Twentieth Century Ethnography, Literature, and Art*, Harvard University Press, Cambridge, MA, 1988, p. 11

42 See also A. Hamilton, 'Spoonfeeding the lizards: culture and conflict in central Australia', *Meanjin*, vol. 43, no. 3, 1984, pp. 341–362, and S. Gunew, 'Denaturalizing cultural naturalisms: multicultural readings of "Australia"', in *Nation and Narration*, ed. H. K. Bhabha, Routledge, New York, 1990, pp. 99–120

43 'Opinion of Brennan, J.', p. 27

44 *Australian*, 14 June 1993, [my emphases]

45 M. Foucault, *The History of Sexuality, Volume 1*, Vintage, New York, 1978, p. 88

46 D. Harvey, *The Condition of Postmodernity: An Enquiry into the Origins of Cultural Change*, Blackwell, Cambridge, MA, 1989

47 See also M. Sahlins, 'Cery cery fuckabede', *American Ethnologist*, vol. 20, no. 4, 1993, p. 864

48 N. Dirks, G. Eley, & S. Ortner, eds, *Culture/Power/History*, Princeton University Press, Princeton, NJ, 1994, p. 5

49 P. Ricouer, *Time and Narration, Volume 1*, University of Chicago Press, Chicago, 1984, p. 15

50 'Opinion of Brennan, J.', p. 27

51 See E. LaClau & C. Mouffe, *Hegemony and Socialist Strategy: Towards a Radical Democratic Politics*, Verso, London, 1985; J. Comaroff & J. Comaroff, *Of Revelation and Revolution*, University of Chicago Press, Chicago, 1992

52 See E. Povinelli, *Labor's Lot: The Culture, History and Power of Aboriginal Action*, University of Chicago Press, Chicago, 1993

53 As the owner of a small business on Aboriginal land once put it to me

Chapter 6   Patent pending

* I would like to thank Peter Langmead for the invaluable research he contributed to this chapter

1   *Oxford English Dictionary*, concise edition
2   Marsha L. Montgomery, 'Building a better mouse—and patenting it: altering the patent law to accommodate multicellular organisms', *Case Western Reserve Law Review*, vol. 41, 1990, pp. 231–265
3   The paper is confined to the discussion of 'utility' patents (which are issued for processes, machines, manufactures, and compositions of matter) as opposed to 'design' patents or 'plant' patents, which are framed in different terms
4   Robert L. Baechtold, Lawrence S. Perry, Jennifer A. Tegfeldt, Peter Knudsen, Patricia Carson, 'Property rights in living matter: is new law required?' *Denver University Law Review*, vol 68, no. 2 1991, pp. 141–172
5   For a detailed background on the legal rulings on the case, which was *Diamond v Chakrabarty*, see Rayan Tai, 'Substantive versus interpretative rulemaking in the United States Patent and Trademark Office: the Federal Circuit Animal Legal Defense Fund decision' *Idea* vol. 32, 1992, pp. 235–249
6   ibid.
7   Recombinant DNA technology involves the insertion of a desired gene of one species into the cells of another species. The host species then aquires the capacity to produce the protein for which the inserted gene is responsible. See for example, Michael S. Greenfield, 'Recombinant DNA technology: a science struggling with the patent law', *Stanford Law Review*, vol. 44, May 1992, pp 1051–1094. Transgenic animals are the outcome of a process called transgenesis. This involves the isolation of a gene from one species and transferring it into the embryonic genetic makeup of another species. See Sue Irvine, 'The patenting of transgenic animals—will it matter at the end of the day?', *Current Developments in Intellectual Property and Trade Practices*, Dec 1990, pp. 6–16, and Elizabeth Joy Hecht, 'Beyond *Animal Legal Defense Fund v Quigg*: the controversy over transgenic animal patents continues', *The American University Law Review*, vol. 41 1992, pp. 1023–1074
8   Articles which discuss such issues include Rebecca Dresser, 'Ethical and legal issues in patenting new animal life', *Jurimetrics Journal*, vol. 28, no. 4 1988, pp. 399–435; Sue Irvine, 'Biotechnology—to patent or not to patent?' *Current Developments in Intellectual Property and Trade Practices*, Feb, 1990, pp. 10–17; Brad Sherman, 'Patent law in a time of change: non-obviousness and biotechnology', *Oxford Journal of Legal Studies*, vol. 10, Summer 1990, pp. 278–287; John Slattery, 'Recent patent law developments affecting biotechnology', *Law Institute Journal*, June 1989, pp. 485–487; William L. Hayhurst, 'Exclusive rights in relation to living things', *Intellectual Property Journal*, June 1991, pp. 171–196

9   For a discussion of the applicability of copyright and patent law to both biotechnology and computer software, see Dan L. Burk, 'Copyrightability of recombinant DNA sequences', *Jurimetrics Journal* Summer 1989, pp 469–532, and 'Can justice keep pace with science?' Gary M. Hoffman and Geoffrey M. Karny, *European Intellectual Property Review*, vol. 10, no. 12 December 1988, pp. 355–358

10 See Giulia Sissa, 'Subtle bodies', trans. Janet Lloyd, in *Fragments For a History of the Human Body*, part three, ed. Michel Feher, Zone, New York, 1989, pp. 132–56

11 For accounts of some of these anomalies, see for example Rosalind F. Atherton, 'Artificially conceived children and inheritance in New South Wales', *The Australian Law Journal*, vol. 60, July 1986, pp. 374–386, and Current Topics, 'The Parpalaix Case and postmortem insemination', *Australian Law Journal*, vol. 58, no. 11 Nov 1984, pp. 627–628

12 For a discussion of the asymmetry between maternal and paternal links see Sissa, 'Subtle bodies', and Rosalind Pollack Pechesky, 'Fetal images: the power of visual culture in the politics of reproduction', *Feminist Studies*, vol. 13, no. 2 1987, pp. 263–292

13 Lewis Hyde discusses patent in terms of these two groups in *The Gift: Imagination and the Erotic Life of Property*, Vintage Books, New York, 1979 pp. 74–84

14 Dr. Jonathan Kind, *Boston Globe*, 3 November 1980, p. 19, quoted in Hyde *The Gift: Imagination and the Erotic Life of Property*, p. 82
    See also Nicholas Wade, 'La Jolla biologists troubled by the Midas factor', *Science* vol. 213, no. 7, August 1981 pp. 623–28

15 *The Gift: Forms and Functions of Exchange in Archaic Societies*, trans. Ian Cunnison, Norton, New York, 1967

16 Jacques Derrida, 'Given time: the time of the king', *Critical Inquiry*, vol. 18 Winter 1992, p. 169

17 Quoted in Montgomery, 'Building a better mouse—and patenting it . . .' p. 240

18 Quoted in Irvine 'The patenting of transgenic animals—will it matter at the end of the day?' p. 7

19 Jacques Derrida, 'Psyche: inventions of the Other', trans. Catherine Porter, in *Reading de Man Reading*, eds Lindsay Waters and Wlad Godzich, Theory and History of Literature vol. 59, University of Minnesota Press, Minneapolis, 1989, p. 28

20 My discussion of the concept of invention in this paper borrows heavily from Derrida, 'Psyche: inventions of the Other' pp. 25–65

21 ibid. p. 28

22 This conclusion is reached by Hugo Delevie, 'Animal patenting: probing the limits of US patent laws', *Journal of Patent & Trademark Office Society*, vol. 74, July 1992, pp. 492–509

23 Lorance L. Greenlee, 'Biotechnology patent law: perspective of the first seventeen years, prospective on the next seventeen years', *Denver University Law Review*, vol. 68, no. 2, 1991 pp. 127–140 (p. 134)

24 Derrida, 'Psyche: inventions of the Other' p. 47

25 Francis Collins, Head of US National Institute of Health, quoted in

Jean Marx 'Genome project plans described', *Science*, vol. 260, 9 April 1993 pp. 152–3. The unsuccessful filing for patents on thousands of gene fragments by the US NIH in 1991 caused immense controversy. The NIH was trying to assert rights in instances where the functions of sequences were unknown. Right to not only the genes but also all possible future uses was being sought. Less broad claims are now being adopted by other groups seeking to patent genes. These claims are restricted to known uses, thus avoiding problems of gene ownership per se. See Christopher Anderson, 'A new model for gene patents?', *Science*, vol. 260, 2 April 1993 p. 23

26 Michel Foucault, *The Birth of the Clinic: An Archeology of Medical Perception*, trans. A. M. Sheridan Smith, Vintage Books, New York, p. 155

27 Derrida, Psyche: inventions of the Other, p. 44

28 Rainer Moufang, 'Patentability of genetic inventions in animals', *International Review of Industrial Property & Copyright Law*, vol. 20, no. 6, Dec 1989, pp. 823–846

29 E. I. du Pont de Nemours & Co

30 See Montgomery, 'Building a better mouse—and patenting it . . .' p. 243

31 See Christopher Anderson 'Researchers win decision on knockout mouse pricing' *Science*, vol. 260, no. 2 April 1993, p. 23

32 Walter Benjamin, 'The work of art in the age of mechanical reproduction' in *Illuminations*, trans. Harry Zohn, Schoken Books, New York, 1968, pp. 217–251

33 Montgomery, 'Building a better mouse—and patenting it . . .' p. 242

34 A comparison between European, US and Australian patent law concerning animals is made by Irvine in 'The patenting of transgenic animals—will it matter at the end of the day?'

35 Montgomery, 'Building a better mouse—and patenting it . . .'

36 See Margaret J. Lane, 'Patenting life: responses of patent offices in the US and abroad', *Jurimentrics Journal,* vol. 32, Fall 1991, pp. 89–100 (p. 96)

37 Hallie Plitman, *21 St. U. L. Rev.* 625, 1991, quoted by Russell H. Walker, 'Patent law—should genetically engineered human beings be patentable?' *Memphis State University Law Review,* vol. 22, 1991 pp. 101–117 (p. 104)

38 See, for example, Robert P. Merges 'Intellectual property in higher life forms: the patent system and controversial technologies. *Maryland Law Review* vol. 47 1988 1051–1075, and Hans Jonas, 'Ethics and biogenetic art' *Social Research*, vol. 52, no. 3, Autumn 1985, pp. 491–504

39 See Walker, 'Patent law—should genetically engineered human beings be patentable?'

40 Michael D. Rivard, 'Towards a general theory of constitutional personhood: a theory of constitutional personhood for transgenic humanoid species', *UCLA Law Review,* vol. 39, 1992 pp. 1425–1510

41 Maurice Merleau-Ponty, 'Working notes' in *The Visible and the*

Invisible, trans. Alphons Lingis, Northwestern University Press, Evanston, 1968, p. 234

42 'Other Selves and the human world' in *The Phenomenology of Perception*, trans. Colin Smith, Routledge & Kegan Paul, London and Henley, 1962, p. 360

43 See 'The intertwining—the chiasm', in *The Visible and the Invisible*, pp. 130–155

44 See Luce Irigaray, 'The invisible of flesh: a reading of Merleau-Ponty, *The Visible and the Invisible*, 'The intertwining—the chiasm', *An Ethics of Sexual Difference*, trans. Carolyn Burke and Gillian C. Gill, Cornell University Press Ithaca, New York, 1993, pp. 151–184; Iris Marion Young, 'Pregnant embodiment: subjectivity and alienation', in *Throwing Like a Girl*, Indiana University Press, Bloomington, 1990, pp. 159–173 and; Judith Butler, 'Sexual ideology and phenomenological description' in The Thinking Muse: Feminism and Modern French Philosophy, eds Jeffner Allen & Iris Marion Young, Indiana University Press, Bloomington, 1990, pp. 85–100

45 Germaine Greer, 'The feminine mistake', *Sydney Morning Herald*, Saturday, May 9, 1992 p. 39

46 Luce Irigaray, 'Why define sexed rights?' in *Je, tu, nous* trans. Alison Martin, Routledge, New York & London, pp. 81–92

47 Luce Irigaray discusses the indeterminacy of the body-medium as the condition of perception in 'The invisible of flesh: a reading of Merleau-Ponty', *The Visible and the Invisible*, 'The intertwining—the chiasm', pp. 151–184

Chapter 7　The gift, sexed body property and the law

* I am grateful to Judith Grbich for her comments on an earlier draft of this chapter

1 The idea that the self owns property in their person, including their body and the products of its labour, is usually attributed to John Locke, *Two Treatise of Government*, P. Laslett (intro), 2nd edition, Cambridge University Press, Cambridge, 1967, 11 s.27, p. 288. While John Stuart Mill takes issue with Locke's contract model of social relations, he does assume Locke's concept of a person in his definition of liberty: 'Over himself, over his own body and mind, the individual is sovereign' in 'On liberty', *Three Essays,* Oxford University Press, 1975 p. 15. For a contemporary version of the idea that autonomy is the capacity of a person, externally related to their body property, to decide how to use this property in their best interests, see D. A. J. Richards, *Sex. Drugs. Death and the Law: An Essay on Human Rights and Decriminalization,* Rowman & Littlefield, Totowa NJ, 1982, p.121. And for a critique of this model of a person see Carole Pateman, *The Sexual Contract*, Polity Press, Cambridge, 1988

2 See Locke, *Two Treatise of Government*, 11 ss. 36 & 54, pp. 292–3 & 304 and Mill, 'On liberty', pp. 16–18. As Russell Scott points out,

the provision that you should not bring harm to yourself places legal limits on the disposal of body property for medical or other purposes. For example, in the United States (and Australia) you cannot consent to being killed. See Russell Scott, *The Body as Property*, Allen Lane, London, 1981, p. 63

3 See Scott, *The Body as Property*, pp. 192–6 for a discussion of the practical and legal problems surrounding the selling of blood in the United States

4 See, for example, Sue Dodds and Karen Jones, 'Surrogacy and autonomy', *Bioethics*, Vol. 3, No. 1, 1989, p. 7.1 single out this particular analysis from the wealth of literature on the topic for its systematic presentation of the most commonly held objections to surrogacy

5 Pateman, *The Sexual Contract*, p. 217

6 See, for example, Dodds and Jones, 'Surrogacy and autonomy', p. 9 and Dr Diana Kikby's submission to the National Bioethics Consultative Committee's Surrogacy Report 1, Commonwealth of Australia, April, 1990, p. 17

7 A notable exception is Carol Pateman whose critique of the surrogacy contract in *The Sexual Contract* is raised in the context of a thoroughgoing critique of contract theory in general. Also Dodds and Jones, to whose critique of surrogacy I have been referring, later modify their arguments against surrogacy to include a wider critique of contract and the idea of the body as property ('Surrogacy and the body as property' in Stephen Darling ed. *Cross Currents: Philosophy in the Nineties*, Flinders University Press, Adelaide, 1991). However, despite the broader application of their criticisms to other contracts I still take issue with these theorists insofar as they locate the source of injustice of the surrogacy contract in the control it is said to secure over women's bodies

8 Maurice Merleau-Ponty, 'The child's relations with others' in *The Primacy of Perception and Other Essays*, ed., J. M. Edie, Northwestern University Press, Evanston, 1964

9 ibid., p. 135

10 ibid., pp. 145–8

11 ibid., p. 151–4

12 Maurice Merleau-Ponty, *The Phenomenology of Perception*, Colin Smith trans., Routledge & Kegan Paul, London, 1962, p. 454

13 Friedrich Nietzsche, *On the Genealogy of Morals*, trans. W. Kaufmann and R. J. Hollingdale, Vintage, New York, 1969, ss. 4, 5 & 8, pp. 62–3 & 70

14 See R. Diprose, 'Nietzsche and the pathos of distance' in ed., P. Patton *Nietzsche, Feminism and Political Theory*, Routledge, London, Allen & Unwin, Sydney, 1993 and R. Diprose, *The Bodies of Women: Ethics Embodiment and Sexual Difference*, Routledge, London, 1994, ch. 5

15 Nietzsche, *Beyond Good and Evil*, trans., R. J. Hollingdale, Penguin, Harmondsworth, 1972, p. 174

16 Nietzsche, *On the Genealogy of Morals*, ss. 9–11, pp. 71–6

17 Merleau-Ponty, 'The child's relations with others', pp. 102–4 & 106

250   THINKING THROUGH THE BODY OF THE LAW

18 Dodds and Jones, 'Surrogacy and autonomy', p. 8 and Christine
    Overall, *Ethics and Human Reproduction*, Allen & Unwin, Winches-
    ter, Mass., 1987, ch. 6
19 Pateman, *The Sexual Contract*, p. 207
20 NBCC, Surrogacy Report 1, pp. 27–8
21 While to many this determination may be better for women than the
    reverse, it tends to trivialise and hide rape. And/or it leads to the
    ludicrous situation exemplified by a manual on sexual conduct at
    Antioch College, Ohio which suggests, according to the *New York
    Times* (reproduced in the *Australian* 6 October 1993, p. 26), that
    'verbal consent should be obtained with every new level of physical
    and/or sexual contact or conduct in any given interaction, regardless
    of who initiates it' and that 'the request for consent must be specific
    to each act'
22 Marcel Mauss, *The Gift: Forms and Functions of Exchange in Archaic
    Societies*, trans. I. Cunnison, Norton Library, New York, 1967
23 ibid., p. 6
24 ibid., p. 10
25 ibid., p. 9
26 Linda Singer, *Erotic Welfare: Sexual Theory and Politics in the Age
    of Epidemic,* eds, J. Butler and M. McGrogan, Routledge, New York,
    1993, p. 94
27 Jacques Derrida, 'Given time: the time of the king', *Critical Inquiry*,
    No. 18, Winter 1992, p. 180
28 ibid., p. 170
29 Drucilla Cornell, *Beyond Accommodation: Ethical Feminism,
    Deconstruction and the Law*, Routledge, New York, 1991, p. 110
30 ibid., pp. 110 & 114
31 Derrida, 'Force of law: the "mystical foundations of authority"',
    Cardozo Law Review, Vol. 11, Nos 5–6, 1990, p. 955

Chapter 8 The taxpayer's body

* I would like to thank Gillian Hewitson, Ian Duncanson and Fiona
Mackie of LaTrobe University for their comments on a draft of this
chapter, and for their support and encouragement. An earlier version of
this chapter was presented at the Canadian Law and Society Conference
at Carleton University, Ottawa, Canada, June, 1993

1 Luce Irigaray, *Marine Lover of Friedrich Nietzsche*, trans. Gillian C.
   Gill, Columbia University Press, New York, 1991, pp. 32, 33
2 Gayatri Chakravorty Spivak, 'Feminism and deconstruction, again:
   negotiating with unacknowledged masculinism' in *Between Feminism
   and Psychoanalysis*, ed. Teresa Brennan, Routledge, London, 1989,
   p. 216
3 Paul Ricoeur, 'Imagination in discourse and in action' in *Rethinking
   Imagination*, eds Gillian Robinson and John Rundell, Routledge,
   London and New York, 1994, p. 118. Ricoeur states that his devel-

opment of a general theory of imagination is part of a wider
investigation of which he earlier 'gave the ambitious title of the
"Poetics of Volition"'

4 Philipa Rothfield 'Backstage in the theatre of representation' *Arena*
vol. 99/100, 1992, pp. 98–111; Vicki Kirby 'Corporeal habits:
addressing essentialism differently' *Hypatia*, vol. 6(3), pp. 4–24; Isabel
Karpin 'Reimagining maternal selfhood: transgressing body boundaries and the law', *Australian Feminist Law Journal*, vol. 2, 1994,
pp. 36–62; Roxanne Mykitiuk 'Fragmenting the body', *Australian
Feminist Law Journal*, vol. 2, 1994, pp. 63–98

5 Elizabeth Grosz 'Bodies and knowledges: feminism and the crisis of
reason', in *Feminist Epistemologies*, eds Linda Alcoff and Elizabeth
Potter, Routledge, New York, 1993, pp. 187–215

6 Michel Foucault *The Order of Things*, Tavistock, Bristol, 1970

7 Judith Grbich 'The tax unit debate revisited: notes on the critical
resources of a feminist revenue law scholarship', *Canadian Journal
of Women and the Law*, vol. 4, 1990–91, pp. 512–538; Judith Grbich
'Writing histories of revenue law: the new productivity research', *Law
in Context*, vol. 11(1), 1993, pp. 57–77; Judith Grbich 'The form of
the tax reform story', (forthcoming)

8 *Income Tax Act* 1895 (Vic)

9 Section 2, *Income Tax Act* 1895 (Vic)

10 Gustav Fechner, *Elements of Psychophysics, vol. 1*, [1860], Holt,
Rinehart and Winston, New York, 1966

11 Thomas G. Beckwith and N. Lewis Buck, *Mechanical Measurements*,
Addison-Wesley Publishing Co., Reading, Mass, 1973, p. 16

12 Ian Hacking *The Taming of Chance*, Cambridge University Press,
Cambridge, 1990, pp. 160–169. Theodore M. Porter *The Rise of
Statistical Thinking 1820–1900*, Princeton University Press, Princeton
NJ, 1986

13 Michel Foucault 'Nietzsche, genealogy, history' in *Language, Counter-
Memory, Practice*, ed. Donald F. Bouchard, Cornell University Press,
Ithaca, 1977, p. 139

14 Richard Jennings *The Natural Elements of Political Economy*, [1855],
Kelley Reprints, New York, 1969

15 Ernest Mach *Contributions to the Analysis of the Sensations*, Open
Court Publishing Co., Chicago, 1897

16 Jennings, *Natural Elements of Political Economy*, p. 112

17 William B. Carpenter *Principles of Human Physiology*, John Chur-
chill, London, 1855, p. 619

18 ibid., p. 616

19 ibid., p. 610

20 Jevons was to argue in 1871 that 'We may approximately measure
the intensity of labour by the amount of physical force undergone in
a certain time, although it is the pain attending that exertion of force
which is the all-important element in Economics', W.S. Jevons, *The
Theory of Political Economy*, [1871], Reprint of 5th edition of 1957,
Kelley Reprints, New York, 1965, p. 204

21 Jennings, *Natural Elements of Political Economy*, p. 209

22 Mach, *Analysis of Sensations*, p. 172
23 These notes on a feminine sexual economy are from Irigaray's essays in, Luce Irigaray *Je, tu, nous: Toward a Culture of Difference*, Routledge, New York, 1993
24 Luce Irigaray, *Je, tu, nous* p. 59
25 'On the maternal order' ibid., pp. 37–44
26 ibid., p. 38
27 Henry T. Buckle, *History of Civilization in England*, [1857], Grant Richards, London, 1903, p. 16
28 ibid., p. 17
29 Mach, *Sensations*, p. 68
30 ibid., p. 79
31 ibid., p. 152
32 ibid., p. 151
33 Gustav Fechner, *Elements of Psychophysics, vol.1*, [1860], Holt, Rinehart and Winston, New York, 1966, p. 60
34 Mach, *Sensations*, pp. v–viii
35 ibid., p. 158
36 ibid., p. 169
37 ibid., p. 171
38 Rom Harre *Personal Being*, Blackwell, Oxford, 1983, p. 185
39 ibid., p. 193
40 Michel Foucault, *The History of Sexuality, Volume I: An Introduction*, Penguin, Harmondsworth, 1979, p. 143
41 ibid.
42 ibid., p. 152
43 ibid., p. 157

Chapter 9 Black man, white woman, irresistible impulse

1 Michel Rosenfeld, 'Deconstruction and Legal Interpretation: Conflict, Indeterminacy and the Temptations of the New Legal Formalism', in Drucilla Cornell, Michel Rosenfeld, David Gray Carlson eds, *Deconstruction and the Possibility of Jutice*, Routledge, New York and London, 1992, p. 175, p. 179
2 Fernand Braudel, *On History*, Fontana, London, 1958, p. 26
3 Peter Goodrich and Yifat Hachamovitch,'Time out of mind: an introduction to the semiotics of the common law' in ed. Peter Fitzpatrick *Dangerous Supplements: Resistance and Renewal in Jurisprudence*, Pluto Press, London, 1991, pp. 174–175
4 Michel Foucault ed. *I, Pierre Riviere, Having Slaughtered My Mother, My Sister and My Brother . . . A Case of Parricide in the 19th Century*, University of Nebraska Press, Lincoln and London, 1975, pp. 272–273
5 Michel Foucault, *The Birth of the Clinic: An Archaeology of Medical Perception*, Tavistock, London, 1973
6 Foucault, *I, Pierre Riviere*

7 Michel Foucault, *Power/Knowledge: Selected Interviews and Other Writings, 1972–77*, Harvester Press, London, 1980, p. 81–82
8 A McHoul and W Grace, *A Foucault Primer: Discourse, Power and the Subject*, Melbourne University Press, Melbourne, 1993, p. 19
9 Michel Foucault, *Discipline and Punish: The Birth of the Prison*, Allen Lane, London, 1977
10 Foucault ed. *I, Pierre Riviere*, p. 215
11 McHoul and Grace, *A Foucault Primer*, p. 20
12 Foucault, *I, Pierre Riviere*, p. 202
13 ibid., p. 285
14 Deborah Cameron and Elizabeth Frazer, *The Lust to Kill*, Polity Press, Cambridge, 1987, pp. xii–xiii
15 Foucault ed., *I, Pierre Riviere*, pp. 205, 206
16 ibid., *p. 208*
17 ibid., p. 209
18 Cameron and Frazer, *The Lust to Kill*, p. xiii
19 Foucault ed., *I, Pierre Riviere*, p. 183
20 ibid., p. 181
21 Cameron and Frazer, *The Lust to Kill*
22 ibid., p. 51
23 ibid., p. 67
24 ibid., p. 68
25 Foucault ed., *I, Pierre Riviere*, p. 148
26 Peter Goodrich, *Reading the Law: A Critical Introduction to Legal Method and Techniques*, Basil Blackwell, Oxford, 1991, p. 174
27 Michel Foucault, 'Politics and the study of discourse' *Ideology and Consciousness*, vol. 3, 1978, pp. 7–26, at 14–15
28 Susan Magarey, Sue Rowley and Susan Sheridan, *Debutante Nation: Feminism Contests the 1890's*, Allen & Unwin, Sydney, 1993, p. xiv
29 ibid., p. xv
30 Claudia Knapman 'Reproducing empire: exploring ideologies of gender and race on Australia's Pacific frontier' in eds, Magarey, Rowley and Sheridan, *Debutante Nation* p. 125
31 See Magarey, Rowley and Sheridan, *Debutante Nation*; Pat Grimshaw, Marilyn Lake, Anne McGrath and Marian Quartly, *Creating a Nation*, McPhee Gribble, Melbourne, 1994
32 Marilyn Lake 'The politics of respectability: identifying the masculinist context' in Magarey, Rowley, and Sheridan eds, *Debutante Nation*
33 Paula Hamilton, 'Domestic dilemmas: representations of servants and employees in the popular press' in ibid.
34 ibid., p. 77
35 Josie Castle and Helen Pringle 'Sovereignty and sexual identity in political cartoons' in ibid., p. 147
36 Castle and Pringle, 'Domestic dilemmas', p. 147
37 Marilyn Lake, in *Debutante Nation*
38 Anne Summers, *Damned Whores and God's Police: The Colonization of Women in Australia*, Penguin, Melbourne, 1975
39 Colin Mercer, 'Regular imaginings: the newspaper and the nation' in eds, Tony Bennett, Pat Buckridge, David Carter and Colin Mercer

Celebrating the Nation: A Critical Study of Australia's Bicentenary, Allen & Unwin, Sydney, 1992, pp. 26–46, p. 28
40 ibid., p. 27
41 Terry Threadgold, 'Stories of race and gender: an unbounded discourse' in eds D. Birch and L.M. O'Toole, *Functions of Style*, Pinter, London and New York, 1987, pp. 169–204
42 *The Sydney Mail*, November 3, 1900
43 Knapman, in *Debutante Nation*
44 ibid., p. 135
45 Castle and Pringle, in *Debutante Nation*, p. 147
46 *Sydney Morning Herald*, 27 July 1900
47 Cameron and Frazer, *The Lust to Kill*, p. 15
48 ibid.
49 *Sydney Morning Herald*, 27 July 1900
50 ibid.
51 Cameron and Frazer, *The Lust to Kill*
52 Frank Clune, *Jimmy Governor*, Horwitz Publications, London, 1959
53 Thomas Keneally, *The Chant of Jimmie Blacksmith*, Fontana Collins Australia, 1972, 1978
54 Bill Hornadge ed. *Old Dubbo Gaol*, Old Dubbo Gaol Restoration Committee, Dubbo NSW, 1974
55 S.G. Ellis, *The Breelong Tragedy*, Fitzpatrick family papers, August 1900
56 Frank Clune, *Jimmy Governor*, p. 27
57 ibid., p. 25
58 ibid., p. 25
59 ibid., p. 30
60 ibid., p. 52
61 Paula Hamilton, 'Domestic dilemmas' in Magarey, Rowley and Sheridan, *Debutante Nation*
62 S.G. Ellis, *The Breelong Tragedy*
63 Clune, *Jimmy Governor*, p. 52
64 ibid.
65 *Sydney Morning Herald*, Friday 23 November 1900, p. 7
66 ibid.
67 ibid.
68 ibid.
69 Clune, *Jimmy Governor*, p. 10
70 Keneally, *The Chant of Jimmy Blacksmith*, p. 177
71 Goodrich and Hachamovitch, 'Time out of mind' in ed. Fitzgerald *Dangerous Supplements*, pp. 159, 160

Chapter 10 The dangerous individual and the social body

* Since I originally wrote this, the case of the Menendez brothers has been decided. In each case, there was a hung jury

1 *The American Heritage*, p. 88

2 Susan Bordo, '"Material girl": the effacements of postmodern culture' *Michigan Quarterly Review,* Fall 1990, p. 692
3 Tristram Hodgkinson, *Expert Evidence: Law and Practice* (Sweet & Maxwell) London, 1990, p. 5
4 Thomas Maeder, *Crime and Madness: The Origins and Evolution of the Insanity Defense* (Harper & Row) New York, 1985, p. 108
5 Jean Francois Lyotard, *The Postmodern Condition,* University of Minnesota Press, Minneapolis, 1984, pp. 24–25
6 ibid., p. 23
7 ibid., p. 18
8 Michel Foucault, 'The dangerous individual', in ed. Lawrence D. Kritzman, *Michel Foucault: Politics, Philosophy, Culture* (Routledge) New York and London, 1988, p. 127
9 ibid., p. 134
10 ibid., p. 132
11 ibid., p. 137
12 ibid., p. 135
13 ibid., p. 135
14 ibid., p. 142
15 ibid., p. 127
16 ibid., p. 127
17 ibid., p. 142
18 ibid., p. 149
19 Michel Foucault ed., *I, Pierre Riviere, Having Slaughtered My Mother, My Sister, And My Brother . . . A Case of Parricide in the 19th Century,* University of Nebraska Press, Lincoln and London, 1975, p. 209
20 ibid., p. 207
21 ibid., p. 210
22 ibid., p. xi. Foucault's analysis at times appears to celebrate Riviere's murder, while stopping short of considering the power relations between the murderer and the murdered. What are the power relations in the domestic space?
23 ibid., p. 210
24 Peter W. Low, John Calvin Jeffries Jr., and Richard J. Bonnie, *The Trial of John W. Hinckley Jr: A Case Study in the Insanity Defense* The Foundation Press, Mineola, New York, 1986, p. 44
25 Lincoln Caplan, *The Insanity Defense and the Trial of John W. Hinckley Jr* Dell New York, 1987, pp. 20–21
26 Foucault, *I, Pierre Riviere,* p. 209
27 Foucault, 'The dangerous individual', pp. 130–131
28 Slavoj Zizeck ed., *Everything You Always Wanted to Know About Lacan (But Were Afraid to Ask Hitchcock),* Verso, New York and London, 1992, p. 227
29 Lyotard, *The Postmodern Condition,* p. 20
30 Michel Foucault, *Discipline and Punish: The Birth of the Prison,* Vintage Books, New York, 1979, p. 191
31 Low, Jeffries and Bonnie, *The Trial of John W. Hinckley,* p. 27

32 My analysis of the trial is based on extended experts of the transcript in Low. Caplan's account is also useful
33 Low, Jeffries and Bonnie, *The Trial of John W. Hinckley*, p. 66
34 ibid., p. 57
35 ibid., p. 56
36 ibid., p. 61
37 ibid., p. 95
38 ibid., p. 95
39 Jean Baudrillard, 'Simulacra and simulations', in Mark Poster ed., *Jean Baudrillard: Selected Writings*, Standford University Press, Palo Alto, 1988, p. 168
40 ibid., p. 168
41 Foucault, *I Pierre Riviere*, p. 287

Chapter 11 Do (only) women have bodies

1 Jane Gallop, *Thinking Through the Body*, Columbia University Press, New York, 1988, p. 19
2 See Frances Olsen, 'The family and the market: a study of ideology and legal reform', *Harvard Law Review*, vol. 96, 1983, p. 1457; 'The myth of state intervention in the family', *University of Michigan Journal of Law Reform*, vol. 18, 1985, p. 835
3 Catriona Mackenzie, 'Simone de Beauvoir: philosophy and/or the female body', in eds, Carole Pateman and Elizabeth Gross, *Feminist Challenges: Social and Political Theory*, Northeastern Series in Feminist Theory, New York, 1986, p. 149
4 Luce Irigaray, *Je, tu, nous: Toward a Culture of Difference*, trans., Alison Martin, Routledge, New York and London, 1993, p. 79
5 ibid., p. 59
6 Roxanne Mykitiuk, 'Fragmenting the body', *Australian Feminist Law Journal*, vol. 2, 1994, p. 63
7 Mackenzie, op. cit., p. 150
8 ibid., p. 155
9 ibid., p. 154
10 Judith Butler, *Gender Trouble: Feminism and the Subversion of Identity*, Routledge, New York and London, 1990, p. 12
11 *Reed v Reed*, 404 US 71 (1971)
12 *Adarand Construction v Pena*, 1995 LW 347345 US
13 Butler, op. cit.
14 Duncan Kennedy, 'Sexual abuse, sexy dressing and the eroticization of domination', *New England Law Review*, vol. 26, 1992, p. 1309
15 Charles Dickens, *David Copperfield*, Chapter 12
16 Anonymous, 'Reductionism (notes to amuse a legal writer)', *Yale Journal of Law and the Humanities*, vol. 1, 1988, p. 157
17 Mary Jo Fug, 'A postmodern feminist legal manifesto an unfinished draft', *Harvard Law Review*, vol. 105, 1991–92, p. 1045

Select bibliography

Amery, J. *At the Mind's Limits*, Schocken Books, New York, 1990

Amis, M. *Time's Arrow*, Penguin, London and New York, 1991

Amussen, S. *An Ordered Society: Gender and Class in Early Modern England*, Basil Blackwell, New York, 1988

Anonymous 'Reductionism (Notes to Amuse a Legal Writer)', Series 1, No. 1, *Yale Journal of Law and the Humanities*, vol. 1, 1988, 157

Baechtold, Robert L., Perry Lawrence S., Tegheldt Jennifer A., Knudsen Peter, Carson Patricia, 'Property rights in living matter: is new law required?', *Denver University Law Review*, vol. 68 (2), 1991, pp. 141–172

Baudrillard, Jean 'Simulacra and Simulations', ed. Mark Poster, *Jean Baudrillard: Selected Writing*, Stanford University Press, Palo Alto, 1988.

Bauman, Z. *Modernity and the Holocaust*, Cornell University Press, Ithaca, 1991

Belaief, G. *Spinoza's Philosophy of Law*, Mouton, The Hague, 1971

Benjamin, Walter 'The work of art in the age of mechanical reproduction', in *Illuminations*, trans Harry Zohn, Schoken Books, New York, 1968, pp. 217–251

Blom, J. *Descartes: His Moral Philosophy and Psychology*, Harvester Press, Sussex, 1978

Bordo, Susan '"Material Girl": The Effacements of Postmodern Culture', *Michigan Quarterly Review*, Fall, 1990

Butler, Judith *Gender Trouble: Feminism and the Subversion of Identity*, Routledge, New York and London, 1990

——*Bodies that Matter*, Routledge, New York and London, 1993

Cameron, Deborah and Fraser, Elizabeth *The Lust to Kill*, Polity Press, Cambridge, 1987

Caplan, Lincoln, *The Insanity Defense and the Trial of John W. Hinckley Jr.*, Dell, New York, 1987

Caputo, John D. 'Hyperbolic justice: deconstruction, myth and politics', *Research in Phenomenology*, vol. XXI, 1991, pp. 3–20

Cairns, H. *Legal Philosophy from Plato to Hegel*, John Hopkins, Baltimore, 1949

Castle, Josie and Pringle, Helen 'Sovereignty and sexual identity in political cartoons' eds, Susan Magarey, Sue Rowley and Susan Sheridan, *Debutante Nation: Feminism Contests the 1890s*, Allen & Unwin, Sydney, 1993

Certeau, Michel de 'Des outils pour ecrire le corps', *Traverses*, vol. 14/15, 1979

——'Tools for body writing', trans Paul Foss and Meaghan Morris *Intervention*, vol. 21/22, 1988, pp. 7–11

Christie, N. *Crime Control as Industry*, Routledge, London and New York, 1993

Clune, Frank *Jimmy Governor*, Horwitz Publications, London, 1959

Collins, Patricia *Black Feminist Thought: Knowledge, Consciousness, and the Politics of Empowerment*, Routledge, New York and London, 1991

Comaroff, J. and Comaroff, J. *Of Revelation and Revolution*, University of Chicago Press, Chicago, 1992

Cornell, Drucilla *Beyond Accommodation: Ethical Feminism, Deconstruction and the Law*, Routledge, New York, 1991

——'The good, the right and the possibility of legal interpretation', *The Philosophy of the Limit*, ch. 4, Routledge, New York, 1992

——*The Philosophy of the Limit*, Routledge, New York, 1992

——'The philosophy of the limit, systems theory and feminist legal reform', *New England Law Review*, vol. 26, Spring, 1992, pp. 783–804

Cover, Robert M. 'The Supreme Court 1982 term—forward: Nomos and narrative', *Harvard Law Review*, vol. 97, 1983, pp. 4–68

——'Violence and the word', *Yale Law Journal*, vol. 95, 1986, pp. 1601–1629

Curtis, Dennis E. and Resnik, Judith 'Images of justice' *Yale Law Journal*, vol. 96, 1987, pp. 1727–1772

Danielsen, Dan 'Representing identities: legal treatment of pregnancy and homosexuality', *New England Law Review* vol. 26, 1992

Davis, Tracy *Actresses as Working Women: Their Social Identity in Victorian Culture*, Routledge, New York and London, 1991

de Beauvoir, Simone, *The Second Sex*, ed. and trans. H.M. Parshley, Vintage Books, New York, 1952

Deleuze, Gilles and Felix Guattari *A Thousand Plateaus*, trans. Brian Massumi, University of Minnesota Press, Minneapolis, 1987

Deleuze, Gilles *Spinoza: Practical Philosophy*, trans. Robert Hurley, City Lights Books, San Francisco, 1988

——*Expressionism in Philosophy: Spinoza*, Zone Books, New York, 1990

——*Difference and Repetition*, trans. Paul Patton, Athlone Press, London, 1994

Derrida, Jacques 'Psyche: inventions of the Other', trans. Catherine Porter, in *Reading de Man Reading*, eds Lindsay Waters and Wlad Godzich,

Theory and History of Literature vol. 59, University of Minnesota Press, Minneapolis

——*Of Grammatology*, trans. Gayatri Spivak, Johns Hopkins University Press, Baltimore, 1976

——*Dissemination*, trans. Barbara Johnson, University of Chicago Press, Chicago, 1981

——'The politics of friendship', *Journal of Philosophy*, vol. 85, 1988, pp. 632–644

——*Of Spirit: Heidegger and the Question*, University of Chicago Press, Chicago and London, 1989

——'Force of law: the "mystical foundation of authority"', *Cardozo Law Review*, vol. 11, 1990, pp. 919–1045

——'Given time: the time of the king', *Critical Inquiry*, vol. 18, Winter 1992

——'Mochlos, or, the conflict of faculties', ed. Richard Rand *Logomachia: The Conflict of Faculties*, University of Nebraska Press, Lincoln, 1992

Descarte, R. *The Philosophical Works of Descartes,* vol. 1, trans. E.S. Haldane and G.R.T. Ross, Cambridge University Press, 1970

Dickens, Charles, *David Copperfield*, ch. 12

Diprose, Rosalyn 'Nietzsche and the pathos of distance', in *Nietzsche, Feminism and Political Theory*, ed. Paul Patton, Routledge, London; Allen & Unwin, Sydney, 1993

——*The Bodies of Women: Ethics, Embodiment and Sexual Difference*, Routledge, London, 1994

Dirks, N., Eley, G. and Ortner, S. eds *Culture/ Power/ History*, Princeton University Press, Princeton NJ, 1994

Doane, Mary Ann *Femmes Fatales: Feminism, Film Theory, Psychoanalysis*, Routledge, New York and London, 1991

Dresser, Rebecca, 'Ethical and legal issues in patenting new animal life', *Jurimetrics Journal*, vol. 28 (4), 1988, pp. 399–435

Duclos, Nitya 'Lessons of difference: feminist theory on cultural diversity', *Buffalo Law Review*, vol. 38, 1990, pp. 325

Duncanson, Ian W. 'Legal education and the possibility of critique: an Australian perspective', *Canadian Journal of Law and Society*, vol. 8, 1993, pp. 59–82

——'Broadening the discipline of law', *Melbourne University Law Review*, vol. 19, 1994, pp. 1075–1093

Dworkin, Ronald *Law's Empire*, Fontana Press, London, 1986

Eisenstein, Zillah *The Female Body and the Law*, University of California Press, California, 1988

Engle, Karen 'Female subjects of public international law: human rights and the exotic other female', *New England Law Review* vol. 26, 1992

Feinberg, Joel, and Gross, Hyman eds *Philosophy of Law* (4th ed) Wadsworth Publishing, California, 1991

Fish, Stanley *Doing What Comes Naturally—Change, Thetoric and the Practice of Theory in Literature and Legal Studies*, Duke University Press, Durham, 1989

Foucault, Michel *The Order of Things*, Tavistock, Bristol, 1970

——*The Birth of the Clinic: An Archaeology of Medical Perception*, Tavistock, London, 1973

——ed. *I, Pierre Riviere, Having Slaughtered My Mother, My Sister, and My Brother . . . A Case of Parricide in the 19th Century*, University of Nebraska Press, Lincoln and London, 1975

——'Nietzsche, genealogy, history', in *Language, Counter-Memory, Practice*, ed. Donald J. Bouchard, Cornell University Press, Ithaca, 1977

——*The History of Sexuality. Volume I: An Introduction* trans Robert Hurley, Pantheon, New York, 1978

——'Politics and the study of discourse', *Ideology and Consciousness* vol. 3, 1978, pp. 7–26

——*Discipline and Punish: The Birth of the Prison*, Vintage Books, New York, 1979

——*Power/Knowledge: Selected Interviews and Other Writings. 1972–77*, Harvester Press, London, 1980

——'The dangerous individual', ed. Lawrence D. Kritzman *Michel Foucault: Politics, Philosophy, Culture*, Routledge, New York and London, 1988

——'Clarifications on the question of power', in *Foucault Live—Interviews 1966–84*, Semiotexte, New York, 1989, pp. 179–192

Freud, Sigmund 'The Ego and the Id', in *The Standard Edition of the Complete Psychological Works of Sigmund Freud*, vol. XIX, trans. J. Strachey, London, Hogarth Press, 1978

Friedman, P. 'The Jewish badge and the yellow star in the Nazi era' *Historia Judaica*, vol. 17, 1955

Frug, Mary Joe, 'A postmodern feminist legal manifesto' (an unfinished draft), *Harvard Law Review*, vol. 105 1991–92, 1045

——*Postmodern Legal Feminism*, Routledge, New York and London, 1992

Gallop, Jane *Thinking Through the Body*, Columbia University Press, New York, 1988

Garber, M. *Vested Interests*, Routledge, New York and London, 1992

Gatens, Moira *Imaginary Bodies and their Practices: Gender, Body, Desire*, Routledge, London and New York, forthcoming

Gerth, H.H. and C. Wright Mills eds *From Max Weber—Essays in Sociology*, Routledge, New York, 1991

Gilman, S. *The Jew's Body*, Routledge, New York and London, 1991

Goldfarb, Phyllis 'From the worlds of "others": minority and feminist responses to Critical Legal Studies', *New England Law Review*, vol. 26, 1992, pp. 683–710

Goodrich, Peter *Reading the Law: A Critical Introduction to Legal Method and Techniques*, Basil Blackwell, Oxford, 1991

Goodrich, Peter and Yifat Hachamovitch 'Time out of mind: an introduction to the semiotics of the common law', ed. Peter Fitzpatrick *Dangerous Supplements: Resistance and Renewal in Jurisprudence*, Pluto Press, London, 1991

Gould, Stephen J. *The Mismeasure of Man*, W.W. Norton & Co., New York, 1981

Grbich, Judith 'The tax unit debate revisited: notes on the critical resources of a feminist revenue law scholarship', *Canadian Journal of Women and the Law*, vol. 4, 1990–91, pp. 512–538

——'The body in legal theory', eds Martha Fineman and Nancy Thomadsen *At the Boundaries of Law: Feminism and Legal Theory*, Routledge, New York, 1991

——'Writing histories of revenue law: the new productivity research', *Law in Context*, vol. 11, no. 1, 1993, pp. 57–77

Grimshaw, Pat, Lake, Marilyn, McGrath, Anne and Quartly, Marian *Creating a Nation*, McPhee Gribble, Melbourne, 1994

Greenfield, Michael S. 'Recombinant DNA technology: a science struggling with the patent law', *Stanford Law Review*, vol. 44, May 1992, pp. 1051–1094

Grosz, Elisabeth 'Bodies and knowledges: feminism and the crisis of reason', in *Feminist Epistemologies*, eds Linda Alcoff and Elisabeth Potter, Routledge, New York, 1993, pp. 187–215

——*Volatile Bodies: Toward a Corporeal Feminism* Indiana University Press, Bloomington, 1994

Gumbert, M. 'Paradigm lost: anthropological models and their effect on Aboriginal land rights', *Oceania*, vol. 52, 1981, pp. 103–123

Gunew Sneja 'Denaturalizing cultural naturalisms: multicultural readings of "Australia"' in *Nation and Narration*, ed. H.K. Bhabha, Routledge, New York, 1990, pp. 99–120

Habermas, J. *The Theory of Communicative Action Vol.1: Reason and the Rationalization of Society*, Beacon Press, Boston, 1984

Halberstam, J. 'From Kant to Auschwitz', *Social Theory and Practice*, vol. 14, 1989

Hall, Thomas S. *Ideas of Life and Matter*, vols 1,2, University of Chicago Press, Chicago and London, 1969

Hamilton, A. 'Descended from father, belonging to country: rights to land in the Australian Western Desert', in *Politics and History in Band Societies*, eds E. Leacock and R. Lee, Cambridge University Press, Cambridge, 1982, pp. 85–108

——'Spoonfeeding the lizards: culture and conflict in central Australia', *Meanjin*, vol. 43, no. 3, 1984, pp. 341–362

Hamilton, Paula 'Domestic dilemmas: representations of servants and employers in the popular press', Magarey, Rowley, Sheridan eds *Debutante Nation: Feminism Contests the 1890s*, Allen & Unwin, Sydney, 1993

Hart, H.L.A. *The Concept of Law* Clarendon Press, Oxford, 1961

Harvey, David *The Condition of Postmodernity: An Enquiry into the Origins of Cultural Change*, Blackwell, Cambridge Mass, 1989

Hayhurst, William L. 'Exclusive rights in relation to living things', *Intellectual Property Journal*, June 1991, pp. 171–196

Hebdige, Dick 'After the masses', in *New Times: The Changing Face of Politics in the 1990's*, eds S. Hall and M. Jacques, Verso, London, 1991

Hegel, *Philosophy of Right* trans. T.M. Knox Clarendon Press, Oxford, 1967

Hiatt, Les R. 'Traditional land tenure and contemporary land claims', in *Aboriginal Landowners: Contemporary Issues in the Determination of Traditional Aboriginal Land Ownership*, ed. L.R. Hiatt, University of Sydney, Sydney, 1984

Hitchcock, Alfred. *Psycho*, 1960
Hooks, Bell *Black Looks: Race and Representations*, South End Press, Boston, 1992
Hyde, Lewis, *The Gift: Imagination and the Erotic life of Property*, Vintage Books, New York, 1979
Irigaray, Luce 'The necessity of sexuate rights', ed. Margaret Whitford *The Irigaray Reader*, Blackwells, London, 1991
——*Marine Lover of Friedrich Nietzsche*, trans. Gillian C. Gill, Columbia University Press, New York, 1991
——'How to define sexuate rights', ed. Margaret Whitford *The Irigaray Reader* Blackwells, London, 1991
——'The invisible of flesh: a reading of Merleau-Ponty', in *An Ethics of Sexual Difference*, trans. Carolyn Burke and Gillian C. Gill, Cornell University Press, Ithaca, New York, 1993, pp. 151–184
——*Je, tu, nous: Toward a Culture of Difference,* trans. Alison Dartir, Routledge, New York and London, 1993
——'Why define sexed rights?', in *Je, tu, nous*, trans. Alison Martin, Routledge, New York and London, 1993, pp. 81–92
——'On the maternal order', in *Je, tu, nous*, trans. Alison Martin, Routledge, New York and London, 1993, pp. 37–44
Jonas, Hans 'Spinoza and the theory of organism', in *Spinoza: A Collection of Critical Essays*, M. Grene, University of Notre Dame Press, Notre Dame, Indiana, 1979
——'Ethics and biogenetic art', *Social Research*, vol. 52, no. 3, Autumn 1985, pp. 491–504
Karpin, Isabel 'Reimagining maternal selfhood: transgressing body boundaries and the law', *Australian Feminist Law Journal*, vol. 2, 1994, pp. 36–62
Keen, Ian 'A question of interpretation: the definition of "traditional Aboriginal owners" in the Aboriginal Land Rights (N.T.) Act', in *Aboriginal Landowners: Contemporary Issues in the Determination of Traditional Aboriginal Land Ownership*, ed. L.R. Hiatt, University of Sydney, Sydney, 1984
Kedourie, E. ed. *Spain and the Jews*, Thames and Hudson, London and New York, 1992
Kennedy, Duncan, 'Sexual abuse, sexy dressing and the eroticization of domination', *New England Law Review* vol. 26, 1992, 1309, also published in Kennedy, Duncan, *Sexy Dressing Etc.* Harvard University Press, Cambridge, Mass, 1993, 126
Kenny, A. ed. *Descartes: Philosophical Letters*, Clarendon Press, Oxford, 1970
Kirby, Vicki 'Corporeal habits: addressing essentialism differently' *Hypatia*, vol. 6, no. 3, pp. 4–24
Kline, Marlee 'Race, racism and feminist legal theory' *Harvard Women's Law Journal*, vol. 12, 1989, pp. 115–150
Knapman, Claudia 'Reproducing empire: exploring ideologies of gender and race on Australia's Pacific frontier' Magarey, Rowley, Sheridan eds *Debutante Nation: Feminism Contests the 1890s*, Allen & Unwin, Sydney, 1993

Laclau, Ernest and Chantal Mouffe *Hegemony and Socialist Strategy: Towards a Radical Democratic Politics*, Verso, London, 1985

Lacoue-Labarthe, P. *Heidegger, Art and Politics*, Basil Blackwell, Oxford and Cambridge, Mass. 1990

Lacoue-Labarthe, P. and J.-L. Nancy, 'The Nazi myth', *Critical Inquiry*, vol. 16, 1990, p. 291

Lake, Marilyn 'The politics of respectability: identifying the masculinist context', Magarey, Rowley, Sheridan eds *Debutante Nation: Feminism Contests the 1890s*, Allen & Unwin, Sydney, 1993

Lash, Scott 'Genealogy and the body: Foucault/ Deleuze/ Nietzsche', *Theory, Culture and Society*, vol. 22, 1984, pp. 1–8

Lauretis, Teresa de *Technologies of Gender: Essay on Theory, Film and Fiction*, Indiana University Press, Bloomington, 1987

Levi-Strauss, Claude *The Savage Mind*, Weidenfeld and Nicolson, London, 1966

Lloyd, Genevieve *The Man of Reason: 'Male' and 'Female' in Western Philosophy*, (2nd ed) Minnesota University Press, Minneapolis, 1993

Low, Peter W. Jr., John Calvin, Jeffries, and Richard J. Bonnie *The Trial of John W. Hinckely Jr: A Case Study in the Insanity Defence*, The Foundation Press, Mineola New York, 1986

Lyotard, Jean Francois *The Postmodern Condition*, University of Minnesota Press, Minneapolis, 1984

——*The Differend*, University of Minnesota Press, Minneapolis, 1988

——*Heidegger and 'the Jews'*, University of Minnesota Press, Minneapolis, 1990

——*The Postmodern Explained to Children*, Power Publications, Sydney, 1992

Mackenzie, Catriona, 'Simone de Beauvoir: philosophy and/or the female body', in (eds) Pateman, Carole and Gross, Elizabeth, *Feminist Challenges: Social and Political Theory* Northeastern Series in Feminist Theory, New York, 1986

McHoul, A. and Grace W. *A Foucault Primer: Discourse, Power and the Subject*, Melbourne University Press, Melbourne, 1993

Maeder, Thomas *Crime and Madness: the Origins and Evolution of the Insanity Defense*, Harper and Row, New York, 1985

Magarey, Susan, Sue, Rowley, and Sheridan, Susan *Debutante Nation: Feminism Contests the 1890s*, Allen & Unwin, Sydney, 1993

Matsuda, Mari 'Looking to the bottom: Critical Legal Studies and reparations', *Harvard Civil Rights and Civil Liberties Law Review*, vol. 22, 1987, pp. 323–399

Massumi, Brian 'Everywhere you want to be: introduction to fear', in *The Politics of Fear*, ed. Brian Massumi, University of Minnesota Press, Minneapolis, 1993

Mauss, Marcel *The Gift: Forms and Functions of Exchange in Archaic Societies*, trans. I. Cunnison, Norton Library, New York, 1967

Mensch, Elisabeth 'The Politics of Virtue', *Georgia Law Review*, vol. 25, 1991, p. 923

Mercer, Colin 'Regular imaginings: the newspaper and the nation', eds Tony Bennett, Pat Buckridge, David Carter and Colin Mercer *Celebrating the*

Nation: A Critical Study of Australia's Bicentenary, Allen & Unwin, Sydney, 1992

Merlan, F. 'Australian Aboriginal conception beliefs revisited', *Man*, vol. 21, 1986, pp. 474–493

——'The limits of cultural constructionism: the case of Coronation Hill', *Oceania*, vol. 61, 1991, p. 351

Merleau-Ponty, Maurice 'Other selves and the human world', in *The Phenomenology of Perception*, trans. Colin Smith, Routledge & Kegan Paul, London and Henley, 1962

——'The child's relations with others', in *The Primacy of Perception and Other Essays*, ed. J.M. Edie, Northwestern University Press, Evanston, 1964

——'Working notes', in *The Visible and the Invisible*, trans. Alphons Lingis, Northwestern University Press, Evanston, 1968

——'The intertwining—the chiasm', in *The Visible and the Invisible*, trans. Alphons Lingis, Northwestern University Press, Evanston, 1968

Minow, Martha 'The Supreme Court 1986 term—foreword: justice engendered', *Harvard Law Review*, vol. 101, 1987, pp. 10–95

Montgomery, Marsha L. 'Building a better mouse—and patenting it: altering the patent law to accommodate multicellular organisms', *Case Western Reserve Law Review*, vol. 41, 1990, pp. 231–265

Morris, Meagan *The Pirate's Fiancee: Feminism Reading Postmodernism*, Verso, London, 1988

Mosse, G. *Nationalism and Sexuality: Respectability and Abnormal Sexuality in Modern Europe*, H. Fertige, New York, 1985

Myers, F. *Pintupi Country, Pintupi Self: Sentiment, Place and Person Among the Western Desert Aborigines*, Smithsonian Institute Press, Washington D.C., 1986

——'Burning the truck and holding the country: Pintupi forms of property and identity', in *We are Here: Politics of Aboriginal Land Tenure*, ed. E. Wilmsen, University of California Press, Berkeley, 1989

Mykitiuk, Roxanne 'Fragmenting the body' *Australian Feminist Law Journal*, vol. 2, 1994, pp. 63–98

Negri, A. *The Savage Anomaly*, trans. Michael Hardt, University of Minnesota Press, Minneapolis, 1991

Nietzsche, Friedrich *The Will to Power*, trans Walter Kauffman Vintage Books, New York, 1968

——*On the Genealogy of Morals/Ecce Homo* trans W. Kaufman Vintage Books, New York, 1969

——*Beyond Good and Evil*, trans. R.J. Hollingdale, Penguin, Harmondsworth, 1972

——'On the uses and disadvantages of history for life', in *Untimely Meditations*, trans. R.J. Hollingdale, Cambridge University Press, Cambridge, 1983

Olsen, Frances, 'The family and the market: a study of ideology and legal reform', *Harvard Law Review*, vol. 96, 1983, 1457

——'The myth of state intervention in the family', *University of Michigan Journal of Law Reform*, vol, 18, 1985, pp. 835–64

——'Feminism and Critical Legal Theory: an American perspective', International Journal of the Sociology of Law, vol. 18, 1990, pp. 199–215

Parker, A., Russo M., Sommer D., Yaeger P. eds Nationalisms and Sexualities, Routledge, New York, 1992

Pateman, Carole The Sexual Contract, Polity Press, Cambridge, 1988

Pateman, Carole and Gross, Elizabeth eds, Feminist Challenges: Social and Political Theory, Northeastern Series in Feminist Theory, New York, 1986, pp. 144–56

Pechesky, Rosalind Pollack, 'Fetal images: the power of visual culture in the politics of reproduction', Feminist Studies, vol. 13, no. 2, 1987, pp. 263–292

Peller, Gary 'The metaphysics of American law', California Law Review, vol. 73, 1985, p. 1151

——'Race consciousness', Duke Law Journal 1990, p. 758

Piaget, Jean Play, Dreams, and Imitation in Childhood, trans. C Gattegno and F.M. Hodgson, Norton, New York, 1962

Povinelli, Elisabeth Labor's Lot: The Culture, History and Power of Aboriginal Action, University of Chicago Press, Chicago, 1993

Proctor, R. Racial Hygiene, Harvard University Press, Cambridge and London, 1988

Rebello, Stephen Alfred Hitchcock and the Making of Psycho, Mandarin Paperbacks, London, 1992

Rhode, Deborah 'Feminist critical theories', Stanford Law Review, vol. 42, 1990, pp. 617–638

Ricouer, Paul 'Imagination in discourse and in action', in Rethinking Imagination, eds Gillian Robinson and John Rundell, Routledge, London and New York, 1994

——Time and Narration, Volume I, University of Chicago Press, Chicago, 1984

Ringelheim, J. 'Women and the Holocaust: a reconsideration of research', Signs, vol. 10, 1985

Rosenfeld, Michel 'Deconstruction and legal interpretation: conflict, indeterminacy and the temptations of the new legal formalism', in Deconstruction and the Possibility of Justice, Routledge, eds Drucilla Cornell, Michel Rosenfeld and David Gray Carlson, New York and London, 1992

Rothfield, Philipa 'Backstage in the theatre of representation', Arena, vol. 99/100, 1992, pp. 98–111

Saussure, Ferdinand de Course in General Linguistics, trans. R. Harris, eds C. Bally et al., Open Court, Chicago, 1986

Sahlins, Marshall 'Cery cery fuckabede', American Ethnologist, vol. 20, no. 4, 1993

Scott, Joan W. 'Deconstructing equality versus difference: or, the uses of poststructuralist theory for feminism', Feminist Studies, vol. 14, no. 1, 1988, p. 44

Scott, Russell The Body as Property, Allen Lane, London, 1981

Schlegel, J. 'Notes towards an intimate opinionated and affectionate history of the conference on Critical Legal Studies', Stanford Law Review, vol. 36, 1984, p. 391

Scorsese, Martin, *Taxi Driver*, 1976

Sherman, Brad, 'Patent law in a time of change: non-obviousness and biotechnology', *Oxford Journal of Legal Studies*, vol. 10, Summer 1990, pp. 278–287

Singer, Linda *Erotic Welfare: Sexual Theory and Politics in the Age of Epidemic*, eds Judith Butler and Maureen McGrogan, Routledge, New York, 1993

Sissa, Giulia, 'Subtle bodies' trans. Janet Lloyd, in *Fragments for a History of the Human Body: Part III*, ed. Michel Feher, Zone, New York, 1989, pp. 132–156

Solan, L. *The Language of Judges*, University of Chicago Press, Chicago, 1993

Spinoza, B. de *The Collected Works of Spinoza*, trans. E. Curley, Princeton University Press, New Jersey, 1985

Spivak, Gayatri Chakravorty 'Feminism and deconstruction, again: negotiating with unacknowledged masculinism', in *Between Feminism and Psychoanalysis*, ed. Teresa Brennan, Routledge, London, 1989

——'More on power/knowledge', *Outside in the Teaching Machine*, Routledge, New York, 1993

Summers, Anne *Damned Whores and God's Police: The Colonization of Women in Australia*, Penguin, Melbourne, 1975

Theweleit, K. *Male Fantasies*, University of Minnesota Press, Minneapolis, 1987

Thompson, J. *Studies in the Theory of Ideology*, University of California Press, Berkeley and Los Angeles, 1984

Threadgold, Terry 'Stories of race and gender: an unbounded discourse', D. Birch and L.M. O'Toole eds *Functions of Style*, Pinter, London and New York, 1987

Tushnet, Mark 'Critical Legal Studies: a political history', *Yale Law Journal* vol. 100, 1991, pp. 1515–1544

Vance, Carole ed. *Pleasure and Danger: Exploring Female Sexuality*, 1983

Wellers, G. 'The existence of gas chambers: the number of victims and the Korherr Report', in *The Holocaust and the Neo-Nazi Mythomania* ed. S. Klarsfeld, The Beate Klarsfeld Foundation, New York, 1978

White, Allon 'Bourgeoisie hysteria as carnivalesque' in *Politics and Poetics of Transgression*, eds Peter Stallybrass and Allon White, Cornell University Press, Ithaca, New York, 1986

Young, Iris Marion 'Pregnant embodiment: subjectivity and alienation' in *Throwing Like a Girl*, Indiana University Press, Bloomington, 1990, pp. 159–173

——*Justice and the Politics of Difference*, Princeton University Press, Princeton NJ, 1990

Yovel, Y. *Spinoza and Other Heretics: The Adventures of Immanence*, Princeton University Press, New Jersey, 1989

Zizeck, Slavoj ed. *Everything You Always Wanted to Know About Lacan (But Were Afraid to Ask Hitchcock)* Verso, New York and London, 1992

Index

www.ingramcontent.com/pod-product-compliance
Lightning Source LLC
Chambersburg PA
CBHW020830210326
41598CB00019B/1862